PARTICIPATION AND POLICY-MAKING
IN THE EUROPEAN UNION

Participation · and Policy-Making in the European Union

Edited by
HELEN WALLACE
and
ALASDAIR R. YOUNG

CLARENDON PRESS · OXFORD
1997

Oxford University Press, Great Clarendon Street, Oxford OX2 6DP

Oxford New York
Athens Auckland Bangkok Bogota Bombay
Buenos Aires Calcutta Cape Town Dar es Salaam
Delhi Florence Hong Kong Istanbul Karachi
Kuala Lumpur Madras Madrid Melbourne
Mexico City Nairobi Paris Singapore
Taipei Tokyo Toronto Warsaw
and associated companies in
Berlin Ibadan

Oxford is a trade mark of Oxford University Press

Published in the United States
by Oxford University Press Inc., New York

British Library Cataloguing in Publication Data
Data available

Library of Congress Cataloging in Publication Data
Participation and policy-making in the European Union / edited by
Helen Wallace and Alasdair R. Young.
Based on a workshop convened in October 1994 to discuss interest
in the linkages between industry and the policy process.
Includes bibliographical references.
1. European Union. 2. Political planning—European Union countries. 3. Pressure
groups—European Union countries. I. Wallace, Helen (Helen S.) II. Young, Alasdair R.
JN32.P37 1997 322'.3'094—dc21 97-20428
ISBN 0-19-828060-2

1 3 5 7 9 10 8 6 4 2

Typeset by Best-set Typesetter Ltd., Hong Kong
Printed in Great Britain
on acid-free paper by
Biddles Ltd, Guildford and King's Lynn

PREFACE

This volume grew out of discussions at Sussex around several concurrent research projects. These were all related directly or indirectly to the development of the Single European Market and the impact of European rules on industry. Alan Cawson, Peter Holmes, and others at Sussex had been engaged in a study of the Interaction of Trade, Competition, and Technology Policy in the Single Market, and Francis McGowan, with Paul Seabright at Cambridge, had been researching regulation and competition in the European airline industry. Helen Wallace and Alasdair R. Young had research under way on the interplay between public and private interests in the European policy process. Each of these projects benefited from support from the Economic and Social Research Council (Awards W113251007, L113251023, and L113251029). Alongside these specific projects Keith Middlemas, supported by the Foundation for Manufacturing and Industry, was engaged in the ambitious task of writing a contemporary history of the European integration process (*Orchestrating Europe: The Informal Politics of European Union 1973–1995*, London, Fontana Press, 1995), with the role of industrial and financial institutions very much in his sights.

With support from the ESRC and FMI we were able in October 1994 to convene a workshop to discuss our interest in the linkages between industry and the policy process. This enabled us to involve colleagues from elsewhere who were engaged in similar research or who were themselves part of the process we were seeking to understand. The end result is this volume.

We are grateful to all those who have helped us bring the volume to fruition, and especially to the ESRC and FMI for financial support. Keith Richardson of the European Round Table of Industrialists encouraged us to persevere with the task, as did many other individuals who belong to the various organizations that appear in the volume. David Mayes and Iain Begg, successive co-ordinators of the ESRC's Single European Market Programme, prodded and prompted us towards rounding off the analysis. We owe much to all of them for their encouragement and their criticism. Of course, the final text and its judgement are the responsibility of the authors.

We would also like to thank Julie Smith and Nina Schou for helping with translation and Elizabeth Assassi for assistance in preparing the manuscript. Alasdair Young owes a huge debt to Paige Weber for forbearance throughout and particularly for being a voice of sanity in the penultimate stages.

H.W.
A.R.Y.
Falmer, Sussex

CONTENTS

LIST OF FIGURES

LIST OF TABLES

LIST OF ABBREVIATIONS

ACEA	European Automobile Manufacturers' Association
ACP	African, Caribbean, and Pacific countries
AEA	Association of European Airlines
AmCham	American Chamber of Commerce
ANEC	European Association for the Coordination of Consumer Representation in Standardization
BEUC	European Consumers' Organization
BDI	*Bundesverband der Deutschen Industrie*
CAP	Common Agricultural Policy
CBI	Confederation of British Industry
CC	Consumer Committee
CCC	Consumers' Consultative Council
CCMC	Common Market Car Manufacturers
CD-i	interactive compact disk
CEG	Consumers in Europe Group
CEN	European Standards Committee
CENELEC	European Electro-technical Standards Committee
CEO	Chief Executive Officer
CEPS	Centre for European Policy Studies
COFACE	Confederation of Family Organizations in the European Community
COPA	Confederation of Agricultural Organizations in the European Community
Coreper	Committee of Permanent Representatives
CPS	Consumer Policy Service
CTV	colour television
DCC	Digital Compact Cassette
DCM	Distributed Computing Model
DG	Directorate General (of European Commission)
DTI	UK Department of Trade and Industry
dTTb	Digital Terrestrial Television Broadcasting

DVB	Digital Video Broadcasting group
DVD	Digital Video Disc
EACEM	European Association of Consumer Electronics Manufacturers
EAIC	European-American Industrial Council
EAGGF	European Agricultural Guidance and Guarantee Fund
EC	European Community
ECJ	European Court of Justice
ECPS	Environment and Consumer Protection Service
ESC	Economic and Social Committee
ECSC	European Coal and Steel Community
EEA	European Economic Area
EEC	European Economic Community
EDF	European Development Fund
EEG	European Enterprise Group
EIAJ	Electronic Industries Association of Japan
EFTA	European Free Trade Association
EHLASS	European Home and Leisure Accident Surveillance System
ELG	European Launching Group
EMEA	European Medicines Evaluation Agency
EMU	economic and monetary union
EP	European Parliament
ERDF	European Regional Development Fund
ERT	European Round Table of Industrialists
ESF	European Social Fund
Esprit	European Strategic Programme for Research and Development in Information Technology
ETSI	European Telecommunications Standards Institute
ETUC	European Trade Union Confederation
ETUI	European Trade Union Institute
EU	European Union
EU Committee	EU Committee of the American Chamber of Commerce
Eureka	European Research Cooperation Agency
EURO-C	consumer unit of the European Trade Union Confederation

EURO COOP	European Community of Consumer Co-operatives
FCC	Federal Communications Commission (US)
FDI	foreign direct investment
GATT	General Agreement on Tariffs and Trade
GNP	gross national product
HD-MAC	high-definition technology
HDTV	high-definition television
IATA	International Air Transport Association
IEC	International Electro-technical Commission
IEIC	European Inter-regional Institute for Consumer Affairs
IGC	Intergovernmental Conference
ISO	International Standards Organization
IT	information technology
ITU	International Telecommunications Union
MAC	Multiplex Analogue Component
MEP	Member of the European Parliament
MITI	Ministry of International Trade and Industry
MNE	multinational enterprise
MVDS	multipoint video distributions systems
NTB	non-tariff barrier
OECD	Organization for Economic Co-operation and Development
OFTEL	Office of Telecommunications
ONP	open network provisions
QMV	qualified majority voting
Race	Research and Development in Advanced Communications Technology for Europe
R&D	research and development
SEA	Single European Act
SECO	European Secretariat for Coordination in Standardization
SEM	Single European Market
SGCI	*Secrétariat Général du Comité Interministériel pour les Affaires Européennes*
SMATV	satellite master antenna
SME	small and medium-sized enterprises
TEU	Treaty on European Union

UEAPME	European Association of Craft, Small and Medium-Sized Enterprises
UNICE	Union of Industrial and Employers' Confederations of Europe
UASG	UNICE Advisory and Support Group
VCR	videocassette recorder

CONTRIBUTORS

IRÈNE BELLIER, Centre National de la Recherche Scientifique, Paris

ALAN CAWSON, University of Sussex

ELIE COHEN, Centre National de la Recherche Scientifique, Paris

MARIA GREEN COWLES, University of North Carolina at Charlotte

PETER HOLMES, Sussex European Institute

BEATE KOHLER-KOCH, University of Mannheim

FRANCIS MCGOWAN, Sussex European Institute

ERNESTO PREVIDI, former Commission official

KEITH RICHARDSON, European Round Table of Industrialists

HELEN WALLACE, Sussex European Institute

WOLFGANG WESSELS, University of Köln

ALASDAIR R. YOUNG, Sussex European Institute

INTRODUCTORY FOREWORD

KEITH RICHARDSON

Big business is not only big; it is complex and constantly changing. The networks by which industry tries to communicate with the rest of society are correspondingly complex and difficult to pin down even within a single nation-state. Add in the international dimension and the whole scene begins to shimmer and dance before your eyes like something painted by the early Impressionists. As an active player in this field, I can only welcome the outside observers who are beginning to cast light on the shadows. I know that sometimes I get things right, and kick the ball squarely into the back of the net, and sometimes I am hopelessly wide of the mark. But I would be delighted if somebody else could explain to me how and why—or even simply keep the score.

To begin with a personal word, all my working life has been spent in various aspects of the communications business, as a financial journalist, as head of public affairs for a giant multinational company, and now helping with the activities of that remarkable club which is the European Round Table of Industrialists (ERT). Experience prompts me to make three general comments.

First, communications work on this scale is always very complicated, far more so than anybody can easily imagine. Neither the insider nor the outsider can really follow what is going on, and certainly we need to know more.

Second, it follows that it is impossible for the players themselves to judge effectiveness. We all make claims, of course. Making claims is part of the game. In a more reflective mood I would put it this way: we push on doors labelled single market, or Uruguay Round, or monetary union. Sometimes we push hard and in close co-operation with other players. And sometimes the doors open. But whether they opened because we pushed or not is impossible to judge, simply because there are always so many other pressures at work, pressures that we are certainly not in a position to measure. So all we can do is to push on doors that we believe are of great importance for the health of the European economy, and, if over time some of the doors open and things do improve, we feel our efforts have been on balance worthwhile. And then we move to the next door.

The third comment is that people in this game are far too busy to remember the past. We are all, at any one moment, handling a score of different activities, and our minds are sharply focused on what we are doing now. When the observers come and tell us what we were doing five years ago the reaction tends to be one of total amazement. Perhaps we played some part in persuading European governments to launch the Competitiveness Advisory Group, or to drop the old form of the European Company Statute, and on other points we conspicuously failed. But the argument has moved on, and the old papers of last week are already gathering dust.

Hence the importance of the observers, whether they act as reporters, analysts, critics, or historians. In particular they help us all to see the bigger picture. The involvement of industry in policy advice at European level may not have a long history, but some trends are already becoming clearer.

I am indebted to Maria Green Cowles (see Chapter 6), for example, for explaining how and why the big companies were kept out of the early phase of construction in Europe, and for spelling out the leading role played by the US companies, which for many reasons were the first to start thinking in multinational, pan-European terms. Credit to them, as well as to the force of circumstances.

The Americans were the pace-setters and continue to play an important role, as is perfectly justified. The big European operators thought for too long that they could do it all from Bonn or Paris, or else they relied, first, on their own strong national federations to spread the message, second, on the specialist European federations which gradually emerged for each of the main industrial sectors, and only third, on UNICE, the all-embracing confederation of industrial federations—which in consequence was for a long time starved of funds and of access to top management.

It was this rather unsatisfactory scene which in turn opened the way for the ERT, operating as a club of individual businessmen at the very highest level, to pick up those strategic issues which crossed both national and sectoral frontiers, such as education or infrastructure, and all those policy issues which are now packaged into the single concept of competitiveness. This was agenda-setting of a high order, driven by the strong personalities of individual members, but without being drawn into the detail that other organizations could better supply. And it is this shifting interplay between all the different organizations, as well as the companies themselves, and the many different political actors involved in European decision-making, that starts to make this a rich field for study.

It follows that all of this is a learning process. We are all finding out how to do things, feeling our way within the complex European political system. Europe very well exemplifies what some observers call 'informal politics' (unless they share my own view that virtually all politics are informal politics). Endless bargaining goes on in Europe. Deals are done and undone, concessions are swapped, positions are constantly redefined as the various players adjust to cope with new pressures and challenges. Five years ago was the stone age in terms of communications tactics as well as the content of policies.

An aspect of this which might merit further study would be the timing of some of the main developments and the interplay between communications activities and other historic trends, especially the economic cycles. We know that the ERT was established and UNICE thoroughly reconstructed in the early 1980s, when business was bleak and Euro-pessimism all the rage. At the same time we had a new president in France, with a radical dash for independence followed by a sharp U-turn which put France centre-stage in the process of European integration.

Business strongly supported the development of the single market (indeed Jacques Delors once went on French television to describe ERT as his first ally in the process), but that cannot be divorced from the extraordinary buoyancy of world trade through the mid- to late 1980s. Governments basked in unearned sunshine, euphoria took hold even of things European, public-sector financial disciplines went to pot—and one day we all woke up with a hangover.

Yet it is again interesting that industrialists maintained or even strengthened their support for the Uruguay Round right through the thick of the recession, when a casual observer might have expected them to back away. The integrated world economy had become the dominant frame of reference, and in different ways the industrial organizations all began to hammer away relentlessly at the theme of competitiveness, with warnings that became no less stern as the recession faded.

When governments would on balance perhaps have been rather happy to let the subject of further integration fade into the background (a British diplomat famously depicted the 1996 Inter-Governmental Conference (IGC) as merely a routine 5,000-mile service) it was industry that drew the critical link between the management of Europe and the competitiveness of its economy. It called for an IGC that would make real progress towards effective decision-making and a successful enlargement. These points were made by the ERT, for example, in an unprecedented series of face-to-face meetings with the German, French, and Spanish governments, as well as the president of the Commission in the spring of 1995.

While industrialists always tend to grumble that they have too little influence on the political process, there are many other groups in society with a somewhat anti-business frame of mind that are quick to claim that industry has too much. Let others judge. But if we assume that these communications activities do have some impact on the real world (for if not the proverbially hard-headed industrialists would surely have found some better way of using their time), then we come straight up against the question of legitimacy.

When I went to work for a multinational company in 1983 this question looked very different. Industry, multinational corporations, and the whole nature of big business was under attack all over the world. Industry went on to the defensive and there seemed to me to be a great deal of sloppy thinking about rather peripheral issues. An era of soft-headedness came and went, and the central legitimacy question in big business is once again perceived quite clearly. I would pose it in the following terms. *The unique function of industry is to generate wealth by driving the process of economic development—is it performing this task successfully at a reasonable cost in terms of other interests?*

That is the measure by which industry would like to be judged. And if industry is performing this service, which is of some value to society, then it is entitled to ask in return that society not put unnecessary obstacles in its way. The rest is detail. Of course society is then entitled to criticize industry and call it to account. It may prefer other objectives to the creation of wealth, or, which amounts to much the same thing, redefine the notion of wealth to give preference, let us say, to a pleasant, healthy environment rather than a multitude of consumer goods. Why not, indeed? Provided that society is willing to live with the implications and accept that when it chooses one thing it has to do with less of the other.

Does that sound too rational? I think not. Industry is, for example, much interested in a more effective transport system. But many quite sensible people object to the building of new roads and motorways. This is a rational view—provided, of course, that people living in towns and villages accept that the traffic will continue to pass their front doors, clog up their streets, and generate more pollution—or that people accept the need to stop travelling as much as they do now, and to pay more for food and consumer goods—or again that they agree to invest huge sums of money in attractive public transport systems. Business could live with any of these choices. We only ask that society should make a clear decision as to what it wants.

But there are other forces at work. The ERT has had its own brush with the protest groups, whose thinking does seem to involve a rather emotional reaction against the forces of big business. We must sympathize. Part of my thesis is that big business is very complex and difficult to understand, and we should try to explain more clearly what it does. Perhaps people do tend to depict a rather oversimplified contrast between economic interests, characterized as narrow or even sinister, and the more general interests of society (broad and attractive).

Essentially this is the contrast between the rather nice things we would like to spend our money on (whether individually or collectively is not the issue here) and the slightly discomforting process of earning the money in the first place. But it is precisely this contrast that I would warn against. Either side of the equation can be treated in broad or narrow terms. Society, as a whole, has an absolutely fundamental interest in the overall process of economic development. Industry, as a whole, has a broad interest in the policies that make this possible. A group such as the ERT exists to pursue those broad policy priorities, which are relevant to the whole European economy and therefore to the entire European population, in the face of narrow interests. Narrow interests can be destructive, however they are defined—narrow industrial, narrow environmental, narrow consumerist, the parochial and the short-termist in every aspect of society.

Yet, let us face it, the narrow interests—the here and now of everyday life—do have their appeal. The anti-business and the anti-Europe movements share a common theme, a yearning for a life that is small in scale and easier to understand. Local decisions made by local communities about local shops, local schools, and cottage hospitals. How attractive it sounds—our golden youth when children played safely in the streets and there was neither crime nor pollution nor homelessness nor unemployment.

To all of which there are some simple answers. The world never was like that, except for a privileged few. Even if it had been, there is no going back. The global economy has taken over whether we like it or not. But one advantage that the simpler world did bring: everybody in the village knew exactly where their economic resources came from. Whether a field or a cotton mill or a coal mine, it was at the end of the street and most people worked there. And if the rains failed, or the wheels stopped turning, people went hungry. Today that link is simply not present in most people's minds, when people can pass their whole lives not even seeing a factory, let alone working in one. Restoring that linkage, between where resources come from and what they are spent on, is a central challenge to the communications professionals today.

The implications can be summed up in a handful of issues. The first is *competitiveness*. Europe is an industry-based society and Europe is dead if its industries are not competitive, by which I mean able to hold their own at the high end of world-wide trade and technology, participating as first-division players. Europe pays itself a first-division wage and it cannot keep doing that unless it produces results. The responsibility for competitiveness lies, first of all, with those who work in industry at all levels. But they cannot achieve their potential unless public policies are supportive. So industry will keep calling for better education and training, priority for innovation, simpler regulations, and lower costs. How to deliver these things is the stuff of argument, but the general claim is legitimate, and, if narrow interests block the policies, then we will all pay the cost.

The second issue is that of *Europe*. Our standard of living is now totally dominated by global competition, global trade, global flows of capital and technology, and none of these can be handled in any sensible way by any nation-state. This is not an ideological remark; it is a statement of fact. Small states survive on their own only as satellite economies, and prosper only if they are ruthlessly more efficient than their neighbours. Hence the European dimension is crucial for industry and it is vital to get it right. So industry seeks to generate pressure for the right policies at the European level. Sometimes we succeed and often we fail. Others must judge whether we could do better. But, without expecting to win every battle, my own judgement is that industry loses too many of them and the health of the European economy suffers as a result. Mass unemployment and the other social evils of modern life are among the results of running an economy badly, and yet so often the interests of the broad economy are pushed into a corner, for reasons that are not always easy to understand.

Which leads us to the third issue, the *politics*. There is a straight line going from European economics to European politics. It is inevitable, and irresistible, and yet I do not think any of us have worked out the full implications. Every step we take to implement some low-key piece of technical harmonization or to round off some obscure corner of the single market is a further step towards political integration. The pure ideal of national sovereignty, that every nation-state can do what it likes within its own territory—an ideal that paradoxically led to endless war and destruction—is being eroded all the time. The implications are enormous, and the politicians are rather foolish, if, for reasons of their own, they try to play this down or to imagine that they can draw a line between economic co-operation and politics. But if this is true, and sovereignty is being eroded by historical forces (not by Jacques Delors or any other individual), what on earth are we going to put in its place?

Here I would draw a rather provocative contrast. Industry has a certain legitimacy at the European level, as I have tried to describe. Society needs the wealth that industry creates, and the individual companies that make up industry are directly accountable to customers, employees, shareholders, bankers, and to political and social pressures of every shape and size. Such direct accountability is curiously absent from Europe's political institutions. When, for example, the European exchange rate mechanism fell apart on a summer's day some years ago it was a waste of time asking, 'Who was in charge? Who was responsible? Who lost his job and is now in the streets begging for his bread?'

When industry talks to political leaders at the European level, it is their legitimacy that presents a problem. Of course politicians are entitled to disagree with industry and reject our ideas. But are they then in a position to accept the costs and shoulder the responsibility for the negative consequences, and to stand up in front of the electorate and say, 'We took this decision, we incurred those costs, and now we ask your backing for the position that we took'?

The European institutions are not yet in such a position, which is what the 1996 IGC should be about. Influence and responsibility are slipping away from the national level and have not yet assumed a very solid shape at the European level. This is part of the reason why decision-making in Europe today is so extraordinarily slow and inadequate, as our American and East Asian friends keep reminding us.

But the European level is certainly where it is going, despite the difficulties that this will cause public opinion in every country, for the reasons specified earlier. Certainly industry would be better able to do its job, if it had a strong political authority with which to conduct its dialogue, an authority which would take its decisions, right or wrong, and answer to the electorate for them. Meanwhile, perhaps for many years to come, industry will deal with the current situation as best it can. We learn, perhaps very slowly, how to communicate and explain and contribute to policy-making. What matters is that we do keep on learning.

1

Introduction

HELEN WALLACE

This volume started out as a mapping exercise, with the aim of identifying the range and variety of actors engaged in efforts to influence European regulatory policy. We were specifically not seeking to answer Robert Dahl's (1961) question about 'who governs' in the European Union (EU), but rather to ascertain 'who participates'. This aim grew out of several concerns. The first was a dissatisfaction with 'either/or' analyses of European policy-making: either the European level or the national level predominates; either member governments or some combination of the Commission and private economic interests determine the outcomes; either European policy is a projection of traditional forms of politics or it represents the end of state-based politics in Western Europe. None of these seems to capture the fluid reality of European governance, that is to say the institutions and processes through which collective European policies emerge.

A second concern was prompted by the findings of those studies which focus on one main actor or group of actors. These too easily imply, or can be read to imply, that the object of study is the centre of the relevant policy arena, or that the other groups not studied are absent or less important, or that activity correlates with influence. We also suffer from the fact that the role of non-governmental actors has been studied in such a haphazard way in the past. The new literature is a welcome additional source of empirical material on interest groups and lobbying, but there is a danger of deducing that the phenomenon is more novel and more recent than is the case. Industrial lobbying, like agricultural lobbying, has been a feature of Brussels life since the 1960s. The lack of a documented historical perspective is thus a real handicap, compounded by the inadequacy of attention paid to individual firms and their behaviour. It is for this reason that the involvement of firms is a particular feature of Chapters 6, 7, 8, and 9.

A third concern was more investigative, namely to check out whether the Single European Market (SEM) process had extended the opportunities for relevant organized industrial interests to influence policy, but limited or closed off access for other kinds of 'civic' interests. There was always a suggestion that 'Brussels', particularly as redefined by the single market process, would disproportionately advantage the big business battalions. We have therefore included a study of the consumer organizations (Chapter 10). All of our contributors were asked to identify the range of participants involved in the terrain that they were surveying and to consider the extent and nature of their access to the policy process.

But, of course, the limitation of a mapping exercise is that it is static. Hence a further aim was to shed some light on the dynamics of the European policy process. What patterns of participation were there? What kinds of issues attracted what forms of participation? What impacts did the participants have on the outcomes? What sorts of preoccupations motivated the various participants? These are all deliberately open-ended questions, set out in the hope of gaining a better informed and more nuanced understanding of the European policy process. To root this in a more substantive setting we have assembled several case-histories of European regulatory and industrial policy. These look at the automobile industry (Chapters 7 and 8), airlines (Chapter 8), and consumer electronics (Chapters 7 and 9). They provide building-blocks to underpin the contributions on the institutional patterns of activity, also mainly focused on aspects of the SEM and European regulation. Chapter 4 provides a practitioner's perspective on the way the European Commission handles regulatory policy, while Chapter 5 draws on a larger anthropological study of the Commission. In Chapter 6 Maria Green Cowles summarizes her major study of big business and its efforts to influence European policy.

The focus of the volume is on the emerging shape of European governance in the fields of market regulation and policies for industry, broadly defined. These are issues that lie at the core of the process of European economic integration, and the old European Community (EC) heart of what is now called the European Union. Many analyses of such issues have focused on the political economy and policy communities attached to particular product sectors, and we retain some material that has sectoral specificity.

But it was also an objective of this volume to reveal something of the horizontal features of policy development alongside the vertical segments. This is partly for the sake of balance, but also for a more important reason. Part of our contention is that the nature of the relationship between producers and entrepreneurs, on the one hand, and public policy-makers, on the other hand, has changed. The increasingly international setting of business makes it harder and harder to establish the boundaries of a national economy or even to separate the European economy from its global context.

As a consequence those firms that operate in more-than-very-local markets have to take an interest in the framing of market-influencing public policy beyond the nation-state, not just in terms of classical trade policy, but also of industrial, technology, competition, and other policies. So, of course, they need to participate in the framing of that policy at whatever level is appropriate and pertinent. In addition some firms have acquired a preference for European-level policy rules as more likely to provide a settled and congenial framework than recurrent arbitrage between abutting national systems. We do not explore in great detail in this volume the implications of this development for the old relationships between governments, producers, and society in individual countries, although we are aware of the potentially unsettling effect of European and global developments for the significantly different patterns and relationships in individual countries. Some comments on this point are included in Chapter 7, with particular reference to France.

This extension and redirection of focus has become part of the dynamic of policy-making in and around the European institutions. Moreover, it can be argued, and is in this volume, that the members of the European institutions have recurrently and deliberately encouraged the participation of firms and business groups in their efforts to develop and to implement policy. In this sense the business concerns are partners of the public policy-makers and on the inside track, not 'outside' interests, some of them also simultaneously able to exploit insider positions retained in their national settings. It is tempting therefore to see the SEM as a paradise for the industrial lobbyist, in which sharply focused and egoistical businesspeople either 'capture' pliant policy-makers, or run rings around the elected officials, or out-influence consumers.

However, the evidence simply does not support so simple a judgement. On the contrary, in specific policy networks or advocacy coalitions, and in the framing of the guiding ideas and doctrines of policy we find the footprints of other sections of society. These are exhibited variously: sometimes explicitly, for example, through the consumer organizations and the environmental lobbies; sometimes in the persistence of different social habits conditioning national regulatory 'tastes'; and sometimes in the search for modernizing intellectual frameworks and ideas around which to reshape policy. It seems that in some instances one can observe the emergence of networks which bring together public policy-makers and some of the relevant interests recurrently in forms of interdependence. On specific issues one can see signs of organized groupings that come together to act as coalitions, mobilized to advocate a particular policy or programme for a sector or an industry, or to insert a particular approach to policy. However, this is not to suggest that each such network, or coalition, embraces the range of relevant interests. There are parallel groupings competing for the ear of the European policy-makers, with these latter providing the filters through which interests are aggregated or one set of interests is privileged.

Hence, as Beate Kohler-Koch argues cogently in Chapter 3, we can see the European process as an experiment in redefining governance so as to stimulate different ways of adjusting public and private actors' relationships and their contributions to the management of an internationalized economy. Indeed this is precisely why the European process is not a replica of established national processes and does not provide a substitute polity, but is rather an extended arena of governance. But also, for precisely the same reason, the emerging European process does not have a fixed and settled shape. Indeed its durability is a function of whether the results that it produces are worthwhile to the participants; the process is more results-dependent than habit-dependent. At least on the evidence of this volume we can argue that some of the outcomes are different from what one might expect in extrapolating from experiences of traditional country-based politics, because they are mediated through this very different European process. One evident contrast is the lack of opportunities for conventional parliamentary engagement and for political parties to engage either programmatically or to defend geographically defined constituencies. Thus the functions of framing political discourse and mediating between private interests or *vis-à-vis* wider social or political concerns are performed through other channels.

Quite how they are performed remains something of a puzzle and is contested in the literature, as well as in the reality of day-to-day European politics. Wolfgang Wessels suggests one way of understanding this puzzle in Chapter 2. He sets out in some detail the extent to which the agents of national political systems are engaged in Community policy-making at a variety of levels, with a range of perspectives, and with a startling intensity of involvement. But, he suggests, this is not so as to create a mysterious and impenetrable Eurocracy (even though to the uninitiated it may seem so), but rather because the European arena is providing the participating member governments (and national political classes) with a new way of regaining control over functions of the modern welfare state which, paradoxically, have escaped the grasp of country-based states. Thus for him there has been a 'fusion' of national and European levels of governance, so much so that one can no longer distinguish the boundaries between them or an inbuilt hierarchy of influence.

IN THE ECONOMIC MARKET PLACE

The substance of this volume is about how the economic marketplace in the EU is regulated and operated. The underlying assumption is that from the early 1980s a coalition was forged between big business, the Commission, and member governments in order to set in place forms of agreed and transnational regulation. The shared aim was to enable economic operators within the EC to maximize their market opportunities within western Europe, but also to have a better chance to compete in international markets.

Cowles (Chapter 6) tells the story of how leading firms endeavoured, with some success, to increase their leverage on the European policy process through the European Round Table of Industrialists, by revamping the Union of Industrial and Employers' Confederations of Europe (UNICE), and, for the American firms, through the American Chamber of Commerce (AmCham) in

Brussels. These efforts were largely directed at broad measures to liberalize the internal European market. They were particularly important in the early years of the SEM programme in giving it concrete definition, in providing the Commission with a supporting network, and in making '1992' a 'yesable' proposition. Whether the member governments were showing far-sighted good judgement or simply defending their national champions in buying the case for the SEM, and whether the big firms had in turn made the governments and the trade associations their champions, or were externalizing their problems of restructuring are questions that can be answered in different ways, as our various authors show. But the net result was to give the SEM a big enough push to get it moving up the policy escalator.

Big firms were active on other fronts too. Faced with intensified international competition, heavy domestic costs of production, technological challenges, and pressures to restructure, firms turned to the European level for forms of sectoral advantage. What advantages they sought differed from case to case. In automobiles, as we show from different angles in Chapters 7 and 8, the firms involved had been cushioned from at least some external competitors, especially the Japanese producers, by trade protection that was inconsistent with the advent of a European market without internal borders. Efforts by the firms to collude in order to find continued collective protection were met by a strengthened battalion of freeish traders, found within the European institutions as well as in some quarters of some member states. Interestingly the edge in the ensuing bargaining went to the more liberal side of the case. It became harder for individual member states to impose national restrictions, even the 'grey' forms of protection that exist as 'voluntary' restraints. Indeed the combination of Commission activism and the ability to rely on Community law helped to shift the policy in a more liberal direction, thus incidentally also offering more choice at more attractive prices to the European consumer. Yet, as Elie Cohen argues in Chapter 7, the EC also provided a useful and usable external pretext for domestic restructuring that would have been hampered if confined by traditional domestic politics.

The airlines industry was very different, since in most EU member states—the UK was an early exception—the national flag-carrier airline has remained very much a national champion, helped in some cases by direct public subsidy (now largely absent from the automobile industry). Thus, although European Court of Justice (ECJ) cases provided grounds for pursuing liberalization, and although individual commissioners sought to improve competition, the forces of inertia have remained strong. Chapter 8 shows that efforts to open up the airlines sector have been slow to bear fruit and have delivered only modest benefits, compared with other deregulatory programmes, to the consumer. This may be in part due to the mixed performance in using its existing powers (noticeably its reluctance to enforce vigorously the rules on state aids) and to problems with establishing a competence in external relations. Also, significantly, member governments retain strong footholds, both as direct stakeholders in the fortunes of national flag-carriers, and through the indirect influence that they seem able to exert within the college of commissioners. Yet economic and financial pressures within the European industry, combined with external pressures, are starting to provide policy-makers with more opportunities to stimulate changes to the industry.

None the less in some sectors it is to the European level that the firms have turned for direct support. As Alan Cawson in Chapter 9, with reference to consumer electronics and high-definition television (HDTV), and with a somewhat different emphasis Elie Cohen in Chapter 7, make clear, the larger European firms reached the conclusion that national programmes would be inadequate to provide the cushions that they thought they needed to be able to compete. What is startling about this story is how ill-judged the ensuing policy was from the perspective of both the firms concerned and the public policy process. By a pattern of collusion to privilege the incumbent European firms with research and development support and accommodating European standards, European policy became based on a version of the technology and a set of expectations about consumer preferences that were to prove hopelessly inappropriate. The temptation to foster European champions was overwhelming, but misplaced. Recognition of the penalties of an overly narrow partnership of firms and policy-makers, combined with technological and market pressures from external competitors, has none the less started to produce a more open-ended approach to the sector (Chapter 9). This is emerging both at the European level and within member states, as Cohen shows in Chapter 7.

THE WORKINGS OF THE REGULATORY PROCESS

As each of the relevant case-histories shows, the firms involved found themselves increasingly caught up in efforts to provoke developments in European public policy that would facilitate their adaptation to the forces of market competition. Reliance on national policy processes simply became misguided and inadequate. A combination of economic, legal, and political factors had shifted the policy process to a more transnational frame of reference. This is not to say that 'Brussels' had become the centre of the firms' policy universe, but rather that those entrepreneurs who operated in more-than-local markets needed to influence as many forums of rule-making and support-provision as they could. This picture is consistent with the arguments set out by both Beate Kohler-Koch (Chapter 3) and Wolfgang Wessels (Chapter 2) about the reshaping and changed setting of governance.

But how does this look viewed from the other side of the fence, from the perspective of the public policy-makers? In Chapter 5 Irène Bellier reports on the anthropological study of the Commission, in which she and a Franco-British group of colleagues endeavoured, from close observation of its internal behaviour, to characterize the Commission as a public policy player. She argues, in line with studies by many political scientists, that there is a clearly identifiable sense of 'European identity' and an increasingly European frame of reference to the Commission's activities. These coexist with the professional and functional affiliations of individual services within the Commission. These differing perspectives induce commissioners and Commission officials to develop their own distinct approaches to European public policy and to develop a range of networks through which to prepare and to develop policy. Thus the Commission, neither a monolith nor an introverted bureaucracy, has set about developing open and often open-ended relationships with external interlocutors, sometimes with direct clients of its attempted policy plans, but also with a wide range of intellectual and political partners.

As Alasdair R. Young argues in Chapter 10, these latter include a range of groups and actors that extend well beyond the industrial entrepreneurs and service-providers. Whether the policy issues engage consumer groups, environmental organizations, or other 'civic interests', the Commission has sought to take other perspectives into account alongside those of the producers. Indeed through its various consultative mechanisms and sometimes with direct support (sometimes financial) for their activities, the Commission has gone to some lengths to take an inclusive approach to defining who has relevant views to express. Thus, although the civic interests have less political muscle and less organized power than the producers, they are constant factors in the debate and seem to have a considerable influence on the outcomes. Here it is important to stress that such influences are often implicit rather than explicit, as much in the mind-sets of Commission (and sometimes national) officials as in the formally identifiable or quantifiable influencing activities of such civic interests.

The role of the Commission as policy formulator, or agenda-setter, in the European system of governance is, of course, crucial; it is thus a kind of magnet for those who seek to influence the policy outcomes. The Commission itself needs those external interlocutors in order to make sensible and focused proposals and subsequently to turn them into operable regulatory arrangements. Commissioners and Commission officials need to judge which of their interlocutors are making pertinent and well-founded interventions and to be able to gather the appropriate information from which to develop sensible policy. Its dependence on external networks is thus great, but so too is its capacity to bring informed judgement to bear. Often it is operating in a vacuum—the gap between inadequate national regulatory systems and the broader European market-place—or in response to regulatory failures. Almost always its efforts to intervene are based on the search for a brokered consensus, a process of dialectic between the European and the national levels, or between different interests, which always obscures who has exerted influence over the outcome and makes it difficult for the citizen or the parliamentarian to scrutinize. Ernesto Previdi sets all of these points out with careful nuances in Chapter 4, his analysis and thoughtful criticism of the process being deeply informed by many years of experience working inside the Commission and latterly as secretary to the Sutherland Committee, the 'high-level group on the operation of the single market', which reported in 1992.

Thus both from the policy practitioners' perspectives and as a hallmark of the behaviour of the organized industrial interests, policy networks can be functional and have emerged as a characteristic form of managing the policy dialogue. There is in addition an array of formalized and institutionalized consultative arrangements, as Chapter 2 indicates. However, at least as pertinent are the informally constituted and flexible networks that are so much present.

Three particular consequences seem to flow from this. First, the networks are rarely closed to new entrants. Their membership changes over time and according to the issues. Sometimes they have developed as advocacy coalitions that mobilize support for particular viewpoints, both in terms of congruent substantive interests and as vehicles to propagate a particular doctrine.

Second, the fluidity of the process militates against the entrenching of strong battalions of adversarial coalitions. Our cases yield little evidence of the successful organization of veto-groups—the airlines case is the closest to this. On the contrary, the relative success of the consumer viewpoint in finding a place in the policy debate—explicitly sometimes, often implicitly—suggests that the process is particularly responsive to the inclusion of a wide range of socio-economic perspectives. Or, at least, the process invites the operation of several parallel or concurrent networks of influence.

Thirdly, it seems harder to establish and sustain hard-edged protectionist coalitions in the European process than one expects, given the political economy characteristics of most of the member states. Such opportunities are greater when the policy process is organized vertically and within a sector. But it is precisely a feature of the European policy bias towards market regulation that much of the policy is framed on a horizontal dimension that necessitates the consideration of more than one sector or industry and requires attention to non-producer concerns.

POLITICAL MARKET-PLACE
OR INSTITUTIONAL REDESIGN?

It would be easy to conclude from these various essays that the policy process operates like a kind of political market-place. There is no clear structure of authority or hierarchy of power. There are no clear ground-rules about who can participate in the policy process, or when, or how. The formal procedures, of course, provide a kind of structure, but it is the informal politics that determine the outcomes. In one sense this sounds like a statement of the obvious; all politics stem from a mix of the formal and the informal, and most political processes in democracies depend on bargaining and brokerage.

In the context of European integration, however, the balance between the two is distinctive. Those formal procedures that exist and that have become increasingly complicated over the years—the dense web of committees that have emerged to advise the Commission, and to help it implement policy, known as comitology, symbolizes this procedural complexity—are contested and contestable. They are subject to recurrent redefinition and constantly vulnerable to the vicissitudes of political and economic context. As a result the informal political processes have to bear rather more weight than in a long-established polity, with entrenched rules and ingrained practices. And even though the national political processes of the component member states have been eroded to an extent by the existence of the EU and by changes in the characteristics of economic markets, they can none the less rely on an inherited form of political territory and some enduring patterns of political allegiance.

Because power in the EU is diffused, bargaining is essential to the development of agreements. Authority has to be earned and confidence retained, both more sustainable if a consensus-based outcome can be found, than when decisions are imposed. Persuasive power is generally more important than imposed power; it is only through definite statements of the law from the ECJ that occasionally the need for bargaining can be short-circuited. More often those concerned with establishing a Community regulation have to build a coalition of support and to back it up with an articulated and informed case for action. Legitimacy has to be achieved by the subsequent readiness of the political agencies and economic operators to comply with the agreed regulation. It is a form of indirect and often invisible legitimation that is particularly hard to demonstrate, not least since smooth implementation is barely noticed, while policy failures—HDTV is a case in point—are easily turned into criticisms of the process itself.

One of the defining characteristics of 'Brussels' is the openness of opportunities for access, opportunities taken by battalions of national officials, by many representatives of organized industrial interests, by regional and local authorities, and a range of other interest groups, even individuals who think that they have something to contribute to the discussion. A question which follows is whether the result is to make policy definition particularly vulnerable to strategic manipulation by those who are able to define their preferences coherently and to bargain them through effectively. Public choice theory suggests that this would be the expected pattern of behaviour, partly because of the substantive economic interests at issue, partly because of the bargaining system (with its segmented tendencies), and perhaps partly because of the absent potential corrective of strong parliamentarism.

Up to a point, some such strategic behaviour can be identified, and is to be seen in our case-histories in the more sectorally confined policy arenas. Segmented policy arenas encapsulate some of the specific and specialized policy issues. Each of these has its own characteristics and attracts a slightly different range of participants; these do sometimes organize themselves into strategic and collusive coalitions. However, the very fluidity of the Brussels networks, backed by the variations in national governments' preferences, and complemented by the intrusion of civic interests, both limits the impact of collusion and makes strategic calculation of behaviour more difficult.

In addition many of the policy issues are defined more horizontally and in broader or more variegated terms. The provision of airline services or the development of automobile production may be an industrial support issue in some member states, but a competition policy issue in others. Trade policy cannot be simply used as the external projection of domestic industrial support. While some firms may be chasing a privileged position for their own technology and technical standards, other European firms may be keen to derive benefit from imported technologies and more appropriate technical standards from outside Europe, as in the consumer electronics case. European public policy-makers may not always recognize this diversity of competing concerns when first defining a policy guideline, but the open access to consultation usually means that they are forced to recognize and take account of such factors. Even within the public policy institutions, notably the Commission and many of the national agencies, one can find a tussle between the protectors of the more traditional industrial interests and the promoters of adaptation and modernization.

Opportunities to participate are not so much determined by the structures of the policy process as by the information, resources, and credibility of particular groups or actors. The variety of the pressure points available provides multiple points of access. A viewpoint that may be regarded as eccentric in one quarter is regarded as mainstream in another, an inevitable consequence of the persistent diversity of cultures, habits, and doctrines (both political and economic) in the heterogeneous context of the EU. Note here that, while lobbying skills as such may well make a difference to levels and intensities of involvement, being recognized as a stakeholder on the issue seems to have more relevance for how loud the voice is heard to be. Also, as Chapter 10 suggests, some groups, such as the consumers, may fare disproportionately well in gaining attention, by being recognized as 'niche-players', and thus offered access to the debate.

Moreover, both national and European policy-makers sometimes identify particular groups as ones that need to be invited to participate, so as to provide balancing evidence against a well-established and well-entrenched lobbying coalition. Indeed the broader canvas of the European policy arena sometimes precisely provides opportunities to escape from the policy cartels that often occupy the ground in traditional policy processess within the member states. The gradual opening up of the European market in automobiles to more external suppliers is one example of this: here the political economy of the European bargaining process has started to shift away from the old patterns of concerted protection. Examples such as this have, of course, as we suggested above, to be set against the contrasting cases where collusion persists. In the airlines case, summarized in Chapter 8, the collusion has been organized country by country between governments and airlines of the same nationality. In consumer electronics, as discussed in Chapters 7 and 9, the collusion was transnational and among a small group of firms. The more segmented and sectorally confined the policy issue, the greater the opportunities for such collusion to persist.

Even so, the patterns of participation and attempts to influence policy are characterized more by competition among the varying interests than by successful collusion. In part this is due to the endemic pluralism of the process. As both Chapters 4 and 5 suggest, the Commission is often a deliberate instigator of pluralism.

Member governments, if taken one by one, are as such less so. However, on any given regulatory issue the member governments will generally represent a broad range of differing preferences, in particular between higher and lower product or process standards, or between different kinds of firms in the same sector, or between producer and consumer interests. Thus the member governments provide footholds in the Council, to which different private and civic interests can attach their own arguments, or act as patrons of different policy preferences. This in part explains the relative success of consumer and environmental interests in getting their voices heard.

NEGOTIATED REGULATION

The chapters that follow are permeated with references to establishing regulation by persuasion and by negotiation. At least in the instances that they cover there is rather little evidence of majorities imposing solutions on outvoted minorities or of concerted efforts by explicit veto groups to mobilize opposition to particular proposals. What the formal recourse to qualified majority voting has mainly done is to remove the scope for isolated dissidents to block legislation on the SEM. The unhappy tend rather to seek to defray the costs or to delay the adjustments that would follow from a policy not of their choosing. It is broadly recognized that, once a European rule is in place, it will not easily be amenable to radical change. Thus much of the policy-influencing effort is spent on securing an acceptable default rule and on opening up opportunities for subsequent marginal adjustment.

Hence those concerned are under pressure not only to explain and to justify their particularist interests defensively, but to suggest a framework or a central idea for the legislation being devised. Indeed a premium of advantage attaches to those who can show themselves to be policy innovators. The HDTV case is an example of an effort to pressure by innovation, in this case without achieving commercial success. The experience of the consumers' organizations, though lagging behind most producers in their levels of participation, suggests that in targeting particular issues they have helped to embed in the European regulatory process two important consumer concerns. The first is that product standards should not, as a point of principle, be set at the minimum imaginable level of performance or of quality. The second is that the development of regulation to increase opportunities for entrepreneurs should be followed by the development of a consumer policy as such, an area in which European legislation is beginning to gather pace. This pattern of influence mirrors what had earlier been achieved by those (both in some governments and in organized groups) pleading the case for strengthening environmental safeguards.

These experiences suggest that the process of European regulation is tied up not only with the questions of who participates and who bargains skilfully, but also with who can develop persuasive ideas and compelling arguments. Kohler-Koch in Chapter 3 stresses the importance of examining how the discourse of policy is developed and how particular ideas gain currency. This is not simply a matter of intellectual coherence, but also of defining and solving recognized policy problems. Hence the implementation of policy is as important as its initial framing in making regulatory measures acceptable and enforceable, a point that Previdi (Chapter 4) also argues to be a crucial feature of the Community process.

This point has particular cogency in the European context, as the Commission recognizes, because of the role of negotiated coalitions at all stages of the regulatory process, both to achieve compliance and to gain a form of legitimation. This effort to generate 'modernizing coalitions' was always a feature of European integration and it has emerged again in the development of SEM regulation. Wessels, for this and other reasons, therefore regards the national and European levels of governance, not as antithetical, but as mutually reinforcing. Hence he has argued, both in Chapter 2 of this volume and elsewhere (1997), that the integration process is a form of 'fusion', as the European arena provides the best available vehicle for adapting the European welfare state to changing economic, political, and social conditions. Kohler-Koch argues (both here in Chapter 3 and, more extensively, with Marcus Jachtenfuchs, 1996*a*) that this new form of European governance has produced a different kind of partnership between public and private actors from that which had grown up in the old polities of the member states. She suggests that in response to the changing context of an internationalized economy the affected interests, inside and outside formal political institutions, have used the availability of those transnational institutions to bring into being a special form of governance. Indeed it is for these kinds of reasons that Giandomenico Majone (1994 and 1996) has characterized the EU so categorically as a new form of regulatory state.

INVENTING EUROPEAN GOVERNANCE

This volume therefore reinforces the case for identifying a new form of European governance that is being invented around the EU institutions. Our somewhat eclectic choice of case-histories cannot of course claim to be comprehensive in its range of examples and evidence. But the cases and the accompanying commentaries on institutional performance show enough evidence to confirm that European regulation is distinctive in its characteristics. The European regulatory process may not quite be a state in the language of Majone; indeed much of our volume questions the term 'state' as a misleading metaphor for the process and its institutional framework. But this collection of essays does confirm the presence of many of the characteristics that Majone and others have identified as being associated with the European pattern of regulation, different from national arenas of public policy-making and with some distinct advantages over them as vehicles for the adaptation of the economy. We would distort the evidence if we tried to summarize the process as either based on the projection of power by the member governments or as their subordination to new European institutions. On the contrary, the process seems rather to be an experiment in finding alternative forms for developing public policy.

This is not to say that the EU has already become a firmly embedded form of governance. Several of our authors draw attention to the fluidity and unpredictability of the process, and we know that there are points of strong resistance to the erosion of more traditional forms of governance, rooted in the component national polities. But then results matter. The European process gains credence to the extent that it can provide effective and sustainable responses to the challenges of the modern European political economy. Here our volume shows a very mixed picture: in its substantive outputs European regulatory policy sometimes works, but sometimes does not. It needs a high and continued level of 'success' in the substance to achieve continued vigour.

2

The Growth and Differentiation of Multi-Level Networks: A Corporatist Mega-Bureaucracy or an Open City?

WOLFGANG WESSELS

INTRODUCTION: A 'STRANGE' POLITICAL SYSTEM

For all those who want to study a political system in full evolution the European Union (EU) is a fascinating object: a political 'space' in the making. The formal and informal networks in the Brussels arena offer much scope for stimulating research and reveal a pattern of the growth and differentiation. As with the study of any political system a crucial aim of research on the EU is to identify and to analyse the several and different groups of political, administrative, economic, and social actors. They form complex networks which make institutions work or fail. The emphasis in studies of new democracies on 'civil society' illustrates that knowledge of constitutions—or, for our purpose, treaties—and their official bodies and institutions is not sufficient to explain how a political system works.

Some broad features demonstrate the relevance of networks in the EU. The number of officially declared interest groups has increased from around 200 (1960) to some 2,200 (1995) (see Table 2.1); differentiated and fragmented forms of involvement led over the 1980s to approximately 10,000 lobbyists working in Brussels in 1990 (Andersen and Eliassen, 1991; Commission, 1992*b*; Kohler-Koch, 1992); and meetings organized by the Commission assemble—again in a very rough approximation—30,000 participants per year (Wessels and Rometsch, 1996). Brussels has thus become an 'open city' for all kinds of intermediary groups. These

TABLE 2.1. *Intermediary groups with offices in Brussels*

Category	Number
1. Corporations	314
2. Trade associations	527
3. Interest groups	147
4. Chambers of commerce	34
5. Business and industry	
from inside EU	20
from outside EU	3
6. Regions	
from inside EU	80
from outside EU	15
7. Think-tanks	12
8. Trade unions	21
9. International organizations	86
10. Law firms	
from inside EU	122
from outside EU	40
11. Political consultants	93
12. Management consultants	28
13. Public relations consultants	19
14. National Associations	
from inside EU	72
from outside EU	21
15. Association of chambers of commerce	
from inside EU	10
from outside EU	3
Total (1–15)	1,640
inside EU	1,558
outside EU	82
16. Press agencies	48
17. Specialized journalists	
from inside EU	219
from outside EU	91
Total Media (16 + 17)	358
18. Diplomatic missions	177
Overall Total	2,175

Source: Fallik (1994).

patterns of quantitative growth prompt some basic questions: is the EU just an area of curiosity, a strange new world, but one without further overall relevance for political systems in Europe? Or do EU experiences reveal permanent trends and perhaps new features of the way in which networks of intermediary actors with different characteristics are evolving in Western Europe (Middlemas, 1995)?

Beyond description and analysis, how should we evaluate this evolution in the European political space? Do we witness the building of a 'Brussels Archipelago', an underground maze with a new European political class defying any standards for transparency and accountability? By linking horizontal and vertical channels of interaction the actors involved are argued by some to form a rather closed circle of decision-shapers and makers. A 'mega-bureaucracy' (Wessels, 1996*b*: 183) would thus be merging with 'neo-corporatist structures' (for the debate see Streeck and Schmitter, 1991), thereby emptying the political space of nation-states. A corporatist mega-bureaucracy in the making might be defined as a closely knit network between civil servants and interest groups, in both cases drawn from several levels of governance. Or is what we observe a new variation of 'representative government'? In this alternative view the broad participation of elected actors from several groups and institutions is establishing some kind of Aristotelian polity (Wessels, 1996*a*), characterized by a mixed 'multi-level governance' (Bulmer, 1994; Rittberger, 1994). These issues have been addressed, at least partly, in the relevant academic literature (see, among others, Bressand and Nicolaïdes, 1990; Héritier, 1993*a*; Jachtenfuchs and Kohler-Koch, 1996*a*; Mazey and Richardson, 1993*a*).

The Approach: European Networks as Essential Components of Fundamental Trends

My approach is to look for the structural factors in the evolution of networks in the EU, what economists might call fundamental trends. Such factors may have been very important stimuli in creating and multiplying trans-border interactions by lobbyists, bureaucrats, and politicians. But these structures are themselves a product of the proliferation of formal and informal contacts among those groups. Relevant basic factors might be of different kinds. One set comprises the shifting attitudinal and behavioural patterns of actors. Here political and administrative cultures (Wessels, 1985) might be seen as important influences on networks and their policy styles, but are not further elaborated here (see for example, Mazey and Richardson, 1993*b*).

My underlying assumption is that the reasons for how and why actors interact at the EU level should be understood as an essential component of the evolution of the West European state since the Second World War. The creation of the EU as a new kind of political system can best be explained by recognizing the link between the welfare and service state, with its increasing use of public functions and instruments, and growing European and global interdependencies. The EU level was not, and is not, an isolated, marginalized arena; it became an integral part and dynamic factor in the overall development of the interaction among governments, administrations, and intermediary groups at different levels and in several configurations. These actors both promote the integration process and are pulled by an in-built dynamic, based on competition for access and influence in the making of public policies. The EU, as it now is, has necessarily to be included in any overall analysis of how states in Western Europe are evolving.

I also assume that formal and informal networks are closely related to each other, at least in the political system of the EU. The formal rules that govern how public functions are performed and how public instruments are used, as laid down in the treaties, induce a widely differentiated and intensively used web of informal interactions. In itself this changes the way the institutions work within these procedures, a phenomenon described elsewhere in this volume as 'co-evolution' between political and intermediary systems (see Chapter 3).

Constitutional, institutional, and procedural provisions and their changes are important incentives and constraints for political networks. The provisions of the Single European Act (SEA) and the Treaty on European Union (TEU) have created additional incentives for several groups of actors to participate more actively at the European level, for example those interested in advancing the single market or environmental policy. The new co-decision procedure (TEU Art. 189b) has certainly induced more actors to pay more attention to the European Parliament (EP). The evolving features of the EU will, due to their legal and political relevance, spill over onto and shape the existing networks.

Thus endogenous and exogenous dynamics lead—and this is my major argument—to a new kind of European political system: this is characterized by the fusion between instruments, procedures, and networks from several levels of public policies (Wessels, 1992).

In contrast to many other analyses this approach is based on a macro-political and dynamic view, making it less appropriate to look at individual groupings and their interactions, and more so to examine the general dynamics of the political system as such. The cost and benefits of such an approach in terms of its validity and explanatory capacity are well enough known not to be repeated here.

THE DESCRIPTION: LONG-TERM TRENDS

The EU as an Emerging Political System

The evolution from the European Coal and Steel Community (ECSC) of the 1950s into the EU of the 1990s can be seen as a multi-faceted process. On a broadening scale and with growing intensity, binding decisions for public policies are prepared, taken, implemented and controlled at the European level (see Table 2.2). Political systems can be defined by their 'authoritative allocation of values' (Easton, 1953) or, in line with this argument, by their output of legally binding acts. Since the early 1960s decisions taken by the Council of Ministers and by the Commission have grown extensively (see Table 2.2). These decisions and the treaties comprise the *acquis communautaire*, which has considerable relevance not least for economic, social, and administrative actors. The EU system also produces what some call 'soft law', which includes action programmes, declarations by the European Council, and decisions taken in the second and third pillars of the EU. Soft law is not subject to the control of the European Court of Justice (ECJ), but has nevertheless a kind of binding character and an impact.

The EU's budgetary resources have also increased. At first sight, the budget of just over 1 per cent of EU gross national product (GNP) looks rather modest compared to member states' public expenditures, which averaged 50 per cent of GNP in 1993 (OECD, 1995). Yet, as only 5 per cent goes towards administrative costs (including staff) (Commission, 1995*b*), a considerable amount of expenditure is available for projects, even though it is spread across 15 countries with 370 million inhabitants.

The fundamental trends in this evolving political system can be measured by four indicators (Grabitz *et al.*, 1988; Lindberg and Scheingold, 1970):

1. the enlargement of policy scope;
2. the transfer of competences towards the European level;
3. institutional growth and procedural differentiation; and
4. the extension and development of patterns of access and influence for intermediary groups.

TABLE 2.2. *The growth of European policy activies, 1960–1990*

	1960	1975	1990	1993 1994 1995	% annual growth		
					1960–75	1975–90	1960–90
1. Meetings with official interpretation	2,132	7,254	9,894	10,647 (1995)	8.3	2.1	5.2
2. Commission expert groups		537 (1985)	602			2.3 (1985–90)	
3. Coreper and Council working groups	602	2,215.5	2,128.5	2,221.5 (1993)	9.1	−0.2	4.3
4. Council working groups	10 (1962)	91	224	263 (1994)	18.5 (1962–75)	6.1	11.7
5. Council days in session	44	67.5	138	119 (1993)	3.3	4.5	3.9
6. Separate compositions of Councils	7 (1967)	12	22	19 (1993)	6.9 (1967–75)	4.1	5.1 (1967–90)
7. Legislative output of Council	10	575	618	468 (1994)	33.6	0.5	16.5
8. Legislative output of Commission	6	838	1,367	2,461 (1994)	40.8	2.5	20.8

Note: The average annual growth rate assumes a constant rate of growth for each year between those identified.

Source: Compiled from General Reports of the European Commission 1960 ff.; Annual Reports of the Council of the European Communities 1960 ff.; Budgets of the European Communities 1960 ff.; Commission; CELEX Databank.

The Enlargement of Policy Scope: Towards a State-Like Agenda

The scope of both traditional and new public policies has increased considerably since the early 1950s and has been evident at the EU level. The breadth of EU policy sectors is approaching that of a Western European state, especially as the TEU becomes fully operational. The range can be seen in the objectives set for the EU

(TEU, Art. B) and even more so in the objectives and policy areas attributed to the EU (TEC, Arts. 2 and 3). Not only the classical issues of the European Economic Community (EEC), such as the common market, but also the historically core areas of national sovereignty—internal order (third pillar), external defence (second pillar), and monetary autonomy (first pillar)—are addressed in the TEU. In addition, newer areas of public concern, such as environmental issues or consumer protection (TEC, Arts. 130r–t and 129*a*, and see Chapter. 10) are dealt with by EU institutions.

One significant indicator of this scope enlargement is the proliferation of ministerial compositions of the Council and its working groups (see Table 2.2). All important ministries, except defence, have 'their' council. The frequency of their meetings indicates that Brussels has become an important focus for 'technical' or 'domestic' issues.

Because of its increasing bite on a growing range of public policies the EU has turned into a 'regulatory state' (Majone, 1994). It has, however, also started to play a role as a 'distributive state'. The budget available to the EU might look rather limited for general welfare purposes, but it has contributed to a considerable increase in the wealth of some countries and—important for our subject—it offers considerable attractions to lobbyists, especially in times of austerity in national budgets. The fact that EU allocations trigger additional national resources has a multiplier effect which makes the EU even more interesting. The EU has certainly not developed into an alternative to or substitute for national welfare states, but its scope and intensity for financial incentives has grown.

Transfer of Competences: The Evolution of a Mixed System

Competences for state-like public policies have increasingly been transferred upwards to the European level. Several legal methods have been used, including treaty reforms such as the SEA and the TEU, agreed under Article 236 (EEC) (now Article N of the TEU), and more limited adaptations using Article 235 (EEC)—34 in 1990—and legal 'mutations' by the ECJ (Weiler, 1991). This overall evolution is not based on a federally inspired blueprint for framing a state-like constitution, but on 'package deals' (H. Wallace, 1990), which 'pool' several national interests (Keohane and Hoffmann, 1990) in a rather incoherent way. This upward trend has not produced the traditional division of competences, known in classical constitutions as 'dual federalism'. We are instead confronted with a messy and ambiguous vertical division of labour between national and European levels, and with a highly differentiated 'mixture' of public policy instruments located at several levels. Among the most significant examples of this fusion are the 'mixed treaties', such as the Europe agreements with the countries of central and eastern Europe. What Commission officials sometimes call 'partnership' among several levels is variously characterized as *Verflechtung* (Scharpf, 1985), *engrenage* (Poullet and Deprez, 1976), or 'fusion' (Wessels, 1992).

Institutions and Procedures: Growth and Differentiation

The clearest indicator of a long-term trend in the integration process is to be found in the creation and development of EU institutions as well as in the increasing differentiation of procedures within the policy cycle (see Table 2.3). An important characteristic of this institutionalization is the comprehensive and intensive participation of national governments and administrations in all phases of the process. Their involvement has increased quite considerably (see Table 2.2). In 1994 the EU's administrative infrastructure extended to roughly 1,400 highly complex and differentiated committees.

The tendency towards procedural differentiation has been striking. Under the TEU, the various combinations of Council voting modalities and the different forms of involvement by the EP in the policy process, have produced more than 23 distinct procedures for taking binding decisions (see Table 2.4). This number excludes 'soft law' extensions and mutations, such as the increasing number of inter-institutional agreements (Monar, 1994). But the considerable role of EU institutions, independent of national governments, is not replacing national actors. Instead we see an intensive and differentiated incorporation of national actors into the emerging process of integration.

In pursuing their strategies for access and influence national civil servants are intensively involved in those phases of the policy cycle—such as the preparation of proposals (see Table 2.3)—where the Commission enjoys certain prerogatives under the treaties. As part of its internal procedure to support its sole right of initiative,

Table 2.3. *EU Decision-making and implementation*

Level	Decision preparation	Decision-making				Decision implementation		Control	
		Pre-parliamentary deliberations	Parliamentary deliberations	Preparation	Decision-making	Transposition	Implementation	Execution	Control
Interstate level (EU level)	Commission (20 members) *Cabinets* DGs (25) Expert groups (around 600)	Committee of the Regions (222 members) ECOSOC (222 members) Municipalities Regions European associations & ferations	EP (626 members) Party groups (10) Committees (20)	Council Secretariat General	Council Presidency A&B points	Commission supervision	Commission implementation Implementation committees	Commission supervision	Commission jurisdiction
Intrastate (national) level	Civil servants Interest groups		National parliaments Political parties	Coreper and working groups (around 250)	National ministries and administrations	National governments, parliaments, and administrations	Around 300 of 7 basic types	National and regional administrations	National courts

TABLE 2.4. *EU decision-making procedures*

	Council voting modalities									
European Parliament Participation	Unanimity + national ratification	Unanimity	Qualified majority of 8 states	2/3 of weighted votes (minus 1)	Qualified majority	Qualified majority including concerned states	Qualified majority at level of heads of government	Simple majority	Governments of member states	No participation
No active participation	*236 acceptance of treaty revisions*	J.4 (3) security and defence	J.3 (2) CFSP joint action	104c/13 public deficits in MS	*113 (3) trade agreement*			J.8 (2) CFSP procedures	129a (2) co-ordination of national health policies	
Opinion	*201 EC own resources*	100c visa policy					109 final stage of EMU	*236 to call inter-governmental conference*		
Co-operation 189c					130w development co-operation	130o research programmes				
Co-decision 189b		128 culture			100a internal market					

Assent with simple majority of votes cast		228 (3) agreements with third countries	158 (2) appointment of European Commission
Assent with absolute majority of members	*237 new members*	*238/228 association*	
Majority of members			*142 i EP's internal procedures*
Majority of members and 2/3 of votes cast		*203 (4) + (5 b) budget*	203 (8) *budget* 144 dismissal of Commission
Majority of members and 3/5 of votes cast			203 (6) *budget*

Notes: The table shows the range of potential procedures according to the EEC Treaty (italic) and the Maastricht Treaty (roman). Columns show the voting modalities of the Council; rows show EP participation.

Procedures based on inter-institutional agreements are excluded.

This table only contains examples of procedures and does not represent a complete survey.

the Commission has established some 600 expert groups. These serve to ensure that the Commission receives extended information and also as a kind of early warning system for all actors involved (see Chapter 4). Similarly, for the implementation of decisions, the Council has forced upon the Commission around 420 committees composed of national civil servants. There are more than ten different formulae for these committees, giving varying opportunities for national civil servants to delay or to block operational decisions by the Commission. The Council would like to see these reduced to seven basic types (see Council Decision 87/373 of 13 July 1987). In addition, national and Commission officials work closely together in preparing decisions by the Council in its 200 or so working groups (see Table 2.3).

Two separate estimates suggest that roughly 30 per cent of all 'A' grade (dealing with policy) civil servants in the German federal government take part in Brussels meetings and are directly involved in one segment or other of the EU policy cycle as part of their everyday duties (Wessels, 1990). These patterns of interaction touch many sectors and levels of the national administration hierarchy. The proportion of officials directly engaged is probably even larger within smaller member countries. In the German case, civil servants from the regions (*Länder*) are also increasingly involved in all stages of the cycle, though not in all policy fields. To these must be added those who are indirectly involved in the national preparation and implementation procedures. These domestic spill-overs are difficult to calculate, not least because each country has different ways of managing EU business domestically (Wessels and Rometsch, 1996).

It would be one-sided to interpret the involvement of national civil servants as just a 'watch-dog function', or to see them as 'Trojan horses' breaching the Commission's own guard; for the Commission and the member states this interlocking (Poullet and Deprez, 1976) is an important component of a jointly managed policy cycle. The bureaucratization of 'Brussels' is often criticized, but it is a reflection of this multi-level administrative interpenetration. This is not an accidental product of personnel mismanagement or just another example of 'Parkinson's law', which assumes, as does the economic theory of bureaucracy, that such expansion is for the personal advantage of the civil servants involved. On the contrary, this trend is an unavoidable result of the propensity of national politicians and civil servants to find ways of participating intensively in the preparing, making, and implementing of those EU decisions that affect them directly.

The Network of Intermediary Groups: Growing Demands for Access and Influence

Interest Groups. The same kind of logic applies for interest groups. Institutional and administrative patterns are much affected by the way in which intermediary groups of different kinds impinge on the policy cycle of each political system. Parties, economic and non-profit interest groups, and increasingly the media have become key actors in the political systems of Western Europe, as the debate about neo-corporatism has demonstrated (Lehmbruch and Schmitter, 1982; Streeck and Schmitter, 1991). In the EU arena we can observe that some segments of all these intermediary groups are involved in all phases of the policy cycle. Often the scope and intensity of their involvement are similar to those of national civil servants, even though the form may be different. Certain policy fields—such as the common foreign and security policy (second pillar) and justice and home affairs (third pillar)—are of less direct interest to such groups. In this sense the involvement is functional depending on direct interests.

It is not surprising that from the outset interest groups were identified as a significant part of the integration process. Early neofunctionalist theory emphasized their role in the anticipated spill-over process towards further integration (Haas, 1968). Indeed the involvement of 'officially recognized' interest groups developed quite considerably. In all sectors where regulatory and distributive activities are pursued by EU bodies, relevant interest groups have established their networks.

Though the formal structures of most of these groups were inspired by a kind of federal organization in Brussels, in practice a different pattern of internal decision-making has become predominant. Real power has shifted away from the representative bodies in Brussels to meetings of the presidents of national member organizations, often twice per year, and of their secretaries-general, often four times per year. This development is partly reflected in changes to the formal statutes. Indeed, the internal evolution of these associations has mirrored the evolution of governmental structures. We can identify bodies and committees analogous to the European Council, to the Council of Ministers, and to the Committee of Permanent Representatives (Coreper). The secretariats in Brussels largely play the role of initiators and administrators of common policies. As in the political institutions, EU business is thus not only the preserve of some Brussels-based secretariats and small European or international desks at national headquarters; the EU's political space has increasingly involved the secretariats and leaders of national associations. EU issues have thus moved into the centre of attention in many national groups. As in public institutions, resources from both levels have been fused in a nested game, which makes it difficult to measure the relative weight of each actor and level (Héritier, 1993a). It would thus clearly be wrong to conclude that European federations as such are powerless.

In conjunction with these internal adaptations, interest groups redefined their 'European space' dramatically during the 1980s. Both specialization and variations in forms of participation increased, producing an even more complex picture. Several coexisting trends can be observed (Commission, 1992b; Fallik, 1994; Grant, 1993; Kohler-Koch, 1992; 1996; Mazey and Richardson, 1993a; Petite, 1989; Streeck and Schmitter, 1991; Sidjanski and Ayberk, 1990a). Fallik (1994) reveals a highly differentiated and specialized network of private, public, and semi-public actors in the EU political system (see Table 2.1). The largest number of intermediary groups are commercial representations: trade associations (527), business and industry (20), and chambers of commerce (34). Some groups are rather small, representing only a few small firms from a couple of countries, while others comprise large industry associations or trade unions. Most of the larger federations have created extensive networks of working groups to monitor the work of the Commission and Council. Some national associations, such as the German *Bundesverband der Deutschen Industrie* (BDI), although members of EU federations, have strengthened their own Brussels offices at the expense of their collective organizations. In 1994 there were 72 offices of national industry associations and ten national chambers of commerce from EU countries in Brussels. Policy decisions in Brussels apparently became too serious to be left to only a few European experts, especially when there were clashes among national outlooks, such as conflicts within the Union of Industrial and Employers' Confederations of Europe (UNICE) between the pro-free trade BDI and its more protectionist French counterpart.

National associations are not, however, always perceived as sufficient for effective lobbying. Many large corporations have opened their own offices, often with more staff than the European federations. The Daimler-Benz office in Brussels, for example, has more employees than does UNICE. In 1994, 314 corporations had some kind of public affairs office in Brussels. Their interests are too specific and too company-oriented for them to rely on generalists, especially as the larger federations find it difficult to recruit 'real' business people as opposed to 'civil servants' from national interest groups.

The same reasoning explains the growth of specialized consultancies. Those organizations that do not see a need for a permanent presence in Brussels turn to professional agencies which offer access to EU decision preparation and implementation. This category of agencies is very varied encompassing 93 political, 28 management, and 19 public relations consultants, as well as 122 law firms.

Also striking is the personal involvement of top business leaders. The European Round Table of Industrialists (ERT) is the clearest, but certainly not the only, example of their direct engagement (see Chapter. 6).

Semi-Public Interest Groups. These patterns of increasing presence in Brussels do not stop at the traditional set of lobbies. Another group of actors that has entered the EU arena is what one might term semi-public intermediary groups. One such association consists of the 80 regions and local authorities from within the EU that have opened offices in Brussels, some of which are quite large. Regional authorities try to pursue a type of strategic triad. First, they seek formalized access to the European policy cycle, especially via the new Committee of the Regions. This provides rights of representation in the Committee under the new Article 146 of the TEC. They also look for opportunities to participate in expert and working groups. Civil servants from the German *Länder* now participate in about 270 Commission and Council bodies. Second, they lobby the Commission and other member governments directly on specific projects. The competition to win support for regional projects and efforts to influence decisions on subsidies are quite often considerable. The Committee of the Regions is an inadequate channel for such concerns. Third, they seek to increase their influence at the national level. The German *Länder* have been especially successful in establishing constitutional rights to influence or even determine the position of the German federal government in Brussels (see especially Art. 23 of the *Grundgesetz*).

Local authorities are also turning increasingly to Brussels (Seele, 1991). About half of the seats of the Committee of the Regions were awarded to representatives from local bodies. Although local authorities have on the whole fewer and smaller offices in Brussels than do the regions, their influence is not negligible.

National governments and administrations which are themselves pushing more and more for specific interests might also be included among the semi-public actors. The line between being a Council member and a 'lobbyist' is becoming blurred. Direct lobbying takes place on issues such as the location of EU institutions, the filling of Commission posts, and on Commission decisions on mergers and acquisitions or state aids. The direct distributive effects of many decisions taken in Brussels are so large that they attract the direct involvement of national politicians even at the level of heads of government. More and more distributive issues are therefore becoming politicized at the European level.

In addition we should note the efforts by governments of third countries and their diplomatic missions in Brussels. Their representations to the EU cover not only external affairs, but an increasing range of internal EU policies. After all, single market legislation has been seen by many third countries as having the potential to veer towards 'fortress Europe'. Third-country representatives are thus constantly engaged in efforts to mitigate such tendencies. The political weight of these direct interventions, for example by the United States, are often considerable. In addition some 86 international organizations (such as the African, Caribbean, and Pacific (ACP) states and the European Free Trade Area (EFTA)) have offices in Brussels, with a major part of their activities directed towards the EU.

Some 80 regions, associations, chambers of commerce, and law firms from outside the EU are also quite active in the EU's unofficial networks. Brussels is thus an 'open city' for the articulation of interests from outside the EU.

Civic Interests, Parties, and Other Intermediary Actors. Another major characteristic of the EU network of policy actors is how widely it is spread. It includes labour unions (21) and issue-oriented groups (147), such as the Young European Federalists, Amnesty International, Greenpeace, and the World Wide Fund for Nature. (For a discussion of consumer organizations see Chapter. 10). Twelve think-tanks are also active.

In contrast to the growth and specialization of groups supposed to articulate interests an analogous process cannot be observed in those structures supposed to aggregate interests. Parties were late-comers to direct involvement in the integration process and have stayed at a secondary level of importance. The trans-European party federations (Gresch, 1978; Jansen, 1995; Niedermayer, 1985) have evolved over the decades into more structured and active organizations; and have particularly developed activities within the EP. In these networks the weight of national political leaders in shaping policy has also grown considerably. These latter constitute additional informal networks around the EU, especially in preparing sessions of the European Council, now regularly preceded by meetings of Christian Democrat and Socialist leaders. The day-to-day role and impact of these federations is, however, marginal. One reason for this limited influence is that the multi-level game is less easy for them. With the members of the EP playing an increasing role in the Brussels arena, but a limited one on the national playing-field, the party federations have trouble making effective links between the two arenas, not least since the relevant active members often have a lower rank in their national parties and low impact in Brussels. The same argument might be applied to national parliamentarians who have quite inadequate access to the European level. They are clearly the losers in the competition to influence EU decisions.

Visits to Brussels by students, parties, and interest groups indicate, however, that EU institutions have become part of political tourism. Brussels is a political arena which attracts interested segments of public life.

Extensive media attention is another signal of this. The media monitor political events in the EU intensively: 48 press agencies have offices in Brussels, as do 219 specialized journalists from EU countries and 91 from outside the EU, representing all of the major newspapers and television channels. Special news services (such as

Agence Europe) and some major—mainly English-language—newspapers have created a a kind of European 'public news market'; it is, however, limited in its audience. 'Real' communication spaces comparable to those in national political arenas have not yet evolved. Public discourses on Europe and on the EU are still mainly national, as is reporting by the media. Thus it does not play the role in the policy cycle of the EU that has become commonplace in the political life of Western political systems at the end of the twentieth century.

Involvement in the Policy Cycle. Another set of questions is raised by the patterns of involvement and participation by these various actors in the EU policy cycle. The body which approximates to what one expects in a neo-corporatist model, the Economic and Social Committee (ESC), is of limited importance (Morgan, 1991). The concerns of its three main groupings are heterogeneous and the members have preferred more direct, less troublesome, and less time-consuming forms of access to decision-makers in the Commission and Council. Tripartite gatherings have so far also proved rather ineffectual in the EU context.

As for the Committee of the Regions it is too early to make an assessment of its impact. However, its internal cleavages seem to reduce its external effectiveness (Clement, 1995; Hrbek, 1995; Tomuschat, 1995*a*). As with the ESC, the actors that it represents prefer other, less labour-intensive forms of influence. Some, especially the German *Länder*, have created and are operating elaborate sets of institutionalized procedures within the national arena and increasingly favour direct access to EU decision-makers. Given this trend, the attention given to the Committee of the Regions might decrease, as might its reputation. Thus a vicious circle of irrelevance might set in.

Issue-related networks have acquired distinct and sometimes quite formalized patterns; these are especially evident in the areas of social and agricultural policies. The frequency and intensity of their activities resembles their counterparts in national political systems. National civil servants, EU civil servants, and the representatives of economic and social interests form 'golden or iron triangles'. From early on the Commission gave privileged access to EU-wide federations, expecting that these groups would put pressure on national governments. The agricultural networks provide the most articulated example, but not an isolated case; this 'symbiosis' is especially evident in individual agricultural product sectors. Such relationships also operate the other way round. Certain directorates general (DGs) of the Commission are often argued to be 'captured' by the relevant sectoral interests. DGV (employment, industrial relations, and social affairs) is said to be closely connected to trade-union interests, while DGVI (agriculture) has strong links with the Committee of Agricultural Organizations in the European Community (COPA), the agricultural lobby. DGXXIII (enterprise policy, distributive trades, tourism, and co-operatives) is close to small and medium enterprises. In these policy fields some evidence can thus be found of a corporatist mega-bureaucracy, in so far as closely knit networks between civil servants and interest groups can be observed.

Such triangles now often embrace other actors. Committees and party groups of the EP play an increasingly important role, given their considerable say in the budget and, since Maastricht, their real power on major items of European legislation. The EP is more heavily lobbied than ever before. Regional, local, and external actors are entering relevant issue networks, with other links being formed on an *ad hoc* basis for specific and occasional purposes. When decisions are pending on certain projects or grants, regional and national governments, concerned industries and trade unions, members of the European Parliament (MEPs), and Commission officials, as well as party federations, merge into transnational and multi-level coalitions. The 'infrapolitical' networks below the surface of public procedures thus deserve specific attention. The informal contacts are quite extensive: daily telephone calls, luncheons, and dinners are difficult to assess, but 'Brussels' is generally described as being very open, a gateway to influence. The very variety of formal, informal, and personal contacts permits a mobilization of influencing activities that is fast and intensive, as and when required.

Identifying participation in the policy cycle is one thing; assessing relative influence is another. One aspect of the 'power' of persons and groups is the capacity to link several networks at several levels of the EU system. The impact of each player within this multi-level network depends on how effectively support can be gathered in all relevant arenas. A voice only in Brussels will not be sufficient: the home power-base must not be neglected. The chances of influence increase, however, for those with a strong presence in Brussels, since a mutually reinforcing or weakening dynamic is at work. A virtuous or vicious circle comes into sight: the game must be played at more than one level and in more than one network. Without a reputation for being able to sell a compromise at home, players lose influence in Brussels, which in turn reduces their capacity to act for their ministry or interest group, a factor which then further reduces their reputational credit in Brussels.

CONCLUSIONS AND PERSPECTIVES: THE ISSUE-REVISITED

Past Trends

If we take a dynamic and macropolitical view, we can identify several general features. First, we witness growth and differentiation in the EU system. The strong aim of gaining access to the Brussels arena was and is a permanent feature for most actors from national political systems. New actors have entered the political space, including semi-public lobbies. In this process the fragmentation and atomization of interest articulation has increased: rough estimates claiming around 10,000 lobbyists in Brussels (Andersen and Eliassen, 1991; Commission, 1992*b*) seem rather conservative, given what can be gauged of the spread of the intermediary groups' activities. Second, it might be argued that the Commission initially tried to create a clearly structured and EU-wide corporatism. Such a development has been displaced by a highly pluralistic, competitive, multi-level system of networks. The market for influence and access is not closed in the way that neo-corporatists would have predicted. Open competition for scare resources leads to shifting coalitions. We observe few 'frozen' cleavages that lead to permanent coalitions.

In terms of the relevance for integration theory it can be argued that these groupings, and the networks in which they are involved, are both products and producers of a fusion process. The 'old' neofunctional assertion of an inherent logic of interest convergence (Haas, 1968; Hallstein, 1979) has been borne out. In the rational pursuit of their interests, faced with situations of increasing interdependence, industrial and social groups have looked to the EU for regulation in their areas or for securing funding for their projects, in much the same way that Commission officials look for areas in which to expand their activities. On the other hand, some issues within the corporatist arena of concern have hardly been 'communitarized' or Europeanized. Neither collective bargaining nor decision-making on major issues of explicit welfare policy takes place in the Brussels arena. Indeed the business community has specifically sought to prevent this kind of scope enlargement.

The third side of the 'triangle' is much engaged at the EU level: national ministers and their civil servants have realized that EU policies can also serve the needs of their governments. They compete among themselves for access to scarce resources, with Brussels as an arena. The increased activity of regional and local governments in lobbying is another illustration.

The growth of the system, especially through scope enlargement and procedural differentiation, results from this behavioural pattern. Competition among the players prevents the evolution towards a multi-level and corporatist mega-bureaucracy of the kind that early Commission efforts might have created. The rather closely knit networks of civil servants and lobbyists, both across several levels of government, are not able to dominate the policy cycle completely or permanently. Other actors, not least politicians, can and do intervene. We can thus characterize the picture as the Europeanization of national actors and networks; the political space of the EU is not an isolated island far away in Brussels. This is not a small-scale extension of national networks, which would be under constant pressure for renationalization. Only by combining presence, knowledge, and access at each level can you multiply your influence. Only by demonstrating a political weight at the other levels will you be considered an important partner. The 'synergy effect' leads to a virtuous cycle of increasing power and participators; the 'one-level-only-player' will be punished by a vicious cycle of losing influence at that level. The EU political system is thus geared to fusing the national and Brussels arenas.

The pluralistic structure is not, however, optimal for representative government in the sense of producing a new polity. The maze of Brussels, with its undercurrents and networks, increases the complexity and lack of transparency so often noted in commentary on EU policy-making. Many national and European interest groups gain access to it and exert some influence. The result, however, seems to be an imperfect oligopolistic competition, one which creates a kind of new political class and merges EU and national actors in a political process that is increasingly distant from the ordinary citizen. Accountability is possible only to a limited extent. The problem is thus not that the Brussels arena is a 'closed shop', but rather that the new political space in which national and European institutions and groups compete is composed of complex and differentiated networks. The fundamental issue is then how far these actors, including intermediary groups, are perceived as real 'representatives' by, of, and for the citizens. The extent of legitimacy is after all an empirical issue: how far do those represented accept the decisions prepared, taken, and implemented in the EU policy cycle?

Future Scenarios

What kind of scenarios might we then sketch for the future of the Brussels networks? One cautionary remark: an extrapolation of past trends has, at least at first sight, a low degree of academic validity and it is politically risky, as the intense dispute about future options for the EU after Maastricht reveals (H. Wallace and W. Wallace, 1995). However, it seems reasonable to propose as a working hypothesis that neither the fundamental upheavals of 1989 nor the controversies about the TEU have changed the need for some common problem-solving by interdependent welfare states. The accession of the EFTA countries to the EU supports this hypothesis.

Three possible scenarios can thus be envisaged and compared. The first, extrapolated from the fusion thesis, starts from the assumption that economic and monetary union (EMU) and eastern enlargement take place. Major elements of macroeconomic policy—on monetary and increasingly fiscal issues—would be decided within EU bodies. The national governments' room for manœuvre on welfare policies would be *de facto* or even *de jure* curtailed. The problem of unemployment might become so dramatic that more efforts, successful or not, would be taken at the EU level. Within a monetary union there would also be strong pressures for equal wages within particular industries across the EU, and therefore collective bargaining at the European level is a conceivable spill-over from EMU. Also eastern enlargement might generate new policy activities, whether to assist new members or to compensate old ones.

Overall the focus of attention would shift to the EU level. Whatever the constitutional lawyer or political scientist would call the resulting system, the EU would acquire major functions of a welfare and service state. In such a scenario we would expect a further spread of 'golden (or iron) tri- (or quadr-) angles', in which officials from the Commission DGs and from national ministries, interest groups, and, increasingly, key leaders from the relevant EP committees (or their officials) would form strong, sector-oriented, inward-looking, and perhaps 'protectionist' (in several senses) policy communities or networks.

The competition for access and influence among these networks would continue, with intensifying fights over scarce economic resources as the EU enlarged further. Also the competition for political and especially administrative capacities and for decision-making time would extend to additional policy areas and actors. Thus we could expect a trend towards a highly pluralist structure, with several partly competing, partly co-operating actors within policy fields (intra-sectoral) and between them (inter-sectoral). With so large an increase in policy functions at the EU level a more corporatist reflex might set in: national actors might at last attempt to find functional equivalents to their old national patterns.

Such an intensification of participation would epitomize the fusion process, in that to lobby successfully in the Brussels 'bazaar' requires a capacity to play on two or even three pianos at the same time. Regional (where strong), national, and European arenas would not be separate frameworks, as in traditional 'dual federalism', but would merge into a multi-level game demanding that interests are both well organized within each arena and effectively link them. The significance of decisions taken in Brussels will increase the efforts of actors to meet both demands under the constant pressure of competing for influence.

The resulting networks would not only dominate 'Brussels' but would also 'spill-down' to national arenas. The competition for access and influence would also affect the national distribution of influence and power. Those who operate only at home would tend to lose out, not only in the European arena but also in relation to those competitors in the national political system who succeed in gaining access at several levels. As the German *Länder* (and other actors) have demonstrated, late-comers can be quite successful in entering the game, provided that they are prepared to invest in monitoring EU business, in their regional and national capitals as well as in Brussels. Networks would thus become even more Europeanized than before in a broad sense (Wessels and Rometsch, 1996*a*). From a comparative perspective this trend also implies that national patterns of intermediary groups are converging in significant respects towards a similar European pattern.

A contrasting scenario is one in which the state retreats from major internal and external functions. Individual European states would increasingly compete with each other for the best chances of adapting to economic globalization. Efforts to regain forms of public policy by co-operation or even integration, such as through the EMU, would be considered inadequate responses to the demands of the international system. 'Brussels' would turn into an empty political space, as intermediary groups lost interest in participating in the European arena.

A third scenario might be public politicization, with Maastricht representing a fundamental shift away from previous trends. Increased public and political attention to the policy process in Brussels would expose EU decisions to public debates. The old 'permissive consensus' for European integration (Inglehart, 1971; Reif, 1993) would be replaced by a broad and intensive politicization; this would include a closer scrutiny from a broader group of political forces, national media, and national parties and parliaments. Though Brussels was always an 'open city', only those directly concerned took it seriously, since high direct entry costs and low direct benefits made it difficult for some actors to move into the Brussels arena. This cost–benefit assessment could change fundamentally, as not only functional considerations about access, but also issues of the 'legitimacy' of the EU provoke participation. Brussels might then turn into a besieged city. The evolution of the 1980s, which produced a maze of networks and procedures, provoked reactions from 'outsiders'. Some actors, such as the regions, may have already successfully invaded (or infiltrated) the web of networks and others, including national parliaments, might follow. Other actors, such as the media, might attack the EU system from the outside.

The legitimacy gap would induce policy actors to vie for public attention. The ability to operate in multi-level committee rooms would no longer suffice; they would now have to master the political market-place and television studios. Thus the trends of the past might continue, but might, under changed conditions, acquire a different nature. In this scenario the fundamental issue would be constitutional, namely how to define an optimal polity for such a multi-level system.

3

Organized Interests in European Integration: The Evolution of a New Type of Governance?[1]

BEATE KOHLER-KOCH

The role of organized interests has changed throughout the long process of West European integration. This is no surprise in that the creation of the European Community (EC) had a deep impact on the two environments, which, it is argued, shape the logic of interest intermediation (Schmitter and Streeck, 1981): the 'logic of membership', the material conditions under which actors are constituted and operate; and the 'logic of influence', i.e., the institutional structure and prevailing processes within the relevant political arena. It is a commonplace that the organization of interest representation has adjusted to the changing conditions of European integration. What is contested is whether this has been just an adjustment process or whether the way private interests have been configured has shaped the polity and politics of Europe as well.

In this chapter I examine three competing propositions. The first is that organized interests have been driving forces of European integration. The second starts from the opposite assumption and argues that the organization of interests simply followed the development of the EC, only recently taking the form of 'co-evolution' (Eichener and Voelzkow, 1994a). The third is that private interests have contributed to the institutional transformation and perhaps to the evolution of a new form of governance in Europe. From the assessment of the behaviour of organized interests we can derive important insights into the character of governance in Western

[1] I would like to thank Rainer Eising for his critical comments.

Europe more broadly. The arguments set out in this chapter find further substantiation when one examines other kinds of political actors.

PRIVATE INTERESTS: DRIVING FORCES OF SUPRANATIONAL INTEGRATION?

From the outset, the interrelation between interests and integration has preoccupied those who wanted to grasp the dynamics of the EC process. In the neofunctionalist debate, élites—and especially the representatives of organized interests—ranked high among the driving forces behind regional integration. Whenever the EC gathered momentum again and analysts asked what had prompted the new initiative or which forces had promoted the process, the neofunctional reasoning about the importance of private interests was adduced. A well received argument to explain the successful launching of the single market programme, for instance, was that 'the effort to reshape the European Communities has so far been guided by three groups'—industrial élites forming a transnational business coalition being one (Sandholtz and Zysman, 1989: 128). These élites were viewed as supporting the Commission's efforts and exercising an 'indispensable influence on governments'.

This is not the place to recapitulate the different ramifications of neofunctional theory. Rather, my intention is to recall some of its original findings in order to answer three very pertinent questions. Have private interests been the driving forces of European integration? What have their objectives been? Which interests have exerted influence?

When Haas defined 'political integration' as 'the process whereby political actors in several distinct national settings are persuaded to shift their loyalties, expectations and political activities toward a new centre, whose institutions possess or demand jurisdiction over the pre-existing national states' (E. Haas, 1968: 16), he assigned an important role in this process to organized interest groups. This did not, however, imply that they made a crucial contribution to the setting up of a 'collective decision-making system'—which is what Lindberg later defined as an equivalent to political integration (Lindberg, 1970: 650).

In his writing, Haas rather describes and systematically elaborates the conditions for the gradual political adjustment of economic élites to a supranational governmental agency 'which is accepted as given, from whom favours must be asked and advantages extracted, or whose policies must be opposed' (E. Haas, 1968: 353 f.). The support (of trade unions) or opposition (of companies and trade associations) was not irrelevant, but the European Coal and Steel Community (ECSC), with its High Authority, was agreed and set up by governments at the strong request of senior political actors. It was a response to a particular constellation of external and internal challenges and was aimed at preserving peace and security as well as strengthening national social welfare through economic reconstruction. International co-operation looked very promising indeed as both efficient and a means of preventing cut-throat competition between neighbouring states. That the ECSC took the form of a supranational organization was, however, due to conditioning factors which were no longer valid when the European Economic Community (EEC) was negotiated only a few years later. In the case of ECSC, these were all conducive to the consensus in support of strong political regulation of market forces, with state planning favoured as the best way to tackle the problems of economic reconstruction. State intervention was considered to be inevitable for two reasons: first, to compensate for market failures, which were endemic in the coal and steel industries; and, second, to counter international private cartels in the sector.[2]

The main function of the High Authority, therefore, was political regulation, operating as an instrument for the member states to internationalize regulatory powers over private industry so as to enhance economic efficiency and stability. The reactions of industry accordingly ranged from outright opposition (especially by the coal- and steel-producing industries) to selective and partial support (notably from steel consumers). The regulated industries learned to accommodate the *fait accompli*, but remained critical of supranational 'bureaucracy' and *dirigisme*. The business world, as well as trade unions, had been in favour of some kind of integration and closer international co-operation, but they had no part in framing the particular institutions for this experiment.

[2] In his famous declaration, Robert Schuman referred explicitly to the danger and shortcomings of those international private cartels (Schuman, 1950).

As for the next question—what kind of interests exert influence—the hard evidence runs counter to much of the conventional wisdom in studies of the role and importance of European-level interest groups. As long as integration is about free trade, the free flow of investment and capital goods, there is limited need for organized collective action. Meeting the challenges of the market is strictly the stuff of company strategies; industrial associations have no place in this except as instruments to deal collectively with political actors.[3] As long as the regulatory powers of the EC remained limited, there was no need to strengthen the institutional structures for concerted action. Most European interest groups were federations of national associations and the few European associations with direct company membership were little more than clubs. Both types of organizations simply set the institutional framework for what at best could be called 'inter-organizational diplomacy' between sovereign members. It was always unrealistic to assume that such organizations could become political actors in their own right and play a major initiating role in the integration process. In past decades it always was the national actors who were the core of the multinational interest organizations and not the rather frail superstructures at the European level that were the driving forces of European integration.

The density of European interest organizations, therefore, cannot in itself be taken as an indicator of the potential dynamics of integration. In his early writings Haas elaborated that point, arguing that the willingness of interest groups to co-operate and support supranational decision-making was 'the result of convergences of separate perceptions of interest and not a spontaneous surrender to the myth of the common good' (E. Haas, 1964: 34). A similar socio-economic milieu and comparable international challenges can predispose economic actors to develop parallel interests and to join in common actions in order to safeguard their individual interests. They would 'outgrow dependence on and loyalty to the national state' (E. Haas, 1968: 354), but this would neither be accompanied by a renunciation of autonomy in favour of concerted action nor

---

[3] The exception proves the rule: the European Association of Saving Banks was from the very beginning quite active in promoting the economic interests of the affiliated companies. It could do so only because, and as long as, the economic activities of saving banks were regionally confined and therefore nobody could gain a competitive advantage which might be to the detriment of others.

with a demand for 'far-reaching series of policies realisable only in the framework of supranational institutions' (E. Haas, 1968: 287).

For that very reason the level of lobbying activities is not a valid indicator of the propensity of interests to support further integration. The present inflationary increase in interest representation at the European level can tell us little about the future deepening of the EC. Thus theoretical reasoning and empirical evidence confirm the proposition that the European organization of interests grew in response to, and not in advance of, integrative steps, and that European interest groups, in particular, were not the driving forces of regional integration.

Even though the organization of European interests has been more a process of adaptation than of system-formation, it has become part of the EC system and influences the daily life of EC policy-making. Organized interests thus also take part in shaping the European polity.

TOWARDS A CO-EVOLUTION OF SYSTEMS?

The question which follows is whether, and to what extent, the organization of European interests has followed the political integration process and adjusted to the institutional development of the politico-administrative system of the EC. In other words, what evidence is there of a 'co-evolution' of the two systems. Several factors support the argument that the European system of interest intermediation is highly dependent on the 'logic of influence' and that interest organizations reacted to political system formation.[4]

Their development in time and space followed the phases of integration. There were two major turning points: at the end of the 1960s, with the change from negative to positive integration; and in the latter half of the 1980s, with the Single European Market (SEM) programme, the Single European Act (SEA), and the Treaty on European Union (TEU).

With the passage from customs union to common market, changes took place at all levels: European federations gradually

---

[4] For a more detailed account see Kohler-Koch (1992) and Eising and Kohler-Koch (1994).

turned from dining clubs into working stations; and national interest groups ceased to regard European affairs as part of their foreign relations, including them instead in the necessary daily routine of each desk officer. Problems of internal co-ordination and control arose within national organizations and, more severely, *vis-à-vis* the European associations, prompting or-ganizational reforms aimed at improving the efficiency and the responsiveness of the European groups to the needs and demands of their national members. Companies which had previously left the monitoring of European policies to their associations began to monitor more closely what was going on in Brussels. Organiza-tional reforms secured big business's direct say in the umbrella and in sectoral organizations of the European industry (see Chapter 6).

With the SEM programme, the transfer of new responsibilities to the EC, and an increase in their decision-making power, the EC institutions attracted an ever larger number of bodies representing European interests. National associations, as well as powerful individual actors, tried to establish direct channels of access. New actors—including public authorities, voluntary organizations, and single issue groups—entered the field. Although the precise patterns varied between sectors, they broadly followed the same logic.

The structures and strategies of interest intermediation have come to exhibit the characteristic features of the EC system: the multi-layer structure; the combination of supranational and intergovern-mental elements in decision-making; the changing participants and constellations of actors during the course of the policy-making cycle; the distribution of decision-making powers among the EC institutions, as well as their individual organizational properties; and the distinctive rules, procedures, and practices of European policy-making. Interest groups adapted to the multi-layer character of the EC by establishing organizations at all levels, building direct channels of contact to supranational as well as to national political actors, and seeking involvement in all the relevant transnational and supranational policy networks. They all pursue a 'dual strat-egy', striving for access through national governments as well as directly to the Community institutions. The combination of multi-ple channels of access is mandatory, because, in the course of the policy-making cycle, the arena changes. Agenda-setting and policy formulation are EC affairs, whereas implementation takes place at the national level. Even though the locus of policy-making may be unequivocal, procedures vary according to subject-matter and distribute the decision-making powers between EC organs in different ways. It would therefore be a short-sighted strategy just to concentrate on one EC institution. In addition, the extended committee system which supports and channels the work of the Commission has a strong component of intergovernmentalism which makes a dual strategy even more compulsory. The resulting omnipresence of interest representatives adds to the complexity of the EC system.

Another key feature of the EC system that is reproduced in the organization of interest representation at the European level is its functional segmentation. It has been brought about by the process of piecemeal integration that has added specific functional tasks to the EC's domain. And it has been aggravated by the functional differentiation of the Council and the increasing autonomy of the Commission's Directorates General (DGs). The specialized councils, just like the individual DGs, have, over time, developed their own policy philosophies, styles of policy-making, and networks of interests. Broadly based interest organizations find it difficult to cope with this system, because they cannot be as closely linked to issue-specific networks as sectoral interest groups. Sectoral organizations more easily gain access and find it more rewarding to become part of the game. The proliferation of interest groups with narrow sectoral interests and the mushrooming representation of individual companies mirror the segmented structure of the EC.

Last but not least, the EC is a technocracy in the sense that political hegemony cannot be established by fighting ideological battles in the political market-place. Success depends much more on the actor's capacity to provide what is most needed to induce acceptance of appropriate solutions to problems: expert knowledge, political insight, and bargaining experience. The Commission disposes of only limited resources and is therefore particularly open to external expert advice. It therefore attracts and organizes a dense net of consultation, including all kinds of interested parties. Inter-expert bargaining is the essence of the game of successful interest intermediation.

The European Parliament (EP) is also much attached to developing good working relations with interest groups. Members of Parliament (MEPs) particularly appreciate the expertise that interest groups can provide.[5] They look to this expertise and support in order to strengthen the EP's position *vis-à-vis* the Council and, if necessary, the Commission.

A *'market without a state'* (Joerges, 1991) may be an exaggerated characterization of the EC, but it is nevertheless pertinent. The basic philosophy of the treaties remains dominant: welfare will be provided by the economic growth accruing from the economics of a common market and not from the regulatory and distributive capacity of governments. The market and economic policies are at the heart of EC policy-making. Consequently, it is the representatives of industry, commerce, and the service sector that can contribute most to the management of the EC. They have to be drawn into the policy networks because they provide necessary expertise and because effective implementation depends on their support. Many structural impediments make it harder for labour, environmental, or consumer interests to organize and represent their interests successfully in a transnational setting (see Chapter 10), as the 'logic of integration' has been detrimental to their case. The contrasting over-representation of producer interests has been shaped, though not determined, by the particular properties of the EC system. Moreover, the evidence, though not presented here in detail, strongly supports the argument that European interest organization depends heavily on the logic of influence. Any transfer of power or change in the institutional system has had a strong impact on the structures and processes of interest intermediation.

A complex system of trans- and supranational interest representation has emerged; this not only shares the characteristic features of the EC system as such, but it seems to reinforce those characteristics and aggravate its weaknesses. Policy analysts have produced a number of detailed studies on how these layers of activity are interconnected, resulting in a very particular type of interest

---

[5] In a recent survey (Kohler-Koch and Schaber, 1996) of MEPs' attitudes to lobbying, 80% of the respondents said that the benefit of interest groups is that they provide expert information. Only a few MEPs value their support for grass-roots activities or in aggregating divergent interests.

intermediation. However, the hypothesis that there is a distinct co-evolution of political, administrative, and associational structures still rests on a rather weak empirical foundation.[6]

It is also an open question whether this co-evolution has been a productive institutional innovation, in the sense of increasing the problem-solving capacity of the EC,[7] or whether it tends to make the decision-making process even more unwieldy. Just as disputed is the idea that, with the growing importance of EC integration, a coherent European system of interest intermediation will emerge. It will be of particular interest to ascertain whether institutional co-evolution is a phenomenon only in the realm of 'low politics' and is confined to regulatory policies. If this were the case, even across a broad range of policy areas, the impact of co-evolution on the shape of the EC system, as well as on the transformation of governance in Europe, would clearly be limited.

MULTI-FACETED ASPECTS OF INTEREST INTERMEDIATION AND GOVERNANCE IN EUROPE

The possible future trends of European interest organizations are still unclear. Because our knowledge is based on scattered case studies, taken from different policy areas and time periods, it is difficult to formulate general conclusions. We can to some extent draw on theoretical perspectives to assess the plausibility of these competing propositions. These approaches are institutional, power-structure, and discursive.[8] Each highlights different aspects of reality and suggests the normative implications from a different point of view.

---

[6] Eichener (1993; 1996) and Voelzkow (1993) have developed this argument based on a thorough investigation of technical harmonization in the fields of labour, consumer, and environmental protection. This is only a narrow field of social regulation which in itself is not at the heart of EC policy-making.

[7] Eichener and Voelzkow (1994*a*) have argued that this 'co-evolution' helped the EC to develop innovative regulations at a high level of protection.

[8] With the introduction of practices of 'lean management' a new discussion about the nature and prospects of *diskursive Koordinierung* (discursive coordination) is evolving in German academic circles (Braczyk and Scheinstock, 1996). The term 'discursive' refers to this discussion.

The Power of Institutions

In EC studies, there is no need for a call 'to bring institutions back in'. Their importance is well acknowledged and has been tested in empirical studies, especially with regard to the organization of interests. Congruent distributions of interests and of power played a role in the formation of European interest representation, but its distinctive form and way of operating were shaped by the power of institutions. This has fostered the evolution of very particular characteristics, which feed back into the EC system and increase its fragmentation and segmentation. The European system of interest intermediation is characterized by the multitude of heterogeneous actors, who have divergent policy styles and lobbying practices, are linked only loosely in overlapping networks, engage in shifting coalitions, and move within and across the different levels of the EC system. These features add to the complexity and to the lack of transparency of the EC policy process.

The deficiencies of such a system—a lack of coherence, efficiency and accountability—are quite obvious. One of the main inferences is that the trends of functional segmentation inherent in the organizational structures of the EC's institutions are reinforced by the emergence of closed policy communities. Those that embrace the relevant representatives of public and private interests from both the European and national levels have a tendency to become exclusive and to ward off any external interference in their efforts at problem-solving. To develop coherent policies among narrow policy areas becomes even more difficult and unwieldy. In areas where encompassing policy communities do not exist, policy outputs are difficult to predict because the policy networks and constellations of actors change from one stage of the policy process to the next.

There is little agreement on whether the fragmentation of the system will decline over time and what role the EC institutions might play in the evolution of the system. Some authors (Andersen and Eliassen, 1991) consider it reasonable to predict that a more structured system with stronger corporatist elements will evolve. Others (Mazey and Richardson, 1993b) predict that it is likely that policy-making within the EC, though still sectorally structured, will become more 'manageable'. They argue that the Europeanization of the policy process will trigger processes of adaptation which will lessen the cross-national differences in interest intermediation, that the increase in interest representation will put pressure on the European policy-makers to introduce some form of institutionaliz- ation so as to make it more manageable, and that the 'European Polity' model, which is based on patterns of co-option, will gain strength (Mazey and Richardson, 1993*b*).

I hold the opposite view. Strong push factors—the eagerness of interests to enter the European arena, to adjust to the rules of the game, and to become accepted and influential players—as well as pull elements—European institutions giving active support to the organization of European interests in order to meet their own functional needs—may well be present. However, it is unlikely that a convergent European system of interest intermediation will emerge, or that strong interest associations will develop at the transnational level with wide and encompassing remits, or that the emergent new structures will adapt smoothly to the functional needs of supranational governance. The main argument for this critical view is that with the growing importance of the EC,* the association of interests in the European context is no longer a supplementary exercise to politics at the local, regional, or national levels. To associate with like-minded groups across borders is an act of integration which, I argue, necessarily provokes disintegra- ting effects in the home environment. Operating across borders is difficult not just because of the high transaction costs. More import- antly, borders contain and stabilize integrated national systems. Interests cannot associate freely; they are bound by the legal and institutional setting which they inhabit. Each European organiza- tion has to devise its own optimal strategy to cope with the disrup- tive effects in the national environments produced by more intense European co-operation. It has to take into account the condition- ing effects of established institutional systems and practices of in- terest intermediation, of traditional modes of behaviour, and of the accumulated capital of mutual trust in and experience with existing relationships among its members.

Therefore it does not follow that the growing importance of European integration will produce a common European system. On the contrary, institutional transformations remain dependent on the persistence of national institutional constellations. The future is path-dependent in the sense that the process of Euro- peanization will take different shapes and create different types of entities. The complexity of the system, therefore, will not vanish with the progress of integration.

This complexity can impede efficient decision-making. Even when decisions can be taken by qualified majority vote, the EC does not actually function according to the rules of a hierarchical system. Decisions continue to be reached through horizontal negotiations in overlapping networks. Indeed it has been strongly argued that a system of this kind easily leads to deadlock because of the 'joint-decision trap' (Scharpf, 1988), and that it is inefficient and produces sub-optimal results. Theoretical reasoning based on game theory (Scharpf, 1994; 1996*b*) and empirical research covering different European policy areas (Eichener, 1996; Grande, 1994; 1996; Héritier *et al.*, 1994) has, however, come to the conclusion that efficiency will not necessarily suffer from the decision-making induced by complex negotiating systems. The co-ordination of multiple players is, after all, not a feature unique to European policy-making. It is prevalent in any federal system and under constitutions with strong checks and balances. It is daily practice even in unitary states based on party government. Welfare states cannot induce powerful corporate actors to behave co-operatively by insisting on majority rule; they rather try to secure support by negotiating mutual commitments. Bringing competing interests into the policy process and negotiating with them over strategies to solve problems is not *per se* detrimental to the efficiency of policy-making. Keeping policy networks open and supporting the capacity of interests to organize and to articulate their demands can even ensure a high level of political responsiveness. In particular, the Commission has actively promoted the organization of the less represented social interests in order to achieve more balanced participation (see Chapter 10).

A broader representation of partisan interests in the policy-making process is not, however, a generally accepted substitute for public political control. Protracted negotiations within networks and committees may enhance responsiveness, but not political responsibility. Formal decisions are taken by governments' representatives in the Council, but in the vast majority of cases this is just a formal act of consent.[9] This is not to say that member

[9] A recent empirical study, based on the minutes of the Council of Ministers for Agriculture, gives strong evidence for the 'rubber-stamping' function of Council decisions at ministerial level (van Schendelen, 1995).

governments have little importance in decision-making. But it is not the politically responsible minister, sitting in the Council, who negotiates the compromise. Rather, agreements are reached on the basis of bureaucratic transnational negotiations and inter-institutional bargaining;[10] and it is usually almost impossible to trace where in the myriad committees a particular compromise evolved. Above all, no single actor can be held responsible. Despite several rulings by the European Court of Justice (ECJ), which has stressed the judicial responsibility and accountability of the EC organs, EC governance functions by committee; 'comitology' predominates.

From a normative point of view, the main objection is the lack of political accountability. The strong criticism is that this kind of system does not meet democratic standards and that European governance will, despite a high level of performance, not produce political legitimacy. It is quite obvious that political control and public participation cannot be introduced according to the rules and procedures of the member states' democracies. Strategies to improve the political accountability of the system cannot, there-fore, be limited to measures increasing the power of the EP, but must start from the realities of the existing system. Political actors within the EC, as well as external observers, often advocate an even closer collaboration between EC institutions and interest groups. The principle of 'partnership' in regional and environmen-tal policies, for example, has been introduced to increase the effi-ciency of EC programmes, as well as to bridge the gap between EC institutions and citizens. To take another example, the Commission advocated strongly that the European standards bodies (CEN and CENELEC) be opened to affected interests. Especially in the field of interest intermediation the Commission has been very active, and has pursued institutional innovations. It has been engaged in active 'networking', that is in encouraging decentralized grass-roots activities within individual member countries and in strength-ening them with transnational links. Numerous case-studies have pointed out that the Commission manages quite well to select and to aggregate interests so as to fight any overload of pluralist pressure or clientelist demand. Steps have also been taken to in-

---

[10] Inter-institutional bargains between the Council and the EP have recently provoked an open debate about the legitimacy of this kind of policy-making (Miller, 1995).

crease the transparency and thereby the accountability of decision-making.

Yet what at first sight looks like the successful strategy of a political entrepreneur to work in favour of greater efficiency, transparency, and accountability, becomes more questionable if one takes a closer look. It was the Council that put pressure on the Commission to increase transparency. The Commission made a procedural response, focused on how it handled information and its relationships with external actors (Commission, 1992*a*; 1992*b*). It is establishing some general rules for structuring its dialogue with interest groups, as is the EP (Greenwood and McLaughlin, 1995). Yet it is unlikely that either development will lead to a restructuring of the European system of interest intermediation. *Ad hoc* responses can have only limited effects if they are not in line with the overarching institutional setting. In any case, both institutions advocate an 'open' dialogue with interest groups (Commission, 1993*a*) and publicly declare that they do not want to put up any 'barriers' (Collins, 1995). The Secretary General of the Commission is on the record as saying that lobbies and interest groups are important for the Commission's work because they 'provide expert advice and through their intermediary functions they provide an opportunity to communicate European policies at grass root level' (Williamson, 1995).

The Commission's active engagement in networking[11] will hardly render the system of interest intermediation more manageable, as this will add new transnational networks, and not replace the existing ones (Kohler-Koch, 1996). Change would be more likely to result from broader institutional reform than from strategies aimed at group representation. It was not, for example, an explicit design on the part of the EP that strengthened groups representing environmental, consumer, and human rights interests, but rather the unintended by-product of the increase in the EP's powers. The EP is the natural ally of such groups, not because MEPs necessarily favour their demands, but because their interests match. MEPs are eager to take up those issues which attract a broad public interest and are grateful for any external support which mobilizes public

---

[11] In addition to the well-known cases of industrial policy, research and technology, and regional policy, there are telling case-studies from such policy areas as health (Altenstetter, 1994), culture (Schubert and Bandelow, 1994), and welfare (Loges, 1994; Schmid, 1994).

attention, because this will increase their political weight in the decision-making process. In the short run this strategy is assumed to increase EP influence on particular policies; in the longer run it is a lever for gaining political power and authority. MEPs and interest groups share an interest in building up their strength and therefore in giving each other support, as numerous case-studies about consumer protection, environmental policies, and animal protection illustrate.[12]

Generalizations from policy analysis have to be seen in proper perspective, because they tend to overemphasize endogenous factors and the 'action-capacity' of EC bodies. There is, in particular, a tendency to attribute an influential role to the Commission as a 'process manager' (Eichener, 1993). Although the Commission is a central player, it often lacks the resources of staff and expertise to live up to expectations of its impact as initiator and broker of EC policies. Moreover, institutional reforms do not result from incremental innovations from within; they are still under the political control of member governments, who remain 'masters of the treaty'.

Another aspect that is easily lost from sight is that the EC system is part of a broader political architecture in that the European Union (EU) rests on three pillars and not just on one. Therefore the question has to be asked whether characteristics particular to the policy process of the EC will persist, as European policies expand into the functional domains of international relations and external and internal security. Would it not be more plausible to expect that intergovernmentalism will encroach upon the *Economic* Community? On issues where a consensus can be found only by striking a bargain across different functional domains, neither the Commission nor a single specialized Council will be in charge. Broad package deals are the business of the European Council, by law and by practice the most intergovernmental body of the EU. There is another reason to question the automatic evolution of institutional dynamics. The common foreign and security policy will require mechanisms of enforcement. Whereas the organization of economic welfare has for decades been considered amenable to collect-

---

[12] This evidence is based on a research project at Mannheim on 'Pressures on the European Parliament', exploring the relationship between interest groups and the EP by means of a written survey and several case-studies (Kohler-Koch and Schaber, 1996).

ive management, the organization of security remains an affair of the state and an expression of national sovereignty. In the context of the EU as a whole, the pattern of inter-bureaucratic networking, which includes organized interests, is only part of the game; it cannot be expected to determine the shape of the polity as a whole.

Power and Interest

For the 'realist' approach intergovernmentalism is the whole picture; 'EC policies are the continuation of domestic policies by other means' (Moravcsik, 1991: 25). The basic assumption is that the result of intergovernmental bargaining is determined by the constellation of national interests and the relative power position of the participating states. Supranational institutions have a role to play, but are limited to 'cementing existing interstate bargains' (Moravcsik, 1991: 56). The role of interest groups is conceived of as that of intermediaries between their members and policy-makers, as dependent on their constituencies as on the distribution of power and interest in the political arena. Associations will be formed on the basis of the rational choices of individual actors, according to their own preferences and capacity to exert effective pressure. The future of interest intermediation and governance in Europe will depend not on the institutionalization of co-operation and conflict, but on the strength of the underlying political forces. It will be shaped by the 'realities' of power structures and by the degree to which interests of governments and influential private actors concur.

State actors and economic actors have parallel interests in so far as the international competitiveness of important economic sectors is decisive for national competitiveness, which is the foundation of international strength and status as well as of domestic welfare and stability. The influence of corporate actors on state policies derives less from their associational strength or the resources that they can mobilize to lobby government, and more from their contribution to the performance of the economy. The nature and extent of government support for industry depends on national traditions of industrial policy and on how economic challenges are faced. If the dominant economic philosophy is in favour of a strong hand for the state in industrial policy, governments are more inclined to back 'national champions'. France has a long record of giving powerful political protection to the interests of French industry, while the UK and Germany, especially in periods of conservative government, apparently prefer a neo-liberal line. However, as soon as an issue is defined as a problem of national industrial competitiveness, the political leaning of a government makes little difference. The French did not abandon their national strategy in the early 1980s because they had converted to a more liberal philosophy, but because, in the face of growing global competition, a national strategy seemed doomed to failure whereas as a European strategy looked more promising (see Chapter 7). In addition, we should note that the Commission, ever since Étienne Davignon held the industry portfolio from 1977 to 1985, has been very responsive to demands from governments and industry to strengthen the competitiveness of European firms.

Large firms find it easy to become privileged interlocutors of the political-administrative system, thanks to their economic importance, while small and medium-sized firms rely more heavily on their collective force. Only a common problem brought collectively to the attention of government will induce political reaction. State support, however, is not dependent on successful lobbying by interest associations. The latters' activities may serve only to make a given problem more public, to stress its urgency, and to put it into the 'right' perspective. Governments generally react when the problem raised is a collective one, because only then will it have consequences for the economy as a whole. In the international economy, small and medium enterprises are even less able to opt out and to go their own way. This is not so much due to their lack of organizational skill and resources for establishing new networks, but rather because their share of the market is too small for their problems to be taken into account by political actors, if they act on their own.

Because associations derive their strength from their constituencies they are not able—from a realist point of view—to gain power of their own. Multinational corporations did not seek to reform the Union of Industrial and Employers' Confederations of Europe (UNICE) in order to exert control over an institution that might have become too self-confident, but rather in order to strengthen it. The reform was brought about, and a new consensus forged, not by the association itself or by its national affiliates, but by the European multinationals. The story told by Maria Green Cowles in this volume (see Chapter 6) is that of a few leading business people endeavouring to manage the collective industrial interest representation in Europe.

Does this imply that 'big business' will outgrow the nation-state and that its predominance at the European level will lead it to favour increased supranationalism? To find the answer one has to take a look at the economic rationality of such a strategy. It can be questioned, because even the enlarged EC is not the optimal space for economic activity. By and large, business interests are not focused on Europe; they have to face international, that is global, competition. Any company that is transnational in character has to ensure that it can meet the technical and legal norms and standards which regulate access to the most attractive markets. For European firms these are necessarily the large and prosperous markets of Japan and the United States, because they have innovative capacities and will be trend-setters for conquering global markets. Especially in high-tech industries, European business has to be present in the most important economic and political arenas abroad to protect its interests. Here too only transnational corporations of considerable economic weight have the resources to build international coalitions or to become important players in their own right. Such associations as they form often rest upon a longer history of industrial collaboration (as in the steel industry) or are based on strategic alliances to develop a new technology (as in the information and electronics industries). The latter tend to be informal and temporary. Companies look for coalition partners especially when public regulations (consumer and environmental protection, and health and safety at work) impinge sharply on business interests, or when firms are heavily dependent on agreed new standards for technologically advanced products. Sometimes they find them in the business community and form a 'grand coalition' between competitors, as was the case in the consumer electronics industry with the establishment of new television systems (Cawson, 1994).

Governments also play a role in such inter-firm collaborations by supporting or even initiating them. It was the Bush administration that decided to ask the Federal Communications Commission (FCC) to take a role in selecting the appropriate new standard for high-definition television (HDTV), and it was at the invitation of the chairman of the FCC's advisory committee that competitors came together to agree on a single common format as a standard

(Cawson, 1994). This case is particularly telling, as it was the US initiative which was finally successful, and not the competing European coalition of public policy-makers and industry, which had pursued a different concept (for a detailed discussion of this episode see Chapters 7 and 9).

The existence of the Single European Market and the European institutions, especially the Commission, is of course relevant. The Commission's role, however, is more that of a facilitator of co-operation and collaboration, in order to propagate and endorse positions taken by governments and industry, than that of a political actor of equal standing. Its influence is enhanced when its role changes from guarantor of specific company interests to that of broker. In the case of advanced television the initiative was left to the private sector. Some national governments gave industry strong backing (with EC subsidies), and the role of the Commission was 'to help to sustain the consensus in order to reduce uncertainty and co-ordinate the investments required for successful innovation' (Cawson, 1994: 8).

In general, national administrations are the main interlocutors of interest groups, because their positions are decisive, even with qualified majority voting in the Council and the co-decision power of the EP. What has changed is that national interest groups can no longer rely on the veto power of 'their' government, but have to gain the support of a blocking minority in the Council. Even under unanimity, interest groups were well advised to win the consent of as many Council members as possible to guard against adverse trade-offs ensuing from package-deals. When organized interests strive for a powerful presence in the EC, it is certainly not to support integration or supranationalism, but rather to find additional channels—such as the EC institutions or governments other than their own—through which to defend their interests.

Organizing at the European level cannot redress the balance of power between interests that stems from differences in economic strength. Just as effective co-ordination mechanisms merely make European multinationals' joint interests and aggregated weight more visible, institutional reforms in favour of weaker interest groups will have only marginal effect. The relative power of capital and labour is not altered by the fact that trade-union bodies are subsidized by the Commission, or granted the opportunity to take part in working groups and committees, or offered a 'social dialogue'. The intensity of international competition, by driving national governments to deregulation and enterprises to engage in 'lean production', has weakened trade unions as badly as the growing social differentiation of the labour force. Economic and social realities cannot be redressed by institutional tinkering; a strong EC trade-union association would not solve this problem (Gorges, 1993).

The only remedy might be to strengthen governments. Subsidiarity, as it is conceptualized in the literature (practice may be different), would give member governments more autonomy in responding to problems as they arise and according to their definitions of public interest, drawing on the assumption that governments really can act as mediators. There is some evidence that, contrary to popular belief, governments and their administrations are not subdued by the forceful actors they meet in European affairs, but that they can take advantage of the 'two level game' (Putnam, 1988) in European policy-making. The loss of freedom of action by governments that results from being entangled in European decision-making networks, has the paradoxical effect that they gain autonomy in relation to their national environment, because joint decision-making allows them to ward off pressures from domestic interests.

The basic assumption of such arguments is that states follow their own political logic which is vested in maintaining system stability. Accordingly—with a few deplorable exceptions—governments tend not to intervene in favour of those partial interests that lack an economic rationale. Public policy has to take account of the functioning of market mechanisms; and in the long run it will never be able to achieve political objectives that run counter to economic forces. Thus, from a normative point of view, the institution of 'intergovernmentalism' is an effective device for keeping partial interests under control and for ensuring that governance in Europe is legitimate and efficient. Governments of the member states are uniquely placed to bridge competing demands from different forces of society. Governments have the legitimacy to make choices and to set priorities, and have the power to produce binding decisions. Strong governmental control of European policy-making might therefore be synonymous with preserving the public good. Supranational institutions provide the framework and cement for effective inter-state co-operation.

The realist analysis always sounds convincing because it is so close to conventional wisdom. But it has two major deficiencies: it is static in terms of taking interests as given, without establishing how preferences are formed; and it is too narrow in that it concentrates on dominant actors, without asking what makes them dominant, under what particular conditions, and in which policy-making contexts. Yet nearly 20 years ago Heclo (1978: 102) argued: 'Looking for the few who are powerful, we tend to overlook the many whose webs of influence provoke and guide the exercise of power'.

The (En-)framing of the Discourse

The importance of interest and power in politics certainly should not be underestimated. It ranks high in rational choice analysis which has gained prominence in the study of interest groups.[13] The more elaborate rational choice approaches take account of 'embedded' rationality, but still find it difficult to predict what kind of 'rationale' is likely to develop. To do so requires some thought about what contributes to the definition of interests and what makes an actor powerful in a co-operative setting.

The definition of interest is a multifaceted process which—for analytical purposes—can be divided into separate stages. Defining the nature of the policy problem is the first step to establish what kind of interests might be affected, since the answer determines in which context the issue is situated. If firms in a given industry jointly develop new technology standards this will be considered as related to industrial competitiveness, and will be dealt with differently from cartelization that is seen as a matter of market closure. The shift from one policy domain to another means a move between divergent regimes, in terms of the ruling principles, norms, and procedures that apply. Other actors within an administration will be in charge, and most probably they will be engaged in different policy networks. How the 'core' problem is defined then has an influence on the delineation of the relevant policy area, as well as on which political agenda the problem will be put. This is not without consequence for the choice of political objectives, strategies, and policy instruments.

---

[13] This is particularly true in economic analyses, which tend to view interest-group behaviour as 'rent-seeking' (Tiedemann, 1994).

HDTV provides an instructive example of how efforts at joint problem-solving may be affected. When the policy debate moved from the issue of consumer electronics manufacture to that of broadcasting service, a new type of game was started (see Chapters 7 and 9). The focus of policy changed 'from the industrial policy concern of creating new technologies to protect Europe's high-tech industry to the competition policy issue of how to regulate the new digital technology to prevent unfair discrimination against new market entrants by established channels' (Cawson, 1994: 8). In the initial stages the DG responsible for telecommunications (DGXIII) had taken the initiative; after the switch other DGs made the running. The inner circle of policy-makers, closed until the policy shift occurred, widened and established coalitions became looser. How could this shift of problem-definition come about?[14] At first, the policy debate was dominated by high expectations of a bright new technological future, a widespread popular concern about a protracted technology gap, and the enthusiasm among political and business circles about an interventionist industrial policy to back European champions. When these high expectations were not realized on the basis of technical consultations, a debate was opened with another kind of reasoning and other participants were able to enlist support for their way of looking at things.

The international debate about the 'greenhouse effect' is another example from a different policy area. The ability to put an issue into a different 'conceptual frame' was again the basis for a policy shift in EC environmental policy (Jachtenfuchs, 1996). Only after having adopted the concept of 'sustainability' could the environmentalists within the Commission present their strategies concerning climate protection in a policy perspective which was also acceptable to their colleagues from DGs with clear-cut economic orientations. The concept provided first of all a platform for understanding within the Commission. Its active propagation by the Commission through both the global and national debates finally brought about consensus among the member governments and secured acceptance of the Community strategy proposed by the Commission.

---

[14] Cawson does not address this question in his paper, but the interpretation offered here is in line with his arguments.

Because the definition of a problem has such far-reaching consequences for the approach that is chosen and thus for the policy
outcome, it is a battle-ground for competing actors. The weapons
used are concepts; these are issue-specific, but reflect broader
notions which are rooted in fundamental belief systems about 'legitimate' objectives, 'proper' rules, and 'good' conduct. Such encompassing belief-systems have always been highly relevant in EC
politics. The process of European integration has, in other words,
been shaped by a particular kind of *Ordnungspolitik*. Precisely
because the EC is not a sovereign polity, but a supranational organization uniting individual political systems, the choice of political
objectives, and of ways and means for pursuing those policy choices,
have been laid down in the treaties. These define the guiding principles of integration, and above all the commitment to gear all political activities to the creation of the common market. The logic of
economic integration certainly did not find unreserved acceptance,
but it gained ideological hegemony, enforced by rulings from the
ECJ,[15] and supported by the academic (legal) discourse. There is no
encompassing economic orthodoxy to which all the different treaty
provisions adhere; individual policy areas are rather characterized
by different economic principles and have developed a philosophy
of their own. The neo-liberal market concept, which is a characteristic feature of the single market for goods and services, certainly
does not apply to agriculture. As individual DGs with the special
Councils are responsible for 'their' policy area, such differences can
become pronounced. Over time these philosophies have become
well established and difficult to contest, giving legitimacy to those
actors whose objectives are in line with the 'conventional wisdom'
and making it more difficult for those who cannot reconcile their
own demands with the 'logic of integration'. For any thorough
analysis of EC politics it is, therefore, most important to figure out
what kind of conceptual frameworks are most relevant in the debate and what conditions are needed to develop and uphold them.
Then we can better understand the functioning of interest politics in
the EC and which interests are successfully promoted.

Many observers have argued convincingly that the integration
process has been shaped to a considerable degree by those basic

---

[15] Recently the ECJ has been more wary of overruling member governments'
interests in favour of the unrestricted development of the common market.

concepts which are firmly rooted in interpretations of the 'philosophy of the treaties'. They have gained political force as part of the
common intellectual good that underpins the EC, and because they
carry normative connotations about 'appropriate' behaviour. To
use this capital to benefit particular interests requires that additional prerequisites are met. For an idea to become a 'common
concept' requires that it have political sex appeal, be relevant to
pressing issues, promise successful problem-solving, and be congruent with broader interests.

It is now widely acknowledged that, especially under conditions
of uncertainty, ideas play an important role.[16] 'Ideas are important
because they communicate the potential gains that may accrue
from exchange, especially in situations in which some change in
behaviour must occur before these gains can be captured' (Garrett
and Weingast, 1993: 204). Even if there is every reason to believe
that there is a functional need for ideas, this does not explain how
and by whom they will be produced or which kind of ideas will
become shared concepts. Ideas are intimately related not only to
interests, but also to capacity. Ideas may flow freely, but they have
to be translated into pragmatic policy regimes that embrace issue-
specific principles, norms, and rules of behaviour. Concepts have to
be produced and therefore are not free goods. To develop and
propagate a preferred concept can be a promising investment. As
long as it is in line with an established conceptual framework its
costs will be minimal, but any departure from shared concepts will
raise the costs. Only those who are willing to bear the costs and who
have the capacity to produce and advertise concepts will be able to
exert influence.

When trying to identify which actors would be likely to try to
frame policy debates one has to look for those who both have an
interest in doing so and have the necessary resources. One group
with an interest in setting the terms of the debate is those industries
most vulnerable to international interdependence. The challenges
of global competition bear particularly on those sectors of industry
that have to be pace-setters in order to prosper economically,

[16] This is one of the basic arguments supporting the important role played by
epistemic communities in international relations which are, by definition, characterized as anarchic, and hence unpredictable (P. Haas, 1992). Richardson (1996*a*)
argues convincingly that this concept may well be applicable to the EC because of
the 'fluidity and unpredictability' of the EC policy process.

especially in high-tech sectors. Hence it is no surprise that these industries have been particularly prominent in shaping the European economic debate. In addition, they have the required capacity, since they command sufficient intellectual resources for such a task, have the knowledge and international experience to propose effective problem-solving strategies, and can draw on well-established contacts to disseminate their strategies widely. The Commission is another candidate for framing policy debates. By nature it is a think-tank rather than an administration (Ludlow, 1991). It has a vested interest in strengthening its own political weight in the policy process and knows that it can do so effectively only if it can offer common solutions to mutual problems. Its ability to develop concepts which may turn into a common view endows it with the potential to exercise policy leadership.

What, then, is the role of interest associations in this context? European associations seem to be conspicuously absent. National interest organizations have time and again exerted leadership by promoting conceptual frameworks which became points of reference for a European-wide debate and consensus.[17] Yet European associations should not be assessed only as shapers of policy, they must also be viewed as providing an institutional framework for the exchange of information and ideas (Kohler-Koch, 1992). In this light their influence depends on how well they succeed in making this a privileged framework for discussion and a centre for networking. Their function thus goes beyond reducing transaction costs and establishing 'diffuse reciprocity' based on mutual trust, since their main contribution is to help to build common conceptual frameworks which may then become the foundations of a European regime. Indeed, in order not to have to rely exclusively on the intellectual resources of their affiliates, European associations have established close relations with existing research institutes or founded institutions of their own. The European Trade Union Confederation (ETUC) and UNICE, for example, both sought to establish European think-tanks, the former successfully, the latter less so (see Chapter 6).

This analytical approach puts the normative question about the 'illegitimate dominance' of private partial interests in public policy-

---

[17] Concerning the role of the Confederation of British Industry see Cowles (1994).

making into a different perspective. Concepts reflect the interplay between interests and ideas; ideas are not determined by interests, but have a life of their own. They are not produced and disseminated simply at the behest of individual actors, but are contained in 'cognitive maps' which rest in complex systems of interpretation shared by social communities. They cannot be used just as the instruments of a particular interest or of a single powerful actor. To control the production and use of knowledge is a power resource in itself (Strange, 1988). The evolution and distribution of knowledge follows its own logic, with competing concepts emerging from international epistemic communities (P. Haas, 1990), transnational issue groups (Ringius, 1992), and the media. The broad acceptance of a concept is not just a matter of content or of the successful management of public affairs. What is indeed an 'optimal solution' varies according to distinct, often national, experiences, firmly rooted, as are actor preferences, in established practices and institutions.

The conclusion from this analysis is that to acknowledge the importance of political concepts does not make redundant a thorough analysis of the role of institutions, power, and interests, but rather puts these variables into a different perspective. It implies in particular a different understanding of power, not as the ability to impose one's will on others, but as the capacity to offer others attractive options. This capacity is unevenly distributed, and does not simply correlate with financial resources or manpower. It is shaped by the actors' environment, especially the challenges that they face, and structured by the institutions that incorporate particular concepts and give them stability.

One of the most fascinating questions is whether it is possible to formulate some plausible hypotheses about who can defuse the conceptual discourse within the EC or who gives direction to specific issues of European policy, thereby shaping a kind of ideological hegemony. It may be assumed that in the era of interdependence many problems are externally induced and require internationally concerted action. Those who are present on a European, or even global, scale and who possess the capacity to develop effective strategies will also have a great say in the process of conceptualization. By producing 'leading conceptions' they exercise an influence on the choice of action and objectives. Hence a 'modernizing coalition' composed of leading European industries and the Commission is a likely alignment.

As governance is about defining the nature of the problem and the aims to be sought, identifying possible strategies, and deciding on appropriate measures,[18] it would be correct to say that leading industries and the Commission co-operate in governing Europe. However, their predominance might produce a dialectic process prompted by the opposition of those who feel left out of this process. The prevalence of technological pace-setters may become increasingly resented by those who are dropping out of the competitive race. Policy options developed by a 'think tank' may provoke even deeper resentments, because the latter may be inclined to follow fashionable new concepts, without taking into account the severe consequences which they entail. The progressiveness of EC propositions may be viewed by those who are close to grass-roots politics as 'cheap talk', not least since it is local politicians who have to bear the brunt of criticism and opposition accompanying the implementation process. If those who have to bear the costs of European innovation align with forces which strive for the strengthening of state power to protect their interests, governments are bound to set tighter limits on the 'modernizing coalition'. It is therefore still an open question whether—irrespective of the development of external and internal security co-operation within the other pillars of the EU—the balance might tip in the direction of halting the process of European integration.

[18] For a more extensive discussion of the concept of governance in the EU see Kohler-Koch (1996*a*).

4

Making and Enforcing Regulatory Policy in the Single Market

ERNESTO PREVIDI

THE ATYPICAL CHARACTER OF THE EU'S REGULATORY SYSTEM

The procedures required to ensure the correct and effective application of the regulatory framework that underpins the single market are difficult to understand. To do so requires an understanding of the unique and complex characteristics of the European Union's (EU) regulatory framework. The following factors define its atypical character, which differs from the classic properties of national regulatory systems, whether they are centralized or federal.

• *The lack of a clear separation of legislative and executive powers.* In the EU legislative power is exercized largely by the Council of Ministers, although it does not have the nature of a parliament containing a majority and an opposition. The Commission, although sometimes called the European executive, does not actually wield executive power. Rather, executive responsibility is exercized by the member governments, the Commission (through its co-ordinating and supervisory roles), and the Council itself, which has a particular role in the adoption of certain implementing provisions.

• *The Commission's monopoly on initiating legislation.* This makes the Commission's participation in the legislative process, as opposed to its limited role in the execution of legislation, particularly significant.

• *The lack of a 'hierarchy of acts' in EU law.* This simply reflects the absence of a real separation of powers. EU legislators do not distinguish in their law-making role between a rule of general scope and one with an implementing function.

• *The lack of a precise separation between EU and national competences*. Devoid of a formal delegation of competences—such as occurs in a federal state or in a country where regulatory powers are devolved to local governments—the Treaty on European Union (TEU) struggles to define this principle of separation of competences, known as subsidiarity. Even before the subsidiarity principle was formally enshrined in the TEU, its influence on the development of the regulatory policy of the EU was substantial in that its scope was considerably limited.

The most obvious example of application of this principle is the new approach to harmonization,[1] which the Commission developed in conjunction with its 1985 White Paper on completing the single market. This strategy represented a minimalist approach, restricting the harmonization of regulations to those fields where the lack of equivalence between national legislative systems made mutual recognition and freedom of movement impossible. Even in such cases, only essential requirements of collective interest would be harmonized. The definition of the technicalities of implementation was left to the voluntary activities of the European standards bodies: the European Standards Committee (CEN), the European Electro-technical Standards Committee (CENELEC), and the European Telecommunications Standards Institute (ETSI). Similarly, in fields not necessarily linked to completing the single market, such as environmental protection and working conditions, provision was made for EU regulatory action only in so far as objectives could be more easily achieved at EU level than at the level of individual member states.

All this shows that the EU's regulatory competence is shared with the member governments and is largely subsidiary to the latter. Practice has also demonstrated that, even with regard to the single market, the principle of the EU's exclusive competence, as potentially based on the letter of the treaties, no longer applies. The entry into force of the TEU is certainly not responsible for this precarious distribution of responsibility but, being based more on political evaluations than on precise legal precepts, it does rein-

---

[1] For an exposition of the new approach see Pelkmans (1990).

force political sensitivity with regard to any fresh initiatives which might jeopardize this fragile balance.

• *The dichotomy between responsibility for regulatory policy formulation and application.* The EU is responsible for much policy formulation, but lacks the authority to implement its regulations. Implementation remains within the jurisdiction of the authorities of the member states. Application covers a wide range of forms of action, including regulatory functions (most single market legislation is not directly applicable and must be transposed into national law), administrative implementing orders, monitoring, and enforcement.

With this distribution of powers, the EU's regulatory apparatus displays a break in the sequence of regulatory management functions: perception of needs leads to assessment of risks; this leads to the development and adoption of standards; then come the monitoring and supervision of implementation, which lead to the detection of any gaps in standards; these induce a reassessment of risks and may lead to the modification or adaptation of standards; and so on.

In a national system a break in this sequence can take place in the context of decentralization, with the distribution of responsibility between central and local powers. However, in such cases the efficacy and uniformity of enforcement throughout the national territory is obtained by the normal provisions of administrative law, by the uniformity of traditions and administrative culture, and sometimes by specific monitoring provisions or sanctions which are within the purview of the central authority.

For a mechanism of this type to function correctly—particularly so that the free movement of goods is not impaired—and to redress the break in the traditional risk-management circuit, it is clearly important that there be a certain degree of EU involvement in the executive functions of the national territorial authorities. This role is assigned to the Commission, but is limited to a supervisory function as the guardian of EU law and to co-ordinating the activities of the national territorial authorities using instruments such as working parties, committees, and exchanges of information.

Even in certain exceptional cases—such as veterinary and plant health controls and food regulations—where the Commission is involved in the monitoring and inspection of activities performed by national authorities, or where it has the power to authorize the marketing of certain products (such as medicines for human use), the Commission's essential aim is to improve the co-ordination of the functions and decisions of national authorities or to provide an EU-level of institutionalised regulation.

In short, the EU's regulatory system can be viewed as the sum (or the synergy or the interaction) of three different sources of competences:

• The division of the regulatory initiative between the EU and the member governments, which results in a dialectic search, based upon the principle of subsidiarity, for an equilibrium in regulation between the European and national levels.

• A rupture in the regulatory cycle, due to the distribution of roles between, on the one hand, the EU framework, which adopts the regulations, and, on the other hand, the territorial authorities of the member states, which apply them.

• The Commission's role in compensating for the effects that arise from the breaking of the regulatory cycle, which essentially consists of co-ordinating and systematizing functions exercized at the national level.

EUROPEAN NETWORKS

These distinctive attributes differentiate the EU's legislative process from the procedures normally followed in the member states. Despite the guarantees of transparency and representative democracy that the EU proffers, its legislative process appears to be a form of intergovernmental negotiation in which the final result is seen as a consensual compromise. Consequently, one can comprehend the criticisms about the deficit of transparency and democratic legitimacy in the EU's regulatory process. It is within this context that compensatory or corrective mechanisms have been gradually introduced to address this deficit. These efforts have focused largely on the establishment of European networks of co-operation among the actors concerned with the proper functioning of the single market.

Within this structure the Commission is the focal point for co-ordination of the decentralized powers ascribed to the national and even the local level. The absence of territorial responsibility (and therefore also of a territorial administrative structure) means that the Commission, in order to play its role in the different phases of the regulatory process, must depend upon external sources for information and expertise, whether these be economic, technical, scientific, or legal. It is not surprising that this support comes from partners (such as public administrations and economic actors) that are already engaged in regulatory policy-making at the national and local levels.

The relevant networks vary in the extent to which they are structured. In their simplest form they develop from a pattern of permanent working relations between Commission officials and experts of different national and professional backgrounds. In these informal networks sometimes representatives of national administrations play the most important role, sometimes representatives of industry, and sometimes experts who are consulted because of their reputation and expertise, depending on the circumstances and the dynamism of the individuals involved. This loosely structured form is often found during the first phase in the development of a new policy area.

In later phases the networks generally become more structured. Even so, they still vary in their degree of formal organization. They take the form of a working group or committee, which is composed of permanent experts who are designated by their administrations, organizations, or socio-professional associations. These participants serve as both representatives of their organizations and issue-experts. The committees' work is organized and directed by the various services of the Commission. This type of network is characterized by the more systematic manner in which information is circulated, which requires each party to practise transparency within its sphere. The Commission's role clearly extends beyond the simple material organization of information flows to influencing the organization and development of these flows according to the EU action in question.

In certain fields this type of network can appropriate a rather considerable degree of functional autonomy, especially when its members collaborate at the EU level to administer activities generated at the national level (as is the case with scientific evaluations for regulatory purposes and in the development of common research programmes). The network's role in these cases is to manage the distribution of tasks among its members, to co-ordinate the execution of the tasks, to permit comparison of results, and, finally, to present the Commission with the elements necessary for it to fulfil its responsibilities. The European standards bodies are examples of European networks that are almost completely autonomous, working beyond the EU's institutional framework (see below).

How effective a network is depends, of course, on the actual power of the participants, but also on the credibility of their constituencies. In other words, what is crucial is the network's capacity to create an interface between the public administrations and the organizations or interest groups which represent concrete economic and social interests. It is not unusual to differentiate between the quality of the members of a single network or between those from different networks.

Although national officials have a rather long history of working in networks under the Commission's co-ordination, sometimes their presence is merely a formality, such as when they lack expertise in the area in question. Since the birth of the European Economic Community (EEC) economic actors have expended considerable energy in creating European structures of co-operation. Their degree of success varies from sector to sector. The stronger, more efficient, and more representative these European structures are, the greater their impact in the networks in which they participate.

One result of this complex structure of co-operation is the 'sectoralization' of regulatory activity. Sectoralization tends to develop increasingly in the context of networks that are highly independent of each other, are firmly anchored in national administrative structures with segregated competences, and in which participants often 'play for the team' on the basis of well-established traditions of co-operation between the public and private sectors. This pattern is particularly evident in fields in which international organizations have long played a major role in drawing up technical safety provisions (such as transport, foodstuffs, pharmaceuticals, and electrical engineering).

Because of its heavy dependence on the contributions made by these various networks, the Commission has great difficulty in co-ordinating effectively inter-sectoral and inter-disciplinary activities in an effort to maintain the overall coherence of the EU's regulatory policy. The Commission's difficulties are not very different from those experienced by the other European decision-making institutions. The Council, in particular, replicates the same vertical sectoral structure and usually relies on the same government experts who worked with the Commission during the preparatory phase of the proposal.

The political coherence of regulatory action, in the sense of choosing the appropriate priorities or meeting the optimal allocation of societal resources, is not always easy to guarantee within a country. It is, therefore, not surprising that the co-ordination, or management, deficit should be even more pronounced at the EU level, given the extreme complexity and fragility of its political and institutional structures.

It is highly likely that this structure, with its watertight compartments and parallel networks, is making it very difficult to limit the scope of European regulation with respect to that of national legislation (the subsidiarity principle). Further, this fragmented structure affects the choice of legal basis under which policies are advanced, which in turn has important consequences for the appropriateness of the measures adopted. According to whether or not the social objective (protection against risks) is combined with that of ensuring the functioning of the single market, the choice of an inappropriate legal basis may either compromise the freedom of movement within the single market or impose uniformity where the treaties have provided only for the setting of minimum thresholds of compulsory protection.

EUROPEAN NETWORKS IN THE DIFFERENT PHASES OF THE REGULATORY PROCESS

The Awareness of Needs

Acknowledgement of a new need for regulation may have differing origins. New research findings may reveal the need to protect society against nuisances that have hitherto been undetected and thus not regulated. Changes in society and new problems arising from them may make existing regulations obsolete. In addition, a new awareness has emerged in society with regard to certain requirements regarding the quality of life (such as a clean environment): these arise from an overall increase in the standard of living and create pressures for regulation in new areas. Political factors also intervene to change the scale of priorities attached to certain social objectives. Many other examples could certainly be cited, but it is impossible to produce an exhaustive list of factors that determine the development of regulatory intervention in any given country.

Whatever its origin, the perceived need for regulation is developed and expressed in a process involving numerous actors, including: organizations and centres for research and technological innovation; public authorities responsible for health, safety, and the environment; monitoring and inspection laboratories and institutions; the media; political parties; and associations representing social groups. All of these actors interact to define a particular attitude towards the quality of life in the country in question. This attitude is also shaped by geography and social traditions, including self-regulation by the socio-economic partners on both sides of industry.

In the EU the existence of different national concepts of quality of life is a constant presence in the continuing debate that runs alongside changes in regulatory policy. Throughout the process, the central problem with drawing up new legislation lies in the radical differences in the way that risks are perceived between member states. This clearly poses a major problem in efforts to agree on common protection measures. Measures to curb chemical pollution; to prevent accidents in the workplace; to protect consumers, particularly children; and to reduce the risk of fire are well-known examples of social regulation and are correspondingly areas in which the drafting and adoption of EU legislation is, or has been, highly controversial.

The danger posed by the inflammability of upholstered furniture is a typical example of fundamental differences in the perception of risks. Draft EU legislation to address the matter was under discussion for several years among experts from the member governments, industry, and research bodies meeting under the auspices of the Commission, before being abandoned by the Commission in early 1993. Only two of the then member states—the United Kingdom and Ireland—had adopted regulation in this field in response to the strength of public opinion. Climate, tradition, and life-styles probably explain why some countries are more sensitive to fire risks and make the use of fireproofing substances compulsory in the manufacture of upholstery, while others seem much more concerned about the risks from pollution caused by the production of precisely those substances.

Finally, there is one perverse factor that contributes to the contentiousness of regulation, which should certainly not be underestimated: the technological edge granted to one country's industry over those of its neighbours. Regulations that reflect this technological edge—for example, the ready availability of substitutes for substances regarded as harmful—can result in a considerable competitive advantage. Even when the perception of a risk is based on objective grounds, the mere existence of a technological advantage in the country calling for new legislation makes this call suspect in the eyes of partner countries.

In light of the diversity of these national situations, it is the Commission's duty above all to verify the feasibility of a regulation and the general direction that should be pursued. The verification of the regulation's merit should in principle be made through a combined consultation of all interested groups and the concerned public. This does not at this stage involve a consultation on precise regulatory acts or on concrete measures, but rather on the policy approach that the Commission might develop in response to the articulation of certain concerns. The method followed, when subjects of particular importance to the public interest are involved, could be to publish documents—communications, memoranda, green papers, white papers—of a broad and general scope, with the widest possible distribution, to which all the interested parties are invited to respond. The broad dissemination of these publications is achieved by their publication in the *Official Journal of the European Community* and by their distribution to the European institutions, member governments, and those socio-professional organizations which have working relationships with the Commission's services.

The Verification of the Fundamental Economic and Technical Bases

On the basis of the results of this general consultation, the Commission initiates efforts to develop new legislation. Its first concern is to make use of economic and technical data, so as better to target its draft regulation. At this stage the submission of information from the economic actors could *inter alia* be particularly important. Such consultations are conducted by the appropriate Commission service, which reports to the relevant European organizations with which it maintains recurrent contacts for co-operation and mutual consultation.

The Scientific Evaluation of Risks

In fields that affect the protection of health, the development of a regulation requires risk-analysis and the consideration of the threshold at which to set the benefit. The scientific expertise required for this type of evaluation is held by the organizations and agencies responsible for the application of these regulations in the member states. Consequently, the Commission must secure the co-operation of these experts. Depending upon the gravity of the risks in question, co-operation among the experts is more or less structured. The simplest form is the creation of working groups composed of national experts, under the supervision of a Commission official. Such groups have no formal status, their existence being justified simply by the Commission's need for assistance in its role as initiator of legislation. Moreover, the Commission can request the input of independent experts or contributions from research institutes or consultants, their information always being intended as a contribution to the debate within these working groups.

A more structured form of network is established in those fields that are more central to the protection of health. To develop regulations in the veterinary, phytosanitary, nutritional, pharmaceutical, toxicological, cosmetic, and related fields, expertise is organized at the European level in scientific committees, composed of experts whose competence is already recognized at the international level, and presided over by one of these experts. Such committees have a formal mandate, which means that they are recognized in the Commission's institutional structures. In certain cases, framework directives specifically oblige the Commission to consult such committees, while in others the initiative is left to the Commission or the member governments to pursue consultations. Formally, these committees possess only the authority to assist the Commission in its regulatory activity, but in practice their formal status and prestige lend them an aura of independence and autonomy depending on the strength of the opinions they produce.

The Development of Technical Specifications

Since the adoption of the 'new approach' to harmonization in May 1995, the development of technical specifications for the design and fabrication of manufactured products has become one of the most significant arenas for the involvement of networks in the EU's regulatory activities. The development of industrial standards is dependent upon contributions from thousands of experts from firms and in the standards bodies which are charged with developing a consensus on standards. The new approach rests upon the premise that a consensus can be reached within the relevant standards body and will reflect the collective interest, because of the open and transparent character of its procedures. Working from this premise, the EU abstains from taking its own direct action, and delegates to the standards bodies the task of setting the technical prescriptions needed to ensure that relevant products conform to the essential safety provisions set by the regulation.

The new approach thus represents an innovative response to the routine problem posed by the inadequacy of the European institutions' resources in relation to the tasks with which they are entrusted. The existence of a well-established tradition for establishing standards, at both national and international levels of cooperation, gave the European institutions the opportunity to transfer systematically this extremely important and substantial function outside their institutional framework, and even beyond the sphere of public intervention. The autonomy of the standards bodies is complete because no recognition of their conclusions is required by the European institutions or member governments, despite the fact that under the new approach European standards acquire a quasi-regulatory status.

The Elaboration of the Legal System

The formulation of a text outlining the legal structure for a regulation is impossible without a perfect understanding of the regulatory mechanisms in use in the member states, as well as the likely effects of its application. Consequently, during this phase the Commission's services work closely with representatives of the national administrations, also assembled within working groups. This phase, which can last one or two years, allows the Commission's services to formulate gradually a proposal which takes into consideration all the situations developing in the member states. The more balance and care that are taken in the formulation of a proposal, the better the chances are that it will be adopted quickly.

When the legal text is sufficiently developed the Commission's services again engage in consultation, expanded to include all of the socio-economic partners concerned. In some spheres—such as foodstuffs regulation, industrial relations, and consumer protection—consultation takes place within permanent committees, which bring together, on an *ad hoc* basis, all the organizations concerned (with respect to consumers see Chapter 10).

Informed by these committees, the College of Commissioners adopts the text and transmits it to the other institutions: the European Parliament (EP), the Economic and Social Committee (ESC), and the Council. The ESC brings together representatives of social and economic organizations, and its opinion is received by the two legislative branches. The Commission's proposals are frequently modified by these two bodies before they are adopted and are occasionally rejected.

The Administrative Implementation of Regulations

Networks also play an important role after the adoption of regulations by compensating for the problems presented by the separation between the making of regulatory policy and its application, which can undermine the homogeneity of results, as the member governments use different procedures for surveillance and control. First, there are the problems of a political nature. If the EU's regulation is ultimately concerned with a political objective (such as environmental, social, or consumer protection), the success of the policy can be undermined by the uneven application of the regulation. Secondly, if the subject of the regulation involves the fulfilment of one or more of the 'four freedoms'—free circulation of goods, services, capital and people—uneven application threatens the functioning of the single market.

The guiding principle underlying the functioning of the single market, in particular the free movement of goods, is that products are inspected in the country of origin. This means that products must not be subjected to double controls, and that the authorities in the country of destination must assume that products originating from another member state have been adequately inspected and comply with EU provisions. The only viable basis for this principle of mutual recognition of controls is confidence on the part of the public authorities in each member state in the capacities, expertise, and effectiveness of the monitoring bodies in the other member states.

Creation of this confidence has been the objective of all EU regulatory policy thus far. The greater the disparities between national situations and the more critical the risks addressed, the more necessary it has been to find solutions capable of bridging the confidence gap. The decision to centralize the evaluation of new medicinal products in a European agency—the European Medicines Evaluation Agency (EMEA)—was thus motivated by the assertion that only a limited number of member governments possessed the scientific capacity required to assess adequately the safety of new medicines, and hence that it would be difficult to apply the principle of mutual recognition to decisions concerning market authorization. In other fields, however, confidence has been achieved either through the extensive harmonization of official control procedures, as in the food sector, or by promoting the development of certification and testing capacities, as with most manufactured goods.

Prior to 1993 frontier controls enabled national authorities to block the free movement of supposedly dangerous products, and constituted a last-resort safeguard against any breakdown in the system of mutual recognition of national controls. The abolition of internal frontier controls therefore had the effect of considerably increasing the need for mutual confidence on the part of national agencies responsible for the implementation of EU regulations. Consequently it also increased the need for co-ordination and co-operation between those agencies in order to reach a real uniformity of monitoring practices throughout the EU.

To meet these requirements (which were new more because of the 1992 context than because of their substance) the Commission has set itself the task of developing mechanisms for administrative co-operation based on the same concept of networks that underlies its regulatory work. Here too the task has been made particularly difficult by the need to find the right balance between, on the one hand, the need for intervention by the Commission as co-ordinator and, if necessary, by further regulation (for example, by legislating to align implementing procedures and methods), and, on the other hand, respect for the responsibility of the member governments in the application of EU law.

The Supervision of Conformity

Another autonomous network exercises duties essential for the smooth functioning of the EU's regulatory system: it comprises private organizations, such as laboratories for analysis and testing, product certification bodies, quality control departments in firms, and accrediting agencies. These assess the conformity of products and services with standards and regulatory prescriptions. This infrastructure for quality control has emerged in each member state as a function of the extent of their industrial development; it tends to be outside the public sphere, even though it is generally promoted and supported by the public authorities. As in the realm of standardization, industry plays a central role in the development of this infrastructure, which responds to the demands of competition.

With the new approach, and more specifically with the policy known as the 'global approach', initiated several years later to foster the assessment of conformity, these quality control networks have acquired an essential role in guaranteeing the smooth application of EU regulations. Their stamps, certificates, and testing reports are considered by official controllers as proof of the conformity of products to the regulations.

MONITORING THE FUNCTIONING OF THE SINGLE MARKET AND ACCESS TO JUSTICE

The way the single market works depends above all on the behaviour of consumers, through their purchases, and of firms, through their marketing and investment strategies.

Consumers who have doubts about the quality of goods from other Member States, or who are not convinced of the effectiveness of the checks carried out on such products, could by their behaviour, reduce the opening-up of markets which should result from the harmonization of rules. Similarly, a lack of interest on the part of suppliers of services in exercising their professions or activities on the territory of other Member States would simply highlight the disparity between the effort which harmonization has entailed and its limited effects on the market.

And if firms were to fail to respond to the opportunities created, for example, by the new procedures for making public procurement transparent (advertising of tender notices and award criteria), they would serve merely to preserve national, or even local, market fragmentation thereby preventing the emergence of competition (Sutherland *et al.*, 1992: 26).

The single market cannot be identified solely with the legal-institutional structure created by the treaties and the accumulation of law derived from them. It becomes an economic reality to the extent that the behaviour of economic actors makes it so. Their initiative, therefore, becomes the motor and dynamic for the market and also the factor which reveals the success or failure of the market. Protectionist or discriminatory actions by certain public administrations, poor efforts to transpose EU law into national law, and the denial of mutual recognition constitute many infractions against EU laws. These would go unpunished if the parties involved did not inform their authorities, the Commission, or the courts.

The economic actors (individuals or firms) acting in isolation and unaware of the broader trend, are unable in the short term to grasp the harmful effects of their actions. For its part, the Commission, which rarely takes the initiative in this arena, could certainly be more aware than it is of specific market circumstances and conditions. Even if it were, however, it would be illusory to presume that an administration that can marshal no more than several dozen bureaucrats to monitor the application of EU law could guarantee the fair and just functioning of a market with almost 370 million consumers.

We find ourselves confronting two impossible demands, which were clearly illustrated in the Sutherland report (Sutherland *et al.*, 1992):

- The creation in each national jurisdiction of conditions that require the public administration and the judiciary to exercize effectively their authority so as to ensure respect for European law and to punish all infringements, which implies the improvement of access to the judicial process; and
- Action by the organizations of economic agents, on the one hand, to disseminate information relating to the opportunities offered by new European legislation, and on the other, to

supervise the development of the single market, and to create the means through which national and European authorities can publicize all infringements.

In order to improve access to justice, the Commission, following one of the many recommendations put forward in the Sutherland Report, envisages a sequence of actions aimed at increasing the sensitivity of the national administrations to the need to provide support and information to economic actors. As always, the essential problem lies in the insufficient understanding of EU law by national judges and lawyers. They are either passive in the face of clear contradictions within the logic of the single market, or turn to the Commission or the European Court of Justice (ECJ), both of which are slow in reaching judgments because they are heavily over-loaded with cases.

The clauses of the TEU concerning judicial co-operation (Article K) should in principle open up new means for creating equal and effective conditions for the application of EU law throughout the single market. The problems—particularly those involving enforcing judgments beyond territorial frontiers, harmonizing sanctions, submitting cases to the competent jurisdiction, and harmonizing judicial aid systems—could be addressed within this framework. Whether these opportunities for concrete solutions are made use of will depend entirely on the political determination of the member governments. For in this domain activity is based solely on intergovernmental co-operation, which, as everyone knows, differs from the Community method in that it carries no obligations regarding enforcement! Certain networks do exist for confronting these two impossible demands. They are promoted by the Commission or created spontaneously within the private sector, as were the Euro-guichets and Chambers of Commerce. The principal difficulties in this domain, however, lie in the opaqueness of EU law and in the weakness of the infrastructures designed to create these networks.

Because *directives*, which constitute the majority of single market measures, must be transposed into national law,[2] EU law loses its visibility. Often a directive translates into a country's law through the modification of a whole sequence of clauses in a number of legal acts. In addition, a directive's content, despite the intensity of the

---

[2] The jurisprudence of the ECJ on the direct effect of directives applies only in very specific cases.

debate over its particular details at the time of its adoption, can undergo profound transformations during transposition into national law, such that its scope can be considerably altered.

Whenever issues such as these are raised, the Commission is always bound to express its regret at the fact that its proposal to the 1991 Intergovernmental Conference (IGC), which negotiated the TEU, to establish a 'hierarchy of acts' was not adopted. As the term indicates, the Commission's proposal sought to order the EU's legislative activities in a comprehensive and coherent way, so as to avoid, among other things, the existing legal vacuums at the European level into which fall national regulatory initiatives relating to the implementation of EU law.

The Commission's proposal for a hierarchy of EU law was based on the distinctions between three levels of provisions:

- *treaties*, which constitute the fundamental law of the EU;
- *laws*, which determine for each issue the fundamental principles, general guidelines, and basic elements of the measures to be taken for their implementation and set down in detail the rights and obligations of individuals and firms, with those provisions that do not call for implementing measures to be directly applicable in all member states; and
- *administrative implementing measures and provisions*, which are adopted, according to the criterion of subsidiarity, at either national or European level, in the latter case being directly applicable in each member state.

Such a structure would have made all elements of EU law transparent and uniform throughout the territory of the EU and would dispense with the *directive*, which has been described as a 'hybrid legal instrument of ambiguous status' (Commission, 1991c: 69). It would also have recognized the position of EU flanking measures, whenever their adoption at national level could compromise the pursuit of the EU's objectives.

One cannot help but regret that within the current debate about the lack of transparency in EU law none of the proposed approaches attacks the heart of the problem. The only measure which so far appears to find a relative consensus is to codify EU law. This technique is already practised with regard to EU legislation in so far as it is achieved by the efforts of many private publishers. However, it does not follow that codification would contribute to making EU law transparent if it is not carried through into national implementing laws. The redressing of this shortcoming is never even considered. The Commission has renewed its proposals on the hierarchy of norms for the 1996 IGC. It remains to be seen, however, whether the member governments will agree to abandon the use of the directive, especially now that their attachment to subsidiarity inspires them to reinforce their autonomy by all means possible.

It is certain that the obscure and esoteric character of EU law has encouraged commercial initiatives to provide information and legal assistance. However, this does more to target special-interest groups and particularly motivated agents than to increase more general awareness. So a few possibilities have been provided for the positive evolution of access to justice through EU law, but in both the short and the medium term the development and deepening of the single market will depend primarily upon the effectiveness of socio-economic networks—producers, consumers, unions, etc.—in monitoring its functioning.

An example serves to demonstrate the type of action that is required, but also the conditions in which it should not take place. In 1993 the Danish employers' organization, assisted by a consultant, examined its member firms' activities to discover how the single market really functioned in several sectors. The results, without being negative, were, however, surprisingly at odds with the clearly positive reports that had been written by the authorities of all of the member states and the Commission. Even though this anomalous situation became the subject of debate within the European institutions and between the representatives of the member governments, no critical analysis of the mass of the *acquis communautaire*, except for the isolated case this investigation represented, was undertaken. The lesson one can derive from this example is that, while initiatives of this sort are certainly necessary, without a European network to support them, they have little chance of changing practice.

CONCLUSIONS

When we look at the precarious balance in the institutional structure, as well as the dialectic between EU and national competences, the EU's regulatory policy appears to be becoming a symbol of a dual illusion. First, there is the illusion of centralization, that ruling powers are exercized at the supranational level and the Commission enjoys a monopoly of initiative, which formally grants it extremely important influence. However, it does not possess any territorial competences for implementation or *a fortiori* any relevant administrative structure and the member governments maintain within their jurisdiction all of the structures of regulatory development (those agencies responsible for evaluation, control, surveillance, and so on). Consequently the Commission must rely upon the contributions of the member governments to fulfil its institutional mission.

The second illusion is that of decentralization. The development and implementation of decisions is the responsibility of national authorities, which control the structures of regulatory development, and which enjoy wide discretionary margins for implementation. Nevertheless, the national governments are progressively losing a large portion of their control over the functioning of the regulations within the framework of a partnership organized at the European level, in which the authorities of one member state are only one component among many.

The sterile institutional debates that, since the birth of the EU, have accompanied the search for this balance, and which gave birth to the new discipline of 'comitology', certainly have this dual illusion as their background. The reality that hides behind these debates is found within the contradiction between, on the one hand, the increasing interdependence (despite all the evidence of the attachment to the notion of subsidiarity) of the states which agreed to share a large part of their regulatory sovereignty, and, on the other, the political obstinacy of the states which refuse to recognize this sharing of sovereignty when it involves the means of enforcement.

To progress harmoniously and play its role to the full, the EU needs this dialectical relationship between its institutions and those of the member states. For this to be a constructive relationship, however, it must not be distorted by untruths and inappropriate claims. As experience has generally shown, progress is possible, in the current context of frequent conflict, only after a significant expenditure of time and resources. Should we not envisage a new legal and institutional framework which takes account of certain realities, such as the incapacity of the Commission and the member governments to perform certain functions autonomously and the close interdependence which is their fate?

The proposal put forward by the Commission in 1991 for the establishment of a hierarchy of acts would certainly contribute to setting up this new institutional framework. It could thus reduce the tensions between the EU and its members which arise, in particular, from the lack of coherence in the application of EU law. It is likely, however, that it would be insufficient without radical and innovative reforms to the framework of EU co-operation. At this level, the 1991 proposal was perhaps less innovative than it might seem, as it was very much based on traditional criteria (the well-know 'comitology') that underlie the Commission's decision-making powers. These criteria tend to highlight, rather than to resolve, the tensions and conflicts which have been in evidence since the origins of the EU.

The consequences of this quasi-permanent climate of conflict weigh heavily on the Commission's principal function, which is to prepare, formulate, and generate policies from the contributions provided by the different European networks and those that put pressure on them. This co-ordinating function certainly suffers from the ambiguity which is a feature of the division of power between the European and national levels. This results in a kind of relationship which is often more closely related to intergovernmental co-operation than to the Community method. Here the Commission has to walk a tightrope, performing a balancing act in the face of the wary actions of national authorities, which challenge its legitimacy whenever they feel that their jurisdiction is being violated.

Complex and cumbersome bureaucratic procedures characterize co-operation within the EU. They are particularly poorly adapted to those crucial aspects of regulatory functions that are related to safeguarding public order; these consequently demand very effective communication, efficient means of evaluation, and rapid decision-making. The inadequacy of resources available for these functions at the European level usually leads to the establishment of a complex partnership between the Commission and the member governments, with a division of responsibilities that is not always clear. The potential liability of the EU institutions that might arise from errors or inadequacies in risk assessment or the risk management process is still largely unexplored. In addition, we

can ask whether the various official bureaucratic and political con-
nections, through which partnerships develop, provide all the guarantees of independence and autonomy that are necessary for them
to function free from pressure and political and economic partisan-
ship? It is precisely to meet these requirements and to avoid these
risks that the United States developed powerful independent federal structures such as the Food and Drug Administration and the
Environmental Protection Agency.

In the EU, as we have seen, in two crucial fields connected with
health protection (foodstuffs and medicines), more advanced solutions for increasing the autonomy of regulators and improving the
organization of resources have been sought. For food products the
solution was found in the establishment of a procedure for co-
operation and mutual technical assistance between member states
and the Commission.[3] This is designed to evaluate new substances
for use in food processing. The procedure has independent resources and its own management methods, but is administered by
the Commission's services. For pharmaceutical products, in contrast, a similar objective has been pursued by the creation of an
agency genuinely independent of the Commission.[4] The EMEA,
based in London, enables national experts to collaborate in evalu-
ating new pharmaceutical products, in preparing decisions about
their introduction to the market (decisions subsequently to be
adopted by the Commission and applied throughout the EU), and
in monitoring the use of these products. Both organizations, although they differ in the extent of their structural autonomy, rest
on the principle of managerial autonomy. It is interesting to note
that these solutions were adopted after all other conventional
means of underlining the functioning of the single market had been
well tried and tested and had proved inadequate to meet the prime
objective of health protection. Indeed, it is thanks to the political
pressure from the countries that are usually the most possessive
about their national prerogatives and most advanced in terms of
scientific evaluation capacity that these solutions were adopted.
In particular, the centralization of authorizations for new medicinal products, provided for in the EMEA, was the response to
those countries—especially France, Germany, and the United

---

[3] Council Decision 93/5 of 25 Feb. 1993, *Official Journal*, L52, 4 Mar. 1993.
[4] Council Regulation 2309/93 of 22 July 1995, *Official Journal*, L214, 9 Sept. 1995.

Kingdom—which would not accept the principle of mutual recognition of national registrations.

In order to organize information or to co-ordinate and promote research in other fields, such as environmental protection and worker safety, other autonomous structures have been set up within the EU framework.[5] At present there are no official plans for these structures to become regulatory agencies as such. It is likely, however, that the EU, under pressure from requirements which could turn out to be spectacularly urgent, will have to envisage further changes in these areas in the very near future.

[5] In May 1990 the Council created the European Environment Agency, which will set up a European information and observation network in fields such as air quality, atmospheric emissions, water quality, land use, waste management, and noise pollution. The European Agency for Safety and Health at Work was established by the Council in July 1994, in order to provide the EU institutions, member governments, and other interested parties, with access to research on safety and health at work. It is also to promote co-operation and exchanges of information and experience among the member governments.

5

The Commission as an Actor: An Anthropologist's View

IRÈNE BELLIER

In the 1950s Jean Monnet envisaged 'a new breed of man . . . being born in the institutions of Luxembourg, as though in a laboratory, it was the European spirit which was the fruit of common labour' (Monnet, 1976: 441). The Commission best embodies this notion, inviting us to analyse it as an actor on the European stage in terms of the character of the individuals and not just of its structure or role. The Commission has changed greatly since its 'youth', when it was established as the small administration of a kind of task-force. Now, as a result of the Treaty on European Union (TEU), it has responsibility for a growing number of tasks while retaining its role as the motor of the construction of Europe.

The history of the Commission has yet to be written, but in 1993, in an anthropological study, a Franco-British team of researchers underlined the importance of memory in the 'culture' of European civil servants (Abélès *et al.*, 1993). It is through an oral tradition that Commission officials pass on the words and actions of the personalities who have left their mark on the construction of the European Union (EU). The discourse about the European 'founding fathers' illustrates the ways the officials perceive the dynamics of the Commission, especially the roles of Walter Hallstein and Jacques Delors, the first and last presidents of the Commission at the time of our study. The oral tradition also feeds the rhetoric about the working practices of the different directorates general (DGs), making explicit references to the 'models' which determined, and sometimes still determine, the operating styles of the administrative units under their direction. Individuals play a much more vital part in this institution—often seen by outsiders as opaque—than do the organizational structures which provide the framework for their actions.

This is the conclusion of our anthropological study, which looked at the working practices of officials in their professional environment. We listened to individual officials in very varied situations, ranging from informal conversations to semi-directed interviews, in the corridors of the institutions, in meeting rooms, and in the relative calm of offices. Self-images and images of others emerged from these numerous conversations, accounts, and written and oral contributions, and have been complemented by the observations of the research team. These images reveal the way in which European civil servants view their social and professional relationships, both within the Commission and with governmental and non-governmental representatives from the member states. In his institutional analysis of the EC, B. Guy Peters (1992: 106) put forward the idea of connected 'games', among which he mentioned the political role of bureaucracies, whether at the national or the European level, and the functional nature of the relationships between the DGs and national administrations. It is in this context that one can understand the logic of action developed by the Commission, which this chapter seeks to underline, drawing on two main factors.

The first factor emerges from what we call the process of conversion from the national into the European, a role the Commission plays as a result of its institutional position, the scope of which is revealed by examining its personnel. The second factor is the way in which the Commission organizes its relationships with its institutional partners, governmental or non-governmental, its patterns of thought, and the development of decisions on policy.

CONVERSION FROM THE NATIONAL INTO THE EUROPEAN

Analysis of the perceptions of European civil servants highlights strands of identification which run through the whole Commission, but which develop in different registers. In another context this could nurture a process of fission; in the Commission it creates a novel dynamic, although it does lead to numerous uncertainties which have a destabilizing influence on officials. This is one of the contrasts with national administrations, where the officials, re-cruited from a culturally and historically stable base, serve a state with firmly-established borders in a politically and socially coher-ent framework. These characteristics are not present in the 'admin-istrative' branch of the EU, which is marked by its fragmented nature, just as much in the division of the responsibilities for devel-oping and implementing polities, as in the diverse components of European culture. Although it presents itself as unique and unit-ary, the Commission is, in fact, riddled with many different currents deriving from outside the institution, and reflecting the national origins, ideologies, and politics of individuals within it. The Commission draws these strands together according to its own distinctive logic.

The Impact of Nationality

It is evident that nationality remains a crucial factor of identifica-tion and of differentiation between individuals. The member gov-ernments nominate members of the Commission itself and continue to consider as their own those in senior positions, the so-called *à drapeaux* posts with national flags. Similarly, individuals may be recruited to the European civil service on the basis of European criteria, but as candidates they have nevertheless been socialized in a national milieu. With the exception of the College of Europe at Bruges in Belgium, there is no specific training institu-tion for careers in the Commission, in marked contrast to those member states where future civil servants are trained in schools of public administration.

Starting with the Commissioners, who take an oath to serve Europe entirely independently, all European civil servants ac-knowledge that they are serving the EU and not their native coun-tries. Yet, in the present state of European integration, European identification does not seem able to overcome the differences of national approach which pre-date the EU. This factor helps to explain certain practices and the occasional eruption of critical comments about colleagues that are based on national stereotypes, which are at odds with the normative discourse which repeatedly sings the praises of 'multicultural enrichment'.

In the European laboratory that is the Commission, nationality does not form the basis of action; it is predicated rather on the 'reduction' of national peculiarities (Abélès and Bellier, 1996: 433). This aim is far from being achieved, although there are shifts in that direction. The marginalizing of national criteria as a way of confirming one's European credentials helps to explain an attitude repeatedly observed in interviews with dozens of European civil servants: they tend to put more weight on their regional than their national identities. Thus one interviewee defined herself as Bavarian rather than German, another as Catalan rather than Spanish, a third as Scottish rather than British and a fourth as coming from the provinces rather than 'French' (in marked contrast to the Parisians).

The desire to minimize the divisive effects of nationality in this body devoted to the construction of Europe accounts for the over-emphasis which many officials place on personality and on the role played by individual character traits, when 'explaining' the political and normative attitudes of their bosses and colleagues. The distinct political and administrative cultures within the Commission mean that officials socialized in twenty-odd national cultures have differing attitudes towards authority and the organization of administration.[1] The evaluations of bosses and colleagues showed large disparities, but this is in line with Peters's work (1989) on bureaucratic structures. This reveals that the British tend to develop contacts based on trust, which leave much to depend on personality; that the Germans tend to accept the principle that the boss exercises authority; while southern Europeans tend to give priority to negotiations among individuals. Hence it is not surprising that personality emerges as the sole common criterion for esteem in an organization in which ideology is part of the basis for achieving integration among its officials.

In the current circumstances, however, nationality cannot be entirely eradicated as a factor in the services of the Commission. It comes into play as an explanatory factor in personal tensions over career advancement. The practice of 'parachuting' members of *cabinets* into the services, and the growing number of national experts on temporary secondment from national administrations to the Commission go against the ideal of a public service working entirely in the European interest, or so it is claimed by those officials who criticize and suffer from such practices. The Commis-

---

[1] When there were 12 member states, 19 nationalities were represented in the Commission.

sion and member states encourage anything which helps to bring national and European civil servants closer together, facilitating, if not a process of osmosis, then at least a better understanding between interlocutors, who in principle are serving the same cause. But the officials in question reveal a contradiction between the ideal, which leads them to work as a team, and the logic of bureaucratic organization, which is pyramidal and hierarchical, governed by the classic norms of the Franco-German model present at the EU's inception and added to by the practices resulting from successive enlargements. Each nationality leaves its own imprint on the functioning of the organization.

Conversion to the European

The professional implication of serving the European cause is to transform individuals to the point where, in the words of one German director in the Commission, 'One no longer thinks of someone else as Spanish, French, or British, but as a colleague'. This feeling of identity is reinforced by the impression that the European civil servants give of using a common language. Without going into the wider issues emanating from the study of socio-professional jargon, we can clearly identify two phenomena concerning the rationality and use of this language.[2]

First, a European jargon (Euro-speak) has emerged from a process of semantic and lexical approximations, tapping the working languages of the Commission (French, English, and German), but often formulated by officials with different mother tongues. This helps to explain the oddities of language followed even by the native speakers of one of the main working languages, when they switch into the mode of thinking and expressing themselves as 'European'. These linguistic habits and shared practices are the result of multicultural tolerance and professional cohabitation. It is a sign of the distance which European civil servants feel from their national contexts.

Second, this jargon and all the linguistic distinctions appearing in the work of the Commission create problems only when the Commission's oral and written discourse involves relations with the outside world, where more conventionally recognized languages

---

[2] For other developments see Abélès *et al.* (1993) and Bellier (1995*a*; 1995*b*).

reign and are redolent of different national identities. While one witnesses a wider phenomenon of 'nationalization' in the upper reaches of the Commission, the Europeanization and sense of speaking the same language is stronger at the base and within the services or operating units of the Commission.

The 'European' can thus be seen in contrast to the 'national' and the distance can be witnessed daily in the activities of the Commission. European civil servants have to defend a 'European' position against the national officials and experts who defend the positions of their member states. To demonstrate their independence, European civil servants, faced with negotiators from their own countries, have to adopt a *modus operandi* or criteria which respond to specifically European points, not to national points of view. This process is driven by a double logic: defence of the *acquis communautaire*; and an emphasis on the 'European interest', which national civil servants, in turn, seek to interpret in relation to their understanding of their national interest.

In the European civil service, if we look at all the institutions together, officials show cultural traits inherited from their previous socialization, as well as talents which they cannot develop freely because of their involvement in pursuing European careers. But they confirm in practice the existence of patterns of thought, logic, allegiances, and fields of interest when they encounter officials and groups affiliated with national interests.

In a context in which geographical and mental frontiers are being redefined, anthropological analysis can reveal that European civil servants have different ways of 'thinking European'. The spectacle emerges of a pattern of identification with the European project, but leaving immense areas of uncertainty, defined 'reactively' in comparison with other cultural areas. So it is, for example, that a European civil servant can have the sense of being 'truly' European when she returns home, or meets people from other national or federal backgrounds or encounters, say, Americans or Japanese. In these last cases, perceptions tend to hinge on notions developed in Europe, and on a kind of identity which results from sense of belonging to a historically defined cultural area, even if it is a composite. Although there are certainly 'national networks' within the Commission, they do not provide sufficient explanation for the way in which individuals work in an administrative organization designed to nurture 'the European'.

The science of administration, or of the sociology of organization, aims to analyse the rationality of an institution, its efficiency, and the means it uses to achieve its aims. The anthropologist will note that the DGs of the Commission are not just frameworks for generating a certain type of action; they are places in which individuals make a professional and personal investment, but, when observed *in situ*, develop contrasting perspectives. The different 'points of view' which emanate from officials in the same institution, ranging across specific sectors of work, put in question the notion of the bureaucracy as unitary, formal, and utilitarian in character.[3] Do these views result from the organization to which they belong adapting to a political game which is fragmented, or are they rather the imprint of a bureaucracy which is more political than executive? That European civil servants are called on to be able to have powerful reflexes leads us to conclude that the latter explanation is correct (Abélès *et al.*, 1993).

Professional identification is becoming a well-recognized theme (Sainsaulieu, 1988), but close observation of the DGs of the Commission reveals several interesting features. Commission officials tend spontaneously to identify their place of work as a 'house'. They say it in English, French (*maison*), Spanish (*casa*), and German (*Haus*). Taken literally, this word—which in theory could be replaced by others (office or institution, for example)—gives a sense of the place of work as a home, suggesting the range of associations which give it this meaning. The variety of contexts in which this term is used underlines the metonymic relationship, which allows individuals to place themselves within a complex grouping. It may refer to the Commission as a whole, the DG, or even sometimes the service, depending on the function of the individual concerned and on the nature of the discourse. The sense of the word is conveyed by contrasts, which allow one to distinguish the 'Commission house' from those of the Council of Ministers, or of the European Parliament (EP), or, within the Commission, one DG from another.

A form of internal identification, which produces differentiation within the grouping, is conveyed by association with the names of the leading personalities. An individual DG may mark its identity

---

[3] 'Normally the "spirit" of rational bureaucracy is expressed in a general fashion by 1) formalism . . . 2) the tendency to treat administrative affairs in a material and utilitarian sense' (Weber, 1971: 23).

through the name of its Commissioner or director-general, while officials from particular services inside the DG associate themselves with their deputy director-general. Since these alignments are based on attitudes and not on social norms, individual officials are not forced into this sort of identification. They are thus further evidence of the personalization on which I commented earlier.

Other factors have to be included to make this mechanism comprehensible. In effect, the way in which these names are used makes sense only because it refers back to styles of action, to ideas put into practice, to distinctive working methods which persist in the Commission independent of changes in the leading personnel. History plays a part and it is the oldest DGs—those concerned with external relations, with co-operation and development, and with agriculture—which are most marked by the working languages adopted when they were created, and by the styles bequeathed to them by their bosses in that early period. The internal organization of the services—the functional divisions of tasks and the relationships between units—can be explained by historic patterns which enable us to understand their relative standing.

As in national administrations, individual DGs play different roles and command different budgets. Some are rich, others poor; some spend money, some collect it, others do not manage any funds. These objective differences are relevant to our argument only in so far as they lead individuals to assess their standing according to their function. The responsibility for managing structural funds—the European Agricultural Guidance and Guarantee Fund (EAGGF), the European Regional Development Fund (ERDF), and the European Social Fund (ESF)—or the European Development Fund (EDF) gives officials in the relevant DGs a sense of power. To an extent the sense of professional standing also varies over time, depending on results attained and on assessments from outside the institution.

The spheres of responsibility show another strong form of differentiation between DGs and between services. There are now some forty DGs or special services through which the Commission tackles its programme each year, in pursuit of a mandate outlined every five years, all within the framework of the treaties, of which the Commission is itself guardian. Some responsibilities are divided between the DGs, but the lines of demarcation are relatively clear, as long as one takes into account that one Commissioner may supervise several DGs, and that a DG may report to several Commissioners. The rule of collegiality governs the whole, and limits the scope for autonomy which all bureaucracies tend to encourage, so that officials do not lose sight of their policy objectives and consider only their own clientele. Charged with serving the EU as such, and without their own political legitimacy, the DGs share out the work of the Commission with a rationale which shifts depending on the agenda set by the member governments, and which periodically prompts the Commission to reorganize itself. It is not my task here to comment on whether the division of responsibilities makes sense, but simply to show that it is part of what defines the identities of those involved.

Although they are all part of the same bureaucratic organization, differences exist between DGs. Each DG has its own area of responsibility, and officials do not feel the need to define themselves with regard to all the others: there are some sharp distinctions, but also some signs of indifference. So, for example, a contrast can be drawn between those who 'build Europe from within' and those 'who defend the ideas of Europe to the outside world', or between those who 'speak the economists' common language' and those 'who do the social stuff'. Features of this kind are intrinsic to the range of tasks falling on the Commission. It is none the less striking how much these distinctions are invoked by European civil servants to justify their own places in the structure, and the judgements which they make on their own work and on that of their colleagues.

How do Commission officials become players in a specific area? The Commission recruits its staff primarily by means of the general competition, which selects economists, lawyers, linguists, and a number of specialists (veterinarians, doctors, agronomists, sociologists, and so on). The researcher has observed the tendency of experts in all fields to club together. The limited mobility of staff, and the nature of their contacts with their various institutional partners, shape Commission officials' behaviour quite quickly. From generalists moulded by their own national cultures, they become specialists in the substantive issues treated by their DGs. Here one reaches the hard core of professional identification: it leads some officials to indifference about activities which fall outside their own remit, often causing ignorance of the overall thrust of the Commission's activities.

A different process of segmentation occurs within the DGs. Our anthropological survey shows that the individuals differentiate themselves according to their areas of responsibility, making manifest clear dividing-lines between the 'conceptual' and the 'operational', the 'political' and the 'sectoral'. These sub-divisions mirror a division which recurs in most administrative organizations between horizontal and vertical responsibilities. The overall impact of this is important because it underpins the strategies that individuals adopt to motivate themselves and to manage their careers throughout the Commission.

The net result is that those who work with the Commission find themselves dealing with highly specialized European civil servants, who are relatively isolated from each other and each much preoccupied with how he or she can steer his or her own dossiers through the organization. Though the Commission appears to be characterized by this fragmentation and the corollary feeling of European officials that they live in a segmented world, it would be wrong to conclude that there is a lack of coherence in time, or cohesion in space. The administrative organization of the Commission is certainly complex, and the DGs are dispersed across some forty different sites. However, the Secretariat-General is responsible for co-ordinating the various services, in order to resolve as early as possible any differences of opinion and to promote a basis for consensus. The aim is to allow the college of Commissioners to take a collective position on the proposals to be transmitted to the Council. The mechanisms for inter-service co-ordination, alongside the general rules governing the work of officials and decision-making within each DG and within the college, produce a form of unity. To the outside world, be it the Council, national partners, or European citizens, the Commission seeks to be united in making its proposals.

RELATIONSHIPS WITH EXTERNAL PARTNERS

If it is to fulfil its role as initiator of European policy, the Commission has to develop real powers of anticipation, in order to suggest policies which have a chance of being accepted after long negotiations and bargaining with the member states (Keohane and Hoffmann, 1991*a*). Commissioners and the officials in the services

are in an unusual situation in two senses: it falls to them to formulate new ideas; and they are engaged in a process of institutional
innovation which leaves to the member states the responsibility for
putting European decisions into practice (Metcalfe, 1994). Elected
members of the European Parliament (MEPs) play little part in
this process: quite apart from the formal limits to their powers,
which extended to co-decision only under the TEU, it is the complexity of the issues addressed that largely accounts for the predominance of 'technocrats' and 'policy experts' in the development
of European public policy. Hence, Peters (1992: 119) observes that
'the linkages that the Directorates have with national governments
tend to be functionally specific, so that professional and technical
criteria often guide decisions more than the national concerns
which may arise in the Council'.

The construction of Europe remains incomplete and the Commission thus lives permanently by making plans for the future.
Anthropological analysis highlights one particular set of difficulties
that follows from this. The continuous focus on the future is a real
constraint on European civil servants: in moments of crisis, when
Euro-pessimism tends to prevail in popular opinion, they are
forced to question the purpose of their activity (Abélès *et al.*, 1996:
52). Yet it is precisely this willingness to look to the future which
qualifies the Commission to be a special kind of administration.
The Commission is not an executive agency, neither in the sense
of implementing the decisions that it proposes, nor in the service
of a political authority, elected on the basis of its programme. It
only has to explain itself to the political authorities: MEPs and
the ministers or their representatives in the Council. No censure
motion has ever criticized its work programme. Its freedom for
manœuvre, so much criticized by Eurosceptics and other national-
ists, is actually constrained by several factors: the budgetary control
exercised by the EP; the practice of consulting the diverse parties
and groups concerned by its activities; a respect for judicial norms
which govern decision-making in the EU; and, finally, the objective
constraints interposed by cultural diversity.[4] While this may not
amount to formal responsibility, in the sense of executive accountability, it would be wrong to assume that the Commission is entirely

---

[4] See the discussion about the preparation of the 1996 IGC in *Agence Europe*
1995.

autonomous (Peters, 1992). Political scientists interested in the 'democratic deficit' and academic experts in management focus on whether the Commission should behave like a classic bureaucracy *vis-à-vis* political authority. Anthropologists, in contrast, are interested in the ways in which European civil servants behave *vis-à-vis* the Council and the EP, the political authorities which subject their proposals to controls.

The Commission involves numerous actors, governmental and non-governmental, in its deliberations on European policies. It commissions studies and plans from innumerable groups of consultants; it seeks out experts from the member states, who deal with the policy issues on which it hopes to produce proposals; and it draws many of its intellectual resources from outside its own ranks. Intellectuals are much engaged in the Commission's deliberations—hence the role of its own Forward Studies Unit, or of the *Carrefours Européens de la Science* (convened by Jacques Delors), or the exchanges between senior officials and academic institutions and specialists in their areas of work. Non-governmental organizations are encouraged to intervene, which endows all kinds of groups with the right to bring their interests to the attention of the formal institutions. These invitations to consult are signals from the Commission of how distinctively it approaches its task of policy formulation.

However, the human resources within the Commission are limited: it has about 14,000 staff, about half the size of the administration of the city of Paris. It has had to increase its mechanisms for consultation with outside interests in some respects, thus transforming the traditional mode of policy-making. A visitor to the nerve-centre of the EC may not realize either how few staff the Commission has or how varied are the origins of the individuals whom they meet in the corridors. It is only when you know the machinery of the Commission well, and the individuals within it, that you appreciate how open the structure is, or that European civil servants receive many lobbyists but do not always view them equally nor allow all to have a hand in drafting proposals.

Given how many interlocutors it has and the patterns of consultation, the Commission could not possibly revert to a method of work which depended solely on its internal resources. If it did, it would become a hive of Eurocrats of which national administrations would necessarily be wary, both because of how they were recruited and because it would become isolated. The only result could then be a reorganization that would turn the Commission into an executive agency.

An essential part of the Commission's activity therefore rests on its collaboration with non-governmental actors and on a continual dialogue with administrations and political authorities, in the member states, in the other European institutions, and elsewhere. This is the logic behind the creation of groups of experts to advise the Commission, the *raison d'être* for the institutional linkage between national and European officials in the procedures known as 'comitology', and the motivation for the countless visits and meetings which European civil servants organize in Brussels and elsewhere (see Chapters 2 and 4).

Relationships with Governmental Actors

The Council has a large number of working groups, charged with preparing the decisions of the Committee of Permanent Representatives (Coreper) and sessions of the Council, with their functional division of labour: political, technical, and geographical. Managed by the Secretariat General of the Council, they bring together partners familiar in terms of their national and sectoral origins, although the individual faces may change. Here the representatives of the Commission's DGs find themselves facing national civil servants, from the capitals or from the permanent representations. The latter stay in post for two to three years on average, although the Germans and the Italians tend to have longer postings, and in certain highly specialized areas such as the Article 113 Committee (dealing with trade policy), the members have mostly known each other for five to ten years, regardless of nationality.

As the discussion shifts from the working groups to the Council, so the negotiation moves from the more technical to the more political, reflecting the status of the individuals involved. At the very senior levels, ministers and Commissioners reach the final settlements which square national and European interests. It is in the course of this process, and the complementing debates in the committees and the plenary session of the EP, that the Commission's propositions can be altered, and, on occasion, abandoned.

The number of expert committees attached to the Commission has become vast, though their creation and extension are governed by various rules and procedures (see Chapter 2). Since 1988 the Commission, through its Secretariat General, has set in train a series of measures to improve the consultative procedures and the budgetary arrangements for these committees, for varying reasons. Some consultative committees are temporary, convened by a DG to explore and to incorporate the views of national administrations and their experts before making formal proposals. Permanent management committees, on the other hand, bring together national experts so as to implement common policies—agriculture, transport, external trade, and so on; they often have specialized sub-committees and take decisions by qualified majority vote (QMV). Permanent technical committees manage aid programmes under the Lomé Convention, notably the EDF Committee, which also takes decisions by QMV. Similar long-term, though not permanent, committees manage other technical assistance programmes, such as Phare for the countries of central and eastern Europe and Tacis for the Commonwealth of Independent States. Alongside these are the mixed consultative committees, which bring European and national civil servants together with representatives from third countries to manage the EU's external relations.

This committee structure underlines that there is partnership between national and European officials in developing policy. However, the European officials differ from their national partners in at least two ways. The first concerns their objectives. While there is no single profile of a European civil servant, their interests converge around the promotion of the 'European cause'. Some come with a vocation to 'build Europe', attracted by the multicultural environment and the challenges posed by operating beyond the nation-state; this used to be more evident than it is today. Others, usually younger officials, are motivated by the career opportunities and the salaries offered by the Commission; their preoccupations are thus different from those of the 'militant Europeans', but they are generally strongly committed to the activities of the institution.

Pluralists by nature, European civil servants are not the obscure bureaucrats that the title 'Eurocrat' implies. Cultural diversity, as well as the rules of the institutional game which give the Council and the EP the power to legislate, make Commission officials well aware of the limits to their powers. Even in those services of the

Commission which manage unambiguously *communautaire* policies no idea, however brilliant, can pass directly from its originator to a decision-maker within a single national or political network, despite the weight of a relatively traditional hierarchy which leaves room for traditional systems of influence. The decision-making process operates as a filter and a means to control both individual and policy plans. Recourse to widespread consultation in the early stages and the continuous lobbying of operational services by interest groups and firms of consultants force senior officials to act as umpires and repeatedly to justify their preferences. It is thus that a European character is attributed to each of the Commission's actions.

Suspicions of national bias are as frequent, but less often demonstrated, and European officials endeavour not to be caught by such distortions. For many of them, 'renationalization' and 'repoliticization' go hand in hand, and are linked to a growing influence of member governments over the Commission, although they are contrary to the principle of defending the European interest. But the game is subtle. On the one hand, they try to resist, knowing that at various points, especially at European Council sessions, some of the links in the chain are weak. On the other hand, it seems that the only way of curbing a dominant interest is to allow a proliferation of all types of influence; thus they encourage officials to echo some of the national demands on them, be they public or private.

The essence of the power of Commission officials rests on their right to formulate the initiatives or choices facing the Community, while producing proposals that can win acceptance at several levels: by the bureaucratic hierarchy; by the college; by Council negotiators; and by MEPs. They also enjoy some forms of control, through which they can impose sanctions on recalcitrant member states. Facing Commission officials, national civil servants defend national positions on the basis of recommendations or, more formally, instructions from ministries and the national units which co-ordinate European policy, such as the *Secrétariat Général du Comité Interministériel pour les Affaires Européennes* (SGCI) in France, or the European Secretariat of the Cabinet Office in the UK (Pappas, 1994). They can sense the difficulties inherent in multilateral negotiations. Generally agreement on a common position can be formulated as such only at the level of the Council; it is a complicated exercise, leaving scope for misunderstandings. In the early stages, negotiators seek to be conciliatory or place their reserves. At the later stages, actual decisions are taken, supposedly in full knowledge of the issues.

Do these decisions serve the public interest? It is difficult to find an answer, if one thinks of the stakes when a national industry seeks to defend itself and the employment that it represents. The way the issue of banana imports was addressed is a particularly telling illustration, even if it illustrates only some of the complexities of policy-making. Within the EC, three different types of banana are traded, and each is treated differently by the Commission's services and within the member governments. The 'dollar banana' is the most prized by the Germans who, being large consumers, prefer the prices charged by the American multinationals, when they gain access to the European market; a service in DGI (external trade relations) deals with this type of banana. The French and Spanish look after their national producers by defending the 'Community banana', which is produced in the Antilles and the Canary Islands, a concern shared by the Portuguese and Greeks as smaller producers; a service in DGVI is responsible. The 'ACP (African, Caribbean, and Pacific) banana' on the other hand is defended by 'Europeans' (principally in this case the British) and by a unit in DGVIII, as part of the Lomé Convention. During the Uruguay Round of the General Agreement on Tariffs and Trade it was essential that these three services agree a common line for the Commission to operate its mandate in this global negotiation. Each deadline in each forum in turn revealed the contradictions. Each time European civil servants had to reconcile a European position with the competing national demands from the member states.

How far can one consider as a wider public interest, a German national interest which depends on satisfying the interests of American multinationals and ship owners? The question became larger, because in the Council negotiations, senior German, Dutch, and Belgian civil servants and ministers defended a shared position in favour of free access for American bananas to the European market, apparently after being lobbied by representatives of these interests. On the other hand the consequence of support for more expensive ACP or EC-produced bananas was to penalize the European consumer. This type of contradiction is recurrent and the nature of the interests to be satisfied by European regulations is more complicated than it appears at first sight.

One need only look at the constraints that regulation of exhaust emissions places on the car industry and at the reactions that they arouse in southern member states, where firms find it harder to meet the standards pushed by the northern governments. Yet European citizens, regardless of nationality, have everything to gain from the cleaner air which is a collective and public good. Caught between the harmonization of technical criteria and political considerations at both national and European levels an incalculable number of adjustments are needed for the creation of an integrated Europe. But a process operates which allows dialogue; it leads some European civil servants to consider themselves to be 'in the service of the Community and its member states, neither for their country of origin nor against the member states'.

The second novel feature of the Commission is the way it organizes its relations with interlocutors in pursuit of its aims. There is an abundant literature on 'comitology', the influence of experts, and the role of pressure groups in the development of European decisions. From a European perspective it is interesting to know what part national civil servants play in the Commission's deliberations and what the role of experts and lobby groups is *vis-à-vis* national and European administrations. Does the Commission have the means to act independently? Apart from the methods of recruitment, a wider pattern of politico-administrative behaviour is in play. On overtly political issues, national administrations have the means to influence the Commission's deliberations, provided that their representatives are well-prepared. The British take the very clear view that it is necessary to know about the Commission's plans at a very early stage in order to influence them on the one hand, and to prepare a national response on the other. The vigilance of the UK's Permanent Representation mobilizes Whitehall departments in an extensive 'clearance' process which produces a government line on policy. It also engages the representatives of various British interests through their contacts with the government departments of which they are the clients (the Department of Trade and Industry, the Department of the Environment, and the Ministry of Agriculture, Fisheries and Food, and so on) (Spence, 1993; H. Wallace, 1995). National administrations lobby the Commission progressively and more or less intensively, or rely on their nationals within the Commission's services to gain access to information, a process which is not straightforward.

There is a fine line between giving out information on its plans, to which the Commission puts up little resistance, and allowing influence over which options are chosen; but it is here that the distinction is drawn between a decision to promote an overall European interest and the satisfaction of narrower concerns, whether national or private. Alongside those decisions influenced by private interests or intended to favour a particular national interest, there are many others which are based on a rounder view, or on a careful planning process, or on an appraisal of the qualities of the firms affected or the consultants being retained. European civil servants are the first to recognize the influence of pressure groups over certain items of European legislation (notably directives), but they tend to be most conscious of the role of national negotiators and the way they are able to promote the preferences of large national consortia from farming, industry, and financial services.

It is a hard distinction to pin down if we want to assess the patterns of influence; it requires us to distinguish between the factors that belong to the policy process and those which arise from the operations of markets. The following case serves as an example. In 1992–3 few Spanish firms were selected in the tendering procedures of DGVIII (Co-operation and Development), in contrast to British, German, French, and Italian firms, all coming from countries marked as former colonial powers. Thanks to the commissioner in charge of this sector, the Spanish set about extending Community co-operation to Latin American countries, a shift which fuelled the debate on the philosophy of development aid. This brought into the open the question of whether national biases, promoted by the nationalities of those responsible for calls for tender, were the cause of a weakness, known in Euro-jargon as the 'rate of return'. This is calculated in relation to member states' financial contributions to a particular budget line, in this case the EDF. According to Commission officials and the Spanish Secretariat of State for European Affairs, enquiries apparently showed that Spanish firms, cushioned by their national markets in the run-up to the Olympic Games and the World Fair, were not competitive.

But this observation feeds further reflection about how Europe itself induces competition between Europeans in both national and international markets and about how choices are made. Commissioners and the president of the Commission have at their disposal the means to influence the Commission's legal service, and also the options chosen in the DGs and the services, as they face the pressures of such competition. But for the anthropologist the scales do not balance on the basis of accounting criteria, which are the domain of financial controllers, the Court of Auditors, and the dozens of inspectors who can intervene at any moment. However, it is evident that this question of who exerts influence is the most sensitive for the Commission, and that the least glorious cases are also the best hidden.

Some of what is involved can be seen periodically when occasional accusations of corruption reach the courts. The remarks that follow here are not based on an in-depth enquiry of this subject. However, the researcher can observe the way in which a problem that arises outside the Commission may find its way into the Commission services via a game of stereotypes. Italian officials, for example, felt that both their colleagues and national administrators were getting at them in 1993 when the word 'corruption' was used. It is the Greeks who are under pressure to assume a particularly heavy moral tone at the word 'inefficiency'. Suggestions of improper behaviour do not have to be legally demonstrated or based on clear evidence; an offence does not need to have been committed for the problem to arise through innuendo. In such a situation, perceptions of Greek and Italian nationals in the Commission come from the simplistic assumption often made by people from the northern countries that illegal practices, laxness, and Mediterranean attitudes are all equivalent. These stereotypes are echoed in the Commission, irrespective of any appreciation of the qualities of individual nationals from southern countries. By way of defence, the latter use the same tones to criticize, for example, the British, French, German, or Danish decision-makers, whom they suspect of 'knowing better how to make use of the Commission for much larger-scale operations'.

It is difficult to conduct a calm debate on a topic which reveals clashes of cultures, given the opaqueness which persists, despite the Commission's quite open instincts. Hence its officials are formally committed to playing the game of 'transparency', just as much as the member governments. In the main, therefore, apart from those control procedures aimed at checking on any illicit actions by the services of the Commission, especially as regards the programmes which it implements itself and in the expenditures from the structural funds, the Commission prefers a line of openness and transparency.

Relationships with Interest Groups

Mazey and Richardson (1995: 95) argue that there is a trend in the EC towards the emergence of a more 'mature' form of bureaucratic behaviour, which places the emphasis on more regularized and predictable relationships with interest groups. The anthropologist notes the overall influence of non-governmental actors in the process of developing European policies. But the question follows of how national and European interests, or public and private interests, are articulated. In general one can observe an increasing influence by those private interests which occupy, both substantively and intellectually, the space between European and national policies and politics. Can one therefore talk of individual DGs having their own distinct clients? A debate on this requires greater knowledge of the relationships which each DG has with the actors and subjects concerned by the policies for which it is responsible.

There is a burgeoning literature devoted to the EU process of negotiation and bargaining, to the reasoning behind the subdivisions between policy areas, and the consequences of the shift from reliance on unanimity to the use of QMV. Yet it remains difficult to follow the way in which an idea progresses in the European fabric to take the form of a policy. On the basis of his fourteen years' experience in the Commission, Robert Hull (1993: 83–4) makes it clear that the influence of lobbyists is all the greater if they are active at the stage when a decision is being prepared. When the Council's negotiations are eventually over, the drafters of proposals will find that 80 per cent of their original ideas remain, hardly an inconsiderable proportion. Yet only 5 per cent of lobbyists, in Hull's experience, are likely to intervene at a really early stage; most address an issue only when the Commission makes it public, that is, as it sets in motion the mechanisms for consultation with the member governments.

Staff in the Commission find it easier to weight the arguments articulated by interest groups the more numerous they are. Given the proliferation of interest groups (over 3,000) and the number of people positioned to lobby the Commission and the EP (over

10,000), the Commission prefers its officials to be open and wel-
coming (Commission, 1992*b*). This policy is justified on two counts.
First, interest groups constitute a real source of information for
European civil servants; and, second, they have widely varying
means of exercising influence. The practice of recognizing the
rights of all groups which want a hearing is one of the ways of
avoiding a situation in which small non-governmental organizations are never heard. It also reduces the temptation for large
multinational firms to put undue pressure on officials to incorporate their aims and to bias in their favour a draft regulation or
directive.

Yet there is an issue about when and how the 'clienteles' of the
individual DGs are informed about work-in-progress, given that
there are special relationships with both individuals and certain
groups outside the Commission. Are the lists of the privileged
closed or intended to be opened up, as European activity reaches
into national life, whether public or private (Sidjanski, 1995)? Besides the activities of DGX (responsible for information about the
Commission), each DG has its own tools for external and internal
communication in the form of bulletins, newsletters, and newspapers targeted at specialized audiences (economic operators, regional actors, partners in third countries, and so on). Just as is the
case with efforts to address European citizens as a whole, so for the
clienteles of DGs, there is a huge problem about the nature of
messages transmitted by European authorities to country nationals, who are marked by their national preoccupations and their own
particular interests when it comes to translation and interpretation
from one style to another. Close contact with European officials
reduces the problem, as lobbyists have realized, but just how open
can the Commission be? The multiplication of points of contact
with European officials, partly on the basis of their nationality,
but also because they are identified by the permanent representations and by the institutional lobbyists as responsible for certain
dossiers, risks compromising more radically the independence of
the institution.

The Council working groups, which examine the Commission's
proposals, and the Commission's committees, in which the most
varied subjects come up for discussion before finally becoming
Commission proposals, offer remarkable scope for the articulation
of different interests affected by European policies. For Mazey and

Richardson (1995), it is the concentration of power within the bureaucracy which makes it a favoured point of entry for lobbyists, in line with a natural tendency well known to national governments. The capacity that these groups have in supplying reliable technical information has a logical outcome: 'it is not surprising that one of the key traits of the EU's political process is the use of committees as instruments for the development of policy' (Mazey and Richardson, 1995: 96).

A nuance must be added; the multiplication of interest groups and the special hearing which the Commission gives them might be due to the lack of human resources in the Commission and to the Commission's desire not to depend on the national administrations, which rely on deliberations with their own public administration. The Commission, while escaping the constraints of national politics, tries to reduce its distance from social realities by getting information from many different sources. The dynamic has a tendency to develop. The process of lobbying the Commission has intensified since the SEA; and those involved have become professionalized to the point where Hull (1993: 83) considers that, under certain circumstances, they could become actual participants in the decision-making process: 'Lobbying and pressure group activity therefore needs to be built upon a sophisticated understanding of, and connection to, each of the Community institutions and Member States'.

The Commission's lack of human resources, with its corollary shortage of internal expertise, is evident every time that the EC embarks on a new area of activity. This is especially so when it is building simply on the treaties' legal base rather than developing its own initiatives. The process launched by the SEA to create the single market by 1993 was made possible by an acceleration in the recruitment of national experts on secondment and of temporary officials, through the policy of 'mini-budgets', which authorized the DGs to acquire the infrastructures, the instruments and the personnel to tackle the new demands made on them. When the Court of Auditors condemned this practice in 1991, the problem was resolved by making the temporary posts into permanent ones, but the demand for experts and temporary officials remains strong. The number of directives to be prepared for the single market brought into the daylight an array of regulations over which interest groups could express their preferences. But we should also note how behaviour adapts to the institutional game: to be able to steer an idea through the jungle which is Brussels, specialists have made themselves indispensable at the stage when a problem is articulated. Their role is to present a solution to the services of the Commission, and then throughout the subsequent process, in order to overcome the institutional fragmentation. The lobbyists adapt to this multi-polar framework, putting pressure on the Commission and the EP, and insinuating themselves into the permanent representations in order to lean on the negotiators in the working groups of the Council.

The fall of the Berlin Wall led to the opening up of a new geographical arena for international co-operation and technical assistance, both in central and eastern Europe and in the Commonwealth of Independent States. The implementation of the Phare and Tacis programmes caused an explosion in the Commission's services dealing with these countries and they became fully fledged directorates, their staff increasing in three years from two groups of twelve people to over five hundred people. Most of the new recruits were taken on as experts, with the skills relevant to the specific needs of these countries in such areas as public health, nuclear safety, and institutional transformation. They all find themselves at the heart of a system subject to pressures from all directions, from national authorities as much as from private enterprises, on issues of access to public markets, the management of study contracts, the construction of hospitals, and the installation of communications networks. The outside pressures can be quite direct and concern either particular markets, in relation to which the DGs have a good deal of latitude in awarding contracts, or public markets in which the requirements can be specified at the short-listing stage in such a way that the contract can be awarded to a particular firm, while respecting the objectively stated criteria. This may have a broader political significance, in that those engaged in tendering have an interest in helping to define policy frameworks favourable to the intervention of market forces.

CONCLUSION

Contrary to the rules of classical theatre—based on unity of time, place, and action—the Commission plays its role in a temporal space oriented towards the future, and characterized by the multi-polarity and the plurality of policies and different methods of decision-making. The Commission is clearly the institution best placed to know the agenda of the Council and to know to the day the calendar of relevant legal, technical, and political developments. Yet it does not have complete freedom of action. The constraints on it stem from the general complexity of the decision-making process and the difficulties of reconciling national and European positions rather than from any obligation to account for itself politically to the representatives of the people or governments. A director can thus state regret at his work being 'subject to the primacy of the "chronogramme"'. This linguistic invention refers to the overall timetable of dates which the Commission must respect in the institutional division of labour in the EC. The term underlines the feeling of the officials involved that they are 'working against the clock', without having enough time to consider fully their policy plans or to think.

The concept of *engrenage* applies to the interwoven relationships between the Commission and its interlocutors. This method of working permeates the Commission's dialogue with national administrations, which is marked by continuous exchanges of information, from the initial to the final stages of policy-making, whether the initiatives start at the EC or national level. When the Commission works on a mandate from the Council, or when it decides to pronounce on a problem which can be addressed only at the European level (for example, the White Paper on Growth, Competitiveness and Employment), or when it puts in order its own methods of management (as, for example in the new regulation on the structural funds), the initiative is *communautaire*. But member governments have the chance to push policy ideas at the Commission, either when they take over the Council presidency or when they request a commissioner to comment on a particular subject. *Engrenage* is thus a feature of the way the Commission proceeds, which is based on external sources of information, studies, evaluation, and the implementation of plans and directives. 'The invention of Europe', characterized by the fact that 80 per cent of national social and economic legislation derives from EC law, is exhibited in the engagement of partners who obey rules different from those practised in national political and administrative cultures.

The Commission plays a leading role in this evolution, but the European stage, which has prompted interest groups to reveal their presence openly, has the peculiarity of increasing the possible types of influencing activities. In the development of standards and laws, British and Nordic cultures attach less importance to the bureaucracy than to the legitimacy of elected representatives and of non-governmental organizations, private or voluntary. Mediterranean culture shows less confidence in individuals, when it comes to regulating collective interests, than in institutional structures and judicial frameworks. The Commission's own approach is affected by both cultures: hence the EC functions with a political administration which defies all the national rules of the states which compose it. Thus we can conclude that the Commission has the traits of a bureaucracy experienced by a society in transition: it behaves like a prism, to use Riggs's term (1964: 44). Although a powerful bureaucracy, without coherent cultural support at the EU level it has developed practices influenced by national cultures, administrations, and policies, with its officials recruited to pursue a broader idea. From the *idea* of Europe to its implementation there is much room for different systems of influence and for widely varying interests to be represented.

6

Organizing Industrial Coalitions: A Challenge for the Future?

MARIA GREEN COWLES

The political activities of multinational enterprises (MNEs) and their industrial coalitions have changed the face of policy-making in Brussels. Today, members of the European Round Table of Industrialists (ERT) spell out their industrial agenda in private meetings with heads of state and government and in public documents. Hundreds of company representatives in the EU Committee of the American Chamber of Commerce (EU Committee)—one of the most powerful lobbying organizations in Brussels—operate a legislative intelligence network. MNEs now occupy key policy positions within the Union of Industrial and Employers' Confederations of Europe (UNICE) and, through the UNICE Advisory and Support Group (UASG), contribute funding directly to the European peak association. Participants of the European Enterprise Group (EEG) quietly co-ordinate the large firms' activities behind the scenes.

Given the perceived power of these big business organizations, it is perhaps surprising that the participation of industrial coalitions in Brussels policy-making is a relatively recent phenomenon in the history of the European Union (EU) (Cowles, 1994). Indeed, one can trace the creation of three major industrial coalitions—the ERT, the EU Committee, and the EEG—to the late 1970s and early 1980s. Why did MNEs organize into industrial coalitions? Why did they mobilize relatively late in the EU's history? How have relations developed between the industrial coalitions and the EU institutions? What implications does their participation have for the efficiency and legitimacy of EU policy and for future participation and policy-making in the EU? This chapter explores why and how these industrial coalitions mobilized in the EU, and high-lights their roles and relationships in Brussels today.[1]

MNES AND THE EARLY YEARS

Following the early research on European interest groups (Haas, 1968; Meynaud and Sidjanski, 1974), many scholars assumed that large firms formed industrial coalitions and participated in EU policy-making from the creation of the European Coal and Steel Community onwards. The fact, however, is that these European firms were largely excluded from direct involvement in the form-ative years of the EU. On the one hand, leading figures, such as Jean Monnet, shunned big business, because they believed that the large companies were too nationalistic in orientation to support the federal idea (Cowles, 1994). Members of the Monnet Action Committee for Europe were Christian and Social Democrats and trade-union leaders whose interests were in important respects antithetical to those of European big business during this period. This was a period when policy-makers preferred to emphasize consultation with 'associations' of firms rather than with individual companies. The preference was reinforced, particularly in the German case, by perceptions about the activities of certain companies during the Second World War (Ehrmann, 1957).

On the other hand, the large companies themselves were preoc-cupied with rebuilding their industries in the post-war era. They demonstrated greater interest in the creation of the General Agreement on Tariffs and Trade (GATT) than in the nascent European project. As a consequence, large firms did not play any significant role at the Brussels level in the formative years of the EU, either because they had other preoccupations or because they were precluded from actively participating in the new European institutions.[2]

---

[1] The material for this chapter is drawn largely from Cowles (1994). I would like to thank Keith Richardson and colleagues for their comments on an earlier draft.

[2] One of the first attempts to bring large companies together at the European level occurred in 1967 when the Groupe des Présidents des Grandes Entreprises Européennes was created. Composed of the CEOs of 12 major European compan-ies, the group never aspired to play a political role in European policy-making. Over the years, the organization gained a reputation as a 'social club'. The group was formally disbanded in 1988, when its membership largely merged with the ERT. See Cowles (1996a).

SEEDS OF CHANGE

Ironically, among the first companies to take a more serious interest were large American firms. During the 1950s and 1960s, these firms invested heavily in Europe in order to take advantage of the newly created common market (Gilpin, 1975; Wilkins, 1974). At first, the American companies and their capital were welcomed on the continent. Over time, however, the dramatic increase in foreign direct investment (FDI) raised concerns in European public and élite opinion over the American MNEs' potential control over the European economy, as well as their potential challenge to European governments' sovereignty (Behrman, 1970; Servan-Schreiber, 1968; Vernon, 1971; 1977). The European public developed a two-sided image of multinational firms; the companies were viewed positively in terms of their technological contribution to the economy, but negatively in terms of their potential threat to democratic society (Peninou *et al.*, 1978).

The size and activities of American MNEs compared to most EU firms also attracted the attention of the Commission, which viewed '"corporate bigness" as a political threat to European society' (Robinson, 1983: 74). To combat the perceived abuses of power by multinational firms, the Commission turned to European competition law and the European Court of Justice (ECJ). Competition policies drawn up in the 1950s to prevent European cartels came to be directed towards American MNEs by virtue of their relative size. Indeed, European case-law developed largely at the expense of American firms.[3]

In addition to taking action through the ECJ, the Commission developed its own policy *vis-à-vis* American and European MNEs alike. In the early 1970s, Altiero Spinelli, then the commissioner responsible for industry, laid out a general plan to address the economic and social problems raised by the activities of the multinationals. The result was a memorandum entitled 'Multinational Undertakings in the European Community', which was sent to the

---

[3] In the first competition case involving Article 86 (EEC), the ECJ ruled in February 1973 against the American multinational, Continental Can, charging the company with abusing its dominant position. This ruling was applied to another American multinational, Commercial Solvents, a year later. The second major extension of the European competition law occurred in February 1978, when the ECJ upheld the Continental Can decision in a case against United Brands, and fined the American multinational approximately one million dollars.

Council of Ministers in 1973. While the uncertainty prompted by the global oil crisis precluded immediate action on the 'multinationals programme', the Commission began to generate a number of specific pieces of legislation called for in the Spinelli memorandum. The resulting measures—including directives on subsidiary accounts, group accounts, group liability, and worker protection—represented the first examples of European cross-sectoral regulatory legislation (Greenwood *et al.*, 1992*a*).

The accession of the United Kingdom to the EC in 1973, along with its national business association, the Confederation of British Industry (CBI), also changed the status of MNEs in EU policy-making. In general, continental business confederations limited their membership to sectoral business associations (Cowles, 1996*b*). The CBI, however, allowed individual firms to participate directly. Consequently, the CBI brought European multinational firms directly into European business groups and EU policy-making for the first time. The CBI also gave a more transnational flavour to the existing European business groups, in that it included the largest number of MNEs of any national business association in the EU.[4]

The access of European companies to the European institutions was altered fundamentally again in the late 1970s by the activities and policy approach of Étienne Davignon, then commissioner for industry. Unlike his predecessors, Davignon gave multinational firms direct access to the Commission and worked closely with leaders of firms to negotiate agreements designed to improve their competitiveness during the economic malaise of the 1970s.[5] He encouraged their participation in European programmes such as the Davignon Plan (Hodges, 1983) for the steel industry and the European Strategic Programme for Research and Development in Information Technology (Esprit) (Sandholtz, 1992). Thus, MNEs began to view the Commission as an honest broker, an organization with which the firms could 'do business'.

[4] The attendance lists of the early CBI Europe Committee meetings (composed of presidents of firms or their representatives) reflected this transnational tone with names such as Chrysler, Banque Nationale de Paris, ICI, and Imperial Tobacco.
[5] Previously Commission officials were reluctant to meet with individual business leaders, because of the Commission's judicial role in competition policy, its traditional strong ties with labour unions, and the negative press coverage that might be provoked. Indeed, several commissioners protested at Davignon's business ties, but Roy Jenkins, then president of the Commission, overruled their objections.

TABLE 6.1. *Major companies with strong and relatively sophisticated public affairs departments for managing European policy issues in 1979*

Avon	Ford	Philips
Bank of Tokyo	General Dynamics	Plessey
BASF	General Foods	Procter & Gamble
BAT	General Motors	Rank Xerox
Bayer	Goodyear	Reid International
British Petroleum	Hoechst	Royal Dutch Shell
Brown Boveri	IBM	Siemens
Caterpillar	ICI	Sperry
Ciba-Geigy	ITT	3M
Continental Group	Mars	Toyota
CPC	Merck Sharp & Dohme	TRW
Datsun	Monsanto	Unilever
Dow Chemicals	National Westminster	Union Carbide
DuPont	Nestlé	United Brands
Esso Chemicals	Pechiney Ugine Kuhlmann	Upjohn
Fiat	Pfizer	UTC
FMC		Volvo

Source: Robinson (1983): 203.

Davignon's tenure, however, also reflected the two-edged approach to MNEs found in European society during the 1970s. While supporting MNE industrial competitiveness, the commissioner also established an MNE policy group to follow through the legislation first outlined in the 1973 Spinelli memorandum. Indeed, global developments, such as the 1976 Guidelines for Multinationals agreed in the Organization for Economic Co-operation and Development (OECD), as well as the 'anti-multinational' movement in the United Nations, placed greater pressure on the Commission to develop its own MNE policy (Robinson, 1983).

As a result of developments during the decade, by 1979 about 50 MNEs had established relatively sophisticated public affairs departments for managing European policy issues (see Table 6.1). While these companies began to follow European developments in greater detail, there was little inter-firm co-ordination to address European regulatory matters.

Regulatory Policy and the Organization of Industrial Coalitions

The catalyst for the organization of industrial coalitions proved to be the Commission's October 1980 'Proposal for a Council Direc-

tive on Procedures for Informing and Consulting the Employees
of Undertakings with Complex Structures, in particular Transnational Undertakings'. It became known as the 'multinationals
directive' or, more commonly, the 'Vredeling initiative' after
its author, Henk Vredeling, then the commissioner for social
affairs.

The Vredeling proposal was designed to institutionalize em-
ployee participation in MNEs. Some observers, however, viewed
it as a vehicle for promoting collective bargaining at the European
level. The directive would require companies to enter into consultations with employees on general company strategies. It
would apply not only to relations between the parent company and
its European subsidiaries, but would also affect the 'relationship
between the parent company and its subsidiaries in the same
Member State' (Blanpain *et al.*, 1983: 5). The Vredeling initiative
also had an extra-territorial dimension: it required multinational
firms whose headquarters were located outside the then EC to
establish consultation procedures between the parent company and
subsidiaries.

The Vredeling proposal did not please most firms, many of which
were looking for more flexibility in dealing with the 1970s economic malaise. Anglo-Saxon companies in particular saw the
Vredeling initiative as further evidence of the dominance of trade
unions in continental western Europe and international affairs
(Blanpain *et al.*, 1983). The proposal marked a turning-point in the
attitudes of MNEs. The Commission was no longer just a benign
body, but an organization apparently capable of restricting and
diluting the management prerogatives of multinational enterprises.
Company representatives now acknowledged that rules made in
Brussels would be binding on governments and 'thus [could] actually change both the national and transnational frameworks in
which international business operates' (Robinson, 1979: 17).

The Vredeling proposal heightened MNE representatives' concerns about their ability to influence the European policy-making
process. At first glance, this is surprising given that the Council of
Ministers largely relied on unanimous decision-making prior to
1987. In theory, the firms needed to convince only one government
to resist legislation. In practice, however, the situation was quite
different. Many MNEs had learned that they could not afford to
rely on the veto power of their 'home' government (Cowles, 1994).
The fact that many government officials continued to regard MNEs

in a negative light was one reason for avoiding reliance on a willingness of individual governments to block legislation.

The package deals often agreed among government negotiators were another reason why big business did not rely on the governments' veto power. As one MNE representative noted, 'We recognized that if it came to a crunch in the Council, and we [the MNEs] were persuading one of the governments to hold their support, there would be a high danger of a trade-off'.[6] Company officials were concerned that a vote on Vredeling could be traded for a vote on agricultural prices or regional funding, for example.

Finally, some MNEs were wary of policy changes resulting from the arrival of new parties to government in their 'home' countries. British companies, in particular, could not be certain that the next election in 1983 would preserve the Tory government. They were concerned that a Labour government might be more inclined to approve an issue like the Vredeling proposal. As a consequence, merely looking to their home government to block the legislation was not a reliable option for companies.

MNE representatives also became reluctant to rely on UNICE, the peak organization of European business, to take strong action *vis-à-vis* certain legislation. Company officials actually viewed UNICE as a weak, inefficient organization incapable of responding to policies in a proactive manner.[7] Moreover, they discovered that, although the organization had some 30 committees, no UNICE official or committee was given overall responsibility for reviewing the Commission's legislation on MNEs. The firms realized that, although the Vredeling initiative imposed considerable financial and cultural costs on their operations, it caused little hardship for the civil servants and national business federations (comprised largely of small- and medium-sized firms) of UNICE.

Consequently, MNEs discovered that they could no longer rely either on the home governments or on the existing European business organizations to represent their interests on European regulatory matters. It became clear to many large companies that they would have to work together if they were to have a voice in the Vredeling initiative. Two industrial coalitions emerged: the European Enterprise Group (EEG) and what became the

---

[6] Interview by author, London, 20 Nov. 1992.
[7] For a discussion of the problems within UNICE over the years see Hammerich (1969).

EU Committee of the American Chamber of Commerce (EU Committee).

The European Enterprise Group

In late 1980 a group of government affairs representatives of leading European MNEs met together in Brussels to discuss how their firms could promote their interests better. The group became known as the European Enterprise Group.[8] Early members of the group included British Petroleum, Fiat, Ford, Hoechst, IBM, ICI, Shell, Solvay, and Unilever.

The EEG began as an ante-chamber, holding pre-meetings before UNICE meetings. Representatives from various MNEs assembled to discuss their positions on legislative matters before meeting with the national business associations. While the original *raison d'être* of the group was to defeat the Vredeling proposal, in time, EEG members decided to work to strengthen the voice of European MNEs across the range of European regulatory policy. As one objective, the EEG sought to establish a kind of think-tank that could develop strategies and initiatives for the companies. Members also envisaged that such a think-tank might provide a means to counter the European Trade Union Institute (ETUI), the research branch of the European Trade Union Confederation (ETUC), which had played an important role in developing what became the Vredeling initiative.[9]

The primary object of the EEG was, however, to improve the existing business organizations. EEG members decided that they did not want to become a lobbying group *per se*. The companies realized that it was not in their interest to ignore UNICE or to snub the national business associations. Indeed, it was desirable to have

---

[8] Representatives from Ford Europe and Fiat convinced John Boyd, then the Brussels-based EC relations executive of Imperial Chemical Industries (ICI), to be the convenor of the group. When Boyd retired in 1981, his successor, Paul Winby, took over the organization. The group's name did not change until the late 1980s. For purposes of clarity, the name EEG is used throughout this chapter.

[9] EEG members thought that they had found 'their' research group in the Centre for European Policy Studies (CEPS). In 1983–4 numerous companies—among them BAT Industries, IBM, ICI, Nestlé, and Siemens—became founding members of CEPS. CEPS did not become the think-tank of the business community, but remained a more broadly based forum. It none the less proved to be an important platform for business issues over the years.

the backing of all industrial groups on some issues, and to allow the large companies to 'hide' behind UNICE on other matters. Therefore, the transformation of UNICE into a more effective organization became the most important objective of the industrial coalition.

With pressure from the MNEs, leadership from the then UNICE president, Lord Pennock (a former ICI executive), and support from certain national business associations, UNICE underwent a remarkable overhaul in the early 1980s. First, the UNICE committee structure was streamlined, its 30-odd groups being honed down to five policy committees. Equally important, new committee guidelines allowed the chairs and vice-chairs of the committees to be selected directly from firms, and not only from national business confederations. Consequently, for the first time, leaders or representatives of individual companies presided over UNICE committees responsible for policy matters. Second, a former senior executive of Royal Dutch Shell, Zygmunt Tyszkiewicz, became the secretary general of UNICE in September 1984. Thus the organization's leadership was in the hands of an official from one of Europe's most powerful MNEs. EEG members were not, however, immediately successful in realizing all their aims. As discussed below, although representatives advocated the creation of a 'high-level group of industrialists' within UNICE to represent the organization, this objective was not achieved until early 1990.

EU Committee of AmCham

The extra-territorial provisions of the Vredeling proposal also launched—or more appropriately, relaunched—what became the EU Committee of the American Chamber of Commerce, an industrial coalition of American MNEs with operations in the EU.[10]

Since the creation of the European Economic Community (EEC), the American Chamber of Commerce in Belgium had convened a small committee (usually composed of US government

[10] The EU Committee also includes law firms and consultant groups among its members, but is largely run and financed by the corporate members. Its formal title has changed over the years from Common Market Panel, to EEC Committee, EC Committee, and eventually EU Committee. For further information see Cowles (1996c).

officials and journalists) off and on to follow EU events and activities. By the mid-1970s, given the development of European competition law and the Commission's multinationals programme, American companies had begun to pay closer attention to European legislation and activities. As a result, American companies were the first MNEs to establish informal groups in Brussels during that period.[11]

Co-ordination among American companies was facilitated by the fact that a number of them had established their European headquarters in Belgium, not because it was the home of many European institutions, but because of the favourable Belgian tax laws in the 1950s and 1960s. Most observers agree that American companies far outnumbered European MNEs in Belgium during this period.

In 1977–8, a revamped committee, composed of representatives from MNEs and consultant groups, was established within the American Chamber of Commerce.[12] Although the companies were worried by much of the Spinelli multinational programme in the 1970s, they also saw aspects of the programme that could be beneficial to American firms. For example, they sometimes supported Commission proposals, such as the Fourth Directive on subsidiary accounts and the Seventh Directive on consolidated accounts, that were 'designed to revamp the public, and particularly the financial, accountability of multinational companies in Europe' (Robinson, 1983: 67). The American companies—which were already subject to wide-ranging reporting requirements under US legislation—welcomed the opportunity to 'see some order and uniformity of approach' in European accounting procedures.[13] The EU Committee contacted the Commission to offer technical assistance on the proposed legislation and discovered that Commission officials welcomed the detailed input and expertise of the Committee members. As one observer noted, 'by the late 1970s, this Committee had arguably become among the most influential of business

[11] The Brussels representative of IBM, for example, established the first such grouping, the Ravenstein Group, in 1975. Other organizations included the Internal Public Affairs Forum and the Industry/Government Ad Hoc Council (Cowles, 1994).

[12] Two indigenous European companies, Fiat and ICI, also participated in meetings. They later left the group when the US Chamber of Commerce in Washington, DC asked that the group include only American companies (Cowles, 1994).

[13] Telephone interview by author, 25 May 1994.

bodies on [European] policy toward multinationals' (Robinson, 1983: 204).

However, the Vredeling proposal turned the tables on the American firms. Companies that had worked closely with Commission officials on accounting legislation were strongly opposed to this new legislation. More specifically, the American companies resisted the Vredeling requirements that workers be informed of matters pertaining to the MNEs' headquarters, even if these were located outside the EU.

The Vredeling episode heightened the EU Committee members' concern to improve their ability to defend the group's positions not only on social, but also on other European regulatory policies—for example, environmental legislation—that would impose significant costs on them. The Brussels-based American MNEs believed that they were at a disadvantage compared with their European counterparts because they did not have a 'patron', a member government with which they could work on European matters. While American companies could try to shape member governments' policies by influencing the national and sectoral business associations, many of these associations restricted the access of US firms. Even when American companies did belong to national associations, their influence was limited by the presence of 'national champions' or prized national firms that could expect preferential government treatment. The American companies realized that if they wished to influence European policy, they would have to do so at the supranational level. Indeed, MNEs found it in their interest to promote policy-making at the level at which they could exercise the most influence. As one Committee member noted, 'We all have clout at the European level. We can't affect things at the national level. So, we have a totally obvious vested interest in having legislation at the European level.'[14]

The EU Committee was confronted with another problem. The extra-territorial reach of the Vredeling proposal had also provoked a great deal of anxiety among American MNEs with no Brussels-based representatives and little prior contact with the EU. Instead of calling on the EU Committee to represent their concerns, these US firms took matters into their own hands. Armed with an aeroplane full of Washington lawyers, the companies descended upon

[14] Interview by author, Brussels, 4 Dec. 1992.

Brussels to confront the Eurocrats.[15] In the view of many European affairs representatives of Brussels-based American MNEs, the Washington approach was a public relations disaster. While it may have been appropriate for the confrontational-style of lobbying common in the US, it was inappropriate for the more discreet, subtle approach used in Brussels. After carefully establishing relations with the Commission, the EU Committee members saw the Washington-led campaign tarnish the image of American big business all over again.

From 1981 the EU Committee therefore undertook a number of initiatives to improve its representation in Brussels. The group sought to influence European policy-making better and to ensure that the EU Committee became the recognized voice for all American companies on European matters. These initiatives enabled American companies to develop stronger ties with both the Commission and the European Parliament (EP). By 1985 the EU Committee had evolved into a quasi-autonomous organization of 40 corporate members, with funding and secretarial staff largely separate from the American Chamber of Commerce in Belgium.

The European Round Table of Industrialists

A third industrial coalition to emerge in the 1980s was the ERT. Like the EEG and the EU Committee, the ERT was also established in response to the debate on regulatory issues. The members of the ERT, however, were not so much focused on an individual piece of EU legislation, as motivated by the lack of the overarching regulatory framework necessary for a truly unified European market (Cowles, 1995). The ERT eventually emerged as an organization when a particular group of industrialists recognized that national and European government officials—as well as the traditional European business groups—were apparently incapable of focusing on the Single European Market (SEM) and its importance.

In many respects, the origins of the ERT can be traced to the economic malaise of the 1970s. While many of the largest MNEs emerged from the 1970s with a positive balance-sheet, their leading

---

[15] While lobbying hard against the proposal in Brussels, the companies also enlisted the support of the American government. The US Congress introduced at least three draft bills designed to protect American firms from the requirements of the Vredeling proposal (Blanpain *et al.*, 1983).

executives had become aware that they could no longer afford to operate their companies as they had in the post-war economic boom. In particular, the internal organization of their subsidiaries across Europe posed problems for European MNE executives. The 'federated national companies' structure employed by some European MNEs was no longer viable in the 1980s.[16] Indeed, the cost structure of maintaining self-contained subsidiaries, with separate R&D facilities, was prohibitive, especially in light of foreign competition that could supply European consumers with quality goods at lower cost.

MNE officials also realized that 'getting a grip on the cost structure is a *political* issue'.[17] Restructuring their firms would require corporate executives to pare back budgets, close factories, combine R&D facilities, and lay off workers. Company officials, therefore, faced political difficulties within individual European countries, especially those with strong traditions of social welfare.

The industrialists believed that changes in government regulation were needed, changes that would require both national and EU involvement. In the area of high technology, for example, no single European firm was financially capable of undertaking on its own major new R&D developments, such as a new generation of computer chip or telecommunications switch. This was because no single national market was large enough to permit recovery of R&D costs, let alone make a profit, at world-market prices. To compete against the Japanese and American giants, industry experts believed that European companies would need to merge with one another or at least to co-produce the new technologies (Sandholtz and Zysman, 1989). Moreover, national public procurement procedures in areas such as telecommunications would need to be liberalized, if companies were to have markets large enough to amortize their costs. Yet, the ideological preferences of national governments (and those of some 'national champions') were slanted against these changes in regulatory laws and policies.

---

[16] As one industry analyst pointed out, several of these companies organized their subsidiaries in a manner similar to the way in which their home country organized its colonial empire. For example, subsidiaries of the Dutch electronics firms, Philips, became 'colonies', each directed by an executive from the metropolitan office. Interview by author, Brussels, 26 Nov. 1992.

[17] Interview by author, Brussels, 26 Nov. 1992.

In 1982 the industrialists began to speak out. Pehr Gyllen-hammar, chief executive officer (CEO) of Volvo, the Swedish auto-mobile manufacturer, promoted what he called a 'Marshall Plan for Europe'. He maintained that an overall scheme was necessary 'to spur growth, and to build industry and infrastructure' in Europe (Gyllenhammar, 1983). The Swedish entrepreneur called on Euro-pean industry to 'play an active and important role in the formula-tion of the industrial strategies for future growth', noting that 'co-operation on a European level will be necessary' (Gyllenhammar, 1982).

In 1983, with active support from Davignon in the Commission, Gyllenhammar formed a cross-sectoral group of leading CEOs to promote industrial strategies. Early members of the group, which became known as the ERT, included Umberto Agnelli (Fiat), Carlo de Benedetti (Olivetti), Wisse Dekker (Philips), Roger Fauroux (St Gobain), John Harvey-Jones (ICI), Olivier Lecerf (Lafarge Coppée), Hans Merkle (Bosch), Wolfgang Seelig (Sie-mens), and Dieter Spethmann (Thyssen). In time the underlying purpose of the ERT was agreed upon: namely, to promote a unified European market.

For the industrialists, a unified market required a broader regu-latory framework. Initiatives were necessary to stimulate invest-ment in technological development and industrial growth while firms undertook painful restructuring operations. Trans-European infrastructure networks were needed to ensure the free flow of goods, services, people, and ideas. In other words, political meas-ures were necessary to promote actively the development of a competitive Europe. A socio-political framework was necessary to develop a more positive business environment in Europe. The ERT strategy was, in effect, to offer a 'new Europe', one that could effectively develop and market high technologies, one that could create jobs through wealth creation, one that could compete suc-cessfully in the world market (Cowles, 1995).

The ERT embarked on a level of transnational political activism unprecedented for European industrialists. The CEOs promoted their single market agenda through widely publicized projects—such as plans to create a European infrastructure (ERT, 1984)—as well as through political contacts with European heads of state and government. The ERT, for example, was a major player in promoting French President François Mitterrand's effort to reinvigorate European integration through a major industrial initiative in 1984.

In January 1985, when national and European officials had still not endorsed a concrete programme for a unified European market, Wisse Dekker, then CEO of Philips, unveiled his own plan, entitled 'Europe 1990' (Philips, 1984). The plan laid out the precise steps needed to create a unified market by 1990 in four key areas: trade facilitation (elimination of border formalities); open public procurement markets; harmonized technical standards; and fiscal harmonization. The ERT publicly endorsed the Dekker plan, which served as an important precursor to the Cockfield White Paper issued six months later.

ERT members also played a vital role in ensuring the acceptance and implementation of what became the single market (or '1992') programme. First, in a practice developed with the Delors Commission in 1985, the CEOs appeared publicly with Commission officials to demonstrate their support for the 1992 project. In effect, the CEOs served as an important constituency and as legitimizers for Commission officials who, as appointed officeholders, held no direct political legitimacy of their own. Second, ERT members actively promoted the single market programme to domestic business organizations and with politicians. In 1986, when member governments were behaving in ways that put the future of the single market programme in doubt, the ERT created a special subgroup of CEOs to lobby governments directly with a simple message: support the single market programme or European industry will invest elsewhere. As Jacques Delors noted, the success of the 1992 programme was due largely to European MNEs who 'made a lot of it happen' (Krause, 1992: 86).

THE BIG BUSINESS TROIKA

Today the industrial coalitions continue to serve as important policy actors in EU regulatory matters. Their roles and relations with EU institutions have evolved considerably, as have their relations with one another. As revealed in Fig. 6.1, a 'big business troika' has emerged in EU policy-making. It is made up of the ERT, UNICE, and the EU Committee, with the EEG serving as an intermediary body among the three. (Membership lists of

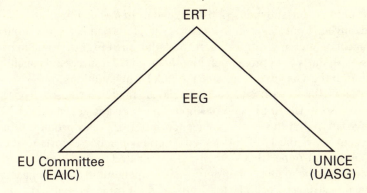

FIG. 6.1. *The big business troika*

the major industrial coalitions are found at the end of the chapter.)

The ERT remains the most powerful industrial coalition in Brussels, largely due to its membership and its established links with EU and national policy-makers. The 45 CEOs represent companies producing a combined turnover of some 500 billion ecus and employing more than three million people world-wide. The ERT has enjoyed easy access to Commission officials, and especially to former President Jacques Delors, who met alone with ERT members on numerous occasions. As one senior Delors *cabinet* official noted, 'There is no doubt that the ERT influences the views of the Commission'.[18] The close relationship between the ERT and the Commission has been maintained beyond the completion of the single market programme and has continued under the presidency of Jacques Santer. Officials credit the ERT with introducing new policy ideas and prompting the Commission to re-evaluate policy directions. Of course, the close relations with the captains of European industry enhance the Commission's status *vis-à-vis* the member governments as well. The relationship between the Commission and the ERT bears a strong resemblance to that between governments and big business at the national level.

The ERT also cultivates regular links with national officials. Indeed, ERT members meet with high-level officials from the incumbent Council Presidency at the beginning of each six-month

---

[18] Interview by author, Cambridge, Mass., 30 Jan. 1993.

term to lay out the industrialists' agenda. *Ad hoc* meetings are also arranged. Fourteen members, for example, attended a two-hour luncheon meeting with Edouard Balladur, then French prime minister, in Paris to impress upon him the need for a successful conclusion to the Uruguay Round of the GATT negotiations.

The ERT views itself as a 'strategic' organization whose purpose is not so much to provide position papers on the specifics of EU legislation, but to serve as an agenda-setter or policy promoter. In recent years the ERT has issued a series of major reports to the European Council that were also disseminated to a wide audience, including the media. Their purpose is to spell out in clear language an industrialist's agenda for Europe: the problems that must be addressed, as well as potential strategies. The reports are designed to promote action at the national level, as well as to influence the debate on the EU's future.

While the ERT aims to be the agenda-setter, UNICE remains the workhorse of the business groups, responding to each piece of EU legislation of general relevance to business. While national industry associations are the 'official' members of UNICE, multinational firms have emerged as leading actors within the organization. In June 1990, after lengthy negotiations with the national business associations, the UNICE Advisory and Support Group (UASG) was created. This coalition is composed of over two dozen large companies which pay dues (1 million Belgian francs/$30,000) directly to UNICE, in addition to their subscriptions to national business associations. While UASG companies do not have 'direct powers' in UNICE, they do have an important say on many UNICE policy matters. In many respects UASG represents the high-level group of MNEs first sought by EEG members in the early 1980s.

Although the national business associations retain the right to determine the policy positions of UNICE, MNEs now play an important role in UNICE's policy committees and working groups, and have helped to transform it into a more proactive organization. Until 1980, the primary function of UNICE was to co-ordinate the differing national associations' views in order to produce collective position papers. Today MNE representatives on UNICE committees not only meet Commission officials to influence the early stages of legislation, they also draft the position papers. UASG members review position papers and, indeed, influence the UNICE policy-making process itself. The perceptions of Brussels-based policy-makers provide an important indicator of the role of MNEs. According to a member of Delors's *cabinet*, UNICE had become 'the multinationals' organization'.[19]

Today the third member of the troika, the EU Committee of AmCham, is composed of some 140 companies with 600 active participants that serve on the 18 sub-committees and 56 issue-based working groups. Like the corporate participants within UNICE,[20] EU Committee members seek to influence the everyday legislative affairs in the EU. In some respects, however, the 'European companies of American parentage' are at a disadvantage in that they do not have the same quality of access to European and national officials as indigenous European companies, which also benefit from national channels of influence. Recognizing their more limited access, EU Committee members have sought to strengthen, and indeed 'create', their own power by developing a 'complex and expert structure of specialist committees [within the organization] which represent an unrivalled network of advance intelligence within the [EU]' (Mazey and Richardson, 1993*a*: 7). With an elaborate database and tracking system, the EU Committee has frequent contacts with Commission officials and suggests policy options even before the drafting stage of the legislative process begins.

In 1993 the EU Committee sought to improve its representative powers in Brussels by creating the European-American Industrial Council (EAIC). The EAIC is, in effect, an American-style ERT, composed of CEOs from the firms' European operations. Today it is evolving into an autonomous organization that seeks to strengthen the American companies' relations with senior European and national officials.

Finally, there is the EEG, a group transformed in recent years by its members from a UNICE ante-chamber into an 'invisible' core for the big business troika. The EEG remains an 'unofficial' group (it has no statutes and no secretariat) of approximately 50 company representatives who meet twice a year. It avoids public visibility as it does not want to be regarded as a discussion partner with EU institutions. Rather, the EEG operates as a central network among existing industrial groups. Believing that there are too many

[19] Interview by author, Cambridge, Mass., 30 Jan. 1993.
[20] Several American firms participate in UNICE working groups and are members of UASG.

business groups in Brussels, EEG members (most of whom belong to other big-business organizations) now use the organization as 'an internal industry co-ordinating platform'.[21] Thus it serves as an 'issue co-ordinator' for the ERT, UNICE, and the EU Committee, bringing in officials from the three organizations so as to make the membership aware of who is responsible for each dossier in each industry group. Efforts are then made to reduce duplication and to 'maximize intelligence'.

IMPLICATIONS FOR THE FUTURE

Understanding the history behind the mobilization of multinational firms and their industrial coalitions allows one better to understand how participation and policy-making in Brussels have evolved over the past two decades. Interest-group activity, for example, did not suddenly re-emerge in the 1980s with the launch of the SEM programme. Rather, as highlighted above, there were considerable changes in industrial representation during the 1970s; a decade once described as the 'doldrums' in EU history. The organization of the EU Committee, the EEG, and the ERT brought new actors, agendas, and dynamics to Brussels. Today, it is difficult to imagine the development of the 1992 project without the leadership activities and support of major European companies.

The organization of industrial coalitions also raises important questions for future participation and policy-making in Brussels. The most important question is that of 'representativeness'. Clearly, multinational firms and their organizations are among the better organized and best funded in Brussels. The EU Committee, for example, sends out approximately 10,000 faxes, documents, reports, and other pieces of information a month to members, national governments, and EU institutions. The large firms also enjoy privileged access to many national and European policymakers. For example, former Commission President Jacques Delors occasionally flew on corporate jets—as the guest of chief executive officers of major European companies—on his visits to member states to promote the SEM programme (Krause, 1992). Today ERT members regularly meet with heads of state and gov-

---

[21] Interview by author, Brussels, 16 Oct. 1992.

ernment to discuss industrial agendas. Representatives from the European Trade Union Confederation (ETUC), however, cannot claim comparable relations with EU policy-makers.

The large firms' resources and access pose considerable challenges not only to environmental, consumer, and labour groups, but also to those national industry associations historically dominated by small and medium-sized enterprises (SMEs). Today European big business can bypass the national industry associations, once the uncontested voices of industry in Brussels. When Daimler Benz opened its Brussels office in 1989, for example, it employed more EU representatives than did the German industry association, the *Bundesverband der Deutschen Industrie*. In a reversal of roles the BDI now meets with large German companies with Brussels-based representatives in order to gather information on EU activities. BDI officials point out that the companies' activities force change not only in Brussels, but also in domestic business–government relations (Cowles, 1996*b*).

Large firms have challenged sectoral industry associations as well. The creation of a multinationals' group within UNICE set in motion the transformation and, in some cases, the takeover of European-level sectoral associations by large companies. For example, the European chemical association, CEFIC, is now divided into two bodies—one for national associations, the other for major companies—which share leadership of the organization.

While large European firms and their industrial coalitions have certain advantages *vis-à-vis* other interest groups, their domination of the Brussels policy-making process should not be overestimated. In recent years a number of factors have mitigated the influence of these industrial actors. First and foremost has been the mobilization of other interest groups seeking to raise their profile in Brussels affairs. Small business organizations, such as the European Association of Craft, Small and Medium-Sized Enterprises (UEAPME) and Eurocommerce, for example, have emerged as important voices in the Brussels industrial debate on some issues. Several national industry associations—which fear losing influence to both the small- and large-firm organizations—are also reinforcing their presence in the European capital. The BDI, for example, will triple the size of its Brussels office over the next five years (Cowles, 1996*b*).

A second factor is the European institutions' recognition that they must listen to—or at least be perceived to listen to—other economic actors. On the one hand, Commission and EP officials are wary of being unduly influenced by large industrial interests. Several Brussels insiders suggest that the EP's lobbying guidelines were drawn up in part to limit the dominance of multinational firms and their organizations in the policy-making process. On the other hand, EU officials also recognize the importance of other groups' interests. A member of Jacques Santer's *cabinet*, for example, points out that 'there is a growing political realization that big companies are not going to create jobs in Europe'.[22] Because the real growth in European employment is likely to occur in small and medium-sized firms, the Commission must focus increasingly on their concerns. Commission officials also find it advantageous to 'play' SME groups off against UNICE or large firm coalitions in order to encourage industry positions closer to the Commission's liking.[23]

The EU's changing legislative agenda is a third factor that tempers large firms' influence. Now that the SEM programme is largely underway, EU policy-makers are turning their attention to issues that were initially too sensitive to tackle (such as energy markets) and to issues that require more specific legislation (such as financial markets). Whereas large firms and their coalitions were able to agree on the broad lines of SEM legislation, the new legislative agenda has demonstrated that European big business is not a monolithic organization. In the debate over the liberalization of the European energy market, for example, key energy producers have been reluctant to give up their national monopolies. To counter the producers' interests, major energy-consuming companies have banded together to form an *ad hoc* industrial group, ENER-G8. The fact that large industrial organizations—representing many different firms—cannot agree on a single position regarding certain new issues has led to the growth of these *ad hoc* coalitions.

In a sense, the MNEs are victims of their own success. The development of company activity and the mobilization of industrial coalitions in the early 1980s have led to a proliferation of industry representations. As one company official noted,

Industry is badly organized because we are working in a very dispersed way. The fact alone that we have several hundred company representa-

---

[22] Interview by author, Brussels, 28 June 1996.
[23] Interview by author, Brussels, 1 July 1996. Recently UNICE has sought to strengthen its ties with and to provide more programmatic assistance to SMEs.

tions either directly or via consultants and law firms, plus sectoral representation, plus UNICE [and the ERT and EU Committee], plus national associations . . . is in fact weakening the power of industry. One clear message with the power behind it would be much better.[24]

Whatever the precise influence of European big business today, it is clear that the mobilization of companies and the organization of the industrial coalitions have transformed traditional forms of representation and participation in Brussels. Large companies have demonstrated their willingness to fund the personnel and facilities necessary to promote MNE concerns, to develop intelligence networks, and to shape European legislation. They have been and will continue to be important players in the EU policymaking process.

APPENDIX

Membership of Main European Business Organizations

TABLE 6A. *Membership of the European Enterprise Group*

Akzo Nobel International	EDS	Motorola[b]
Alcatel Alsthom[a]	European Public Affairs Office	Norsk Hydro[a]
Asea Brown Boveri Europe[a]	Exxon Chemical Europe[b]	Olivetti[a]
BASF	Ford of Europe[b]	Pechiney
BAT Industries[a]	General de Banque	Philips Electronics[a]
Bayer[a]	General Motors Europe[b]	Rhône-Poulenc[a]
Bertelsmann[a]	Hoechst	Robert Bosch[a]
BP Europe[a]	IBM Europe[b]	Shell[a]
Ciba-Geigy	ICI Europe[a]	Siemens[a]
CMB Packaging	Lyonnaise des Eaux[a]	Solvay[a]
Daimler-Benz[a]	Marks & Spencer	Squire, Sanders & Dempsey[b]
Diekmann Associates	Mars Incorporated- Master Foods[b]	Texas Instruments[b]
Du Pont de Nemours[b]	Monsanto[b]	Time Warner Europe[b]
Eastman Kodak[b]		Unilever[a]
		Waste Management International[b]

[a] = ERT member
[b] = EU Committee member

Source: EEG (1996) and personal research.

[24] Interview by author, Brussels, 16 Oct. 1992.

TABLE 6B. *ERT Membership, January 1997*

Helmut MAUCHER (Chair)	Nestlé (Swit)
André LEYSEN (Vice-Chair)	Gevaert (B)
David SIMON (Vice-Chair)	BP (UK)
Américo AMORIM	Amorim Group (P)
Percy BARNEVIK	ABB (UK)
Jean-Louis BEFFA	Saint-Gobain (F)
Marcus BIERICH	Robert Bosch (G)
Peter BONFIELD	BT (UK)
Simon CAIRNS	B.A.T. Industries (UK)
Cor BOONSTRA	Philips Electronics (NL)
Bertrand COLLOMB	Lafarge (F)
François CORNÉLIS	PetroFina (B)
Alfonso CORTINA DE ALCOCER	Repsol (Sp)
Gerhard CROMME	Fried. Krupp (G)
Etienne DAVIGNON	Sté Générale de Belgique (B)
Carlo DE BENEDETTI	Olivetti (I)
Casimir EHRNROOTH	UPM-Kymmene (Fn)
Jean-René FOURTOU	Rhône-Poulenc (Fr)
José Antonio GARRIDO	Iberdrola (Sp)
Fritz GERBER	Hoffmann-La Roche (Swit)
Ronald HAMPEL	ICI (UK)
Ulrich HARTMANN	Veba (G)
Cornelius HERKSTRÖTER	Royal Dutch/Shell (UK/NL)
Daniel JANSSEN	Solvay (B)
Jak KAMHI	Profilo Holding (T)
David LEES	GKN (UK)
Flemming LINDELØV	Carlsberg (DK)
Pietro MARZOTTO	Marzotto (I)
Jérôme MONOD	Lyonnaise des Eaux (F)
Egil MYKLEBUST	Norsk Hydro (N)
Harald NORVIK	Statoil (N)
Theodore PAPALEXOPOULOS	Titan Cement (Gr)
Heinrich von PIERER	Siemens (G)
Lars RAMQVIST	Ericsson (Swed)
Edzard REUTER	Airbus Industrie (multi)
Nigel RUDD	Pilkington (UK)
Richard SCHENZ	OMV (A)
Manfred SCHNEIDER	Bayer (G)
Jürgen SCHREMPP	Daimler-Benz (G)
Louis SCHWEITZER	Renault (F)
Michael SMURFIT	Jefferson Smurfit (Ir)
Morris TABAKSBLAT	Unilever (UK/NL)
Serge TCHURUK	Alcatel Alsthom (F)
Marco TRONCHETTI PROVERA	Pirelli (I)
Mark WÖSSNER	Bertelsmann (G)

Country Key: (A) = Austria, (B) = Belgium, (DK) = Denmark, (F) = France, (Fn) = Finland, (G) = Germany, (Gr) = Greece, (Ir) = Ireland, (I) = Italy, (N) = Norway, (NL) = Netherlands, (P) = Portugal, (Sp) = Spain, (Swed) = Sweden, (Swit) = Switzerland, (T) = Turkey, (UK) = United Kingdom

Source: ERT.

TABLE 6C. *1996 EU Committee Members*

Abbott Laboratories
Adamson Associates
Airtouch
Akin, Gump, Strauss,
  Hauer, Feld & Dassesse
Albemarle
Allied Signal
American Express
Amway
Apple
Arthur Andersen
Ashurst Morris Crisp
AT & T
Avon Products
Baker & McKenzie
Bankers Trust Company
Baxter World Trade
Becton Dickinson
Bellsouth
Belmont
Betz
Boden de Bandt de Brauw
  Jeantet Lagerlof & Uria
Bristol-Myers Squibb
Browning-Ferris
Burlion, Bolle, Houben &
  Co.
BW & Partners
Cargill
Caterpillar
Charles Barker
Chiron
Chubb Insurance
Citibank
Clifford Chance
Coca Cola
Colgate Palmolive
Compaq Computer
Coopers & Lybrand
Corning
Coudert Brothers
Covington & Burling
CPC Consumer Foods
Crummy Del Deo, Dolan,
  Griffinger & Vecchione
Debevoise & Plimpton
Dechert Price & Rhoads
DHL
Digital Equipment

Disneyland Paris
Donaldson
Dow Corning
Dow Europe
Dun & Bradstreet
Du Pont de Nemours
EDS
Eli Lilly
Enron
Ernst & Young
Exxon Chemical
Exxon Company
Federal Express
Ford
General Electric
General Motors
Gillette
Goldman Sachs
GPC Market Access
Hercules
Hewlett Packard
Hill & Knowlton
Hogan & Hartson
Honeywell
Hunton & Williams
IBM
Intel
International Paper
ITT
Johnson & Johnson
Jones, Day, Reavis &
  Pogue
JP Morgan
Kellogg's
Kimberly-Clark
Kodak
KPMG
Kraft Jacobs Suchard
Law Offices of S.G.
  Archibald
Levi Strauss
Lovell White Durrant
Lubrizol
Lucent Technologies
Mars
McDonald's
McKinsey & Co.
Merck Sharp & Dohme
Microsoft

Mobil
Monsanto
Morgan, Lewis &
  Bockius
Morgan Stanley
Morrison & Foerster
Motorola
Nalco
Nike
Northern Telecom
NYNEX
OMC
Oppenheimer, Wolff &
  Donnelly
Pioneer
Pennzoil
Pfizer
Philip Morris
PPG
Price Waterhouse
Proctor & Gamble
Rank Xerox
Salomon Brothers
Shandwick
SJ Berwin
Skadden, Arps, Slate,
  Meagher & Flom
SmithKline Beecham
Sonoco
Sprint
Squire Sanders &
  Dempsey
Texaco
Texas Instruments
3M
Time Warner
Trenite Van Doorne
Union Carbide
UNISYS
United Parcel Service
United Technologies
US West
Van Bael & Bellis
Viacom
Warner Lambert
Waste Management
Whirlpool
Wilmer, Cutler &
  Pickering

Source: EU Committee (1996).

TABLE 6D. *UNICE Advisory and Support Group*

Bayer	Mondial
BP	Norsk Hydro
Coca-Cola	Philip Morris
Danone	Philips
Dow Europe	Procter & Gamble
Esso	Sevillana De
Ferrer	Electricidad
ICI	Shell
IDV/Grand Metropolitan	Solvay
Iveco Fiat	Time Warner Europe
Kone	Unilever
Mars	Veba

Source: UNICE (1996).

7

The Interplay of Corporate, National, and European Interests

ELIE COHEN

This chapter addresses the way in which corporate strategies, national policies for industry,[1] and European policies have evolved since 1985, with particular reference to the French experience.

At first sight one might conclude that the French 'normalized' their economic policy, by creating an orthodox free market, under pressure from the European Community (EC). However, the shift in macroeconomic policy was in 1982–3 and the massive reorganization of French industry began in 1983–4, thus preceding the liberalization propelled by the 1985 Single European Market (SEM) programme and the 1986 Single European Act (SEA). This shift from a state-led financial system to a market-led one in 1982 had much to do with the rapid failure of the socialist experiment. The tremendous change in the behaviour of 'national champions', switching from Colbertist strategies to global ones, was due mainly to the abandoning of national *grands projets* (Cohen, 1995) and to the need to expand in the United States and East Asia.

European integration had a different effect. In some instances—such as the 1991 agreement between the EC and Japan on automobile imports, the Commission's intervention to prevent the acquisition of de Haviland by a Franco-Italian aeronautical consortium, the development of High Definition Television (HDTV), and the recapitalizations of Bull and Air France—there was a natural conflict between a national logic and supranational authority.

---

[1] I deliberately define policies for industry as the range of macro-, meso-, and micro-economics which impinge on global competitiveness in specific sectors, so as to circumvent the debate over the term industrial policy. I also retain a distinction between the politics of industry, in the broad sense of general competition, and industrial policy, in a more restrictive sense limited to specific sectors.

Hence I highlight corporate, national, and European roles, in the light of the imbalance in European policies between those led by the market (competition, trade, state aids) and those targeting specific sectors (technology policy, industrial policy, and so on).

The aim is not to test the relevance of general theories of economics, politics, or law on the basis of a loose understanding of the Community dimension, as is often done in academic studies. Instead evidence is drawn from a careful examination of specific sectoral cases and the decision-making processes actually followed. Cases as varied as the agreement on car imports and the development of HDTV provide the basis for a more fundamental understanding of the European process. This empirical and inductive approach is designed to shed light on the nature of integration.

TWO STYLES OF EUROPEAN POLICY FOR INDUSTRY

European policies built around market principles are markedly different from the technology and industrial policies developed for particular sectors within individual EC countries. In the former, the initiative is political, while the implementation is driven by quasi-automatic pilot. In the latter, political engagement must be retained throughout. Experience suggests that market-led policies have been more successful than interventionist ones. None the less, contrary to what is often argued, there is no independent dynamic that erodes national political authority. A nation does not lose its sovereignty simply through inadvertence, and developments that coincide should not be confused. The imposition of an external rule is not the same thing as the invocation of an external rule in order to constrain which solutions can be addressed to a particular problem. European integration is a multi-level process, driven not only by the Commission or the Council of Ministers, but also by the strategic games played by firms and national bureaucracies in order to capture resources and to achieve domestic political objectives.

The disequilibrium between market-led policies and interventionist policies raises several issues. First, is the disequilibrium structural, or the result of lobbying, or a sequence, with liberalization first, to be complemented by interventionist policies? Second, how should we explain industrial collaboration, such as on Ariane and Airbus, developed outside the EC framework? Is it that policies of *juste retour*, negotiated between firms and states, are more rewarding? Third, why should the French institutional model, such an influence on the European model, have proved so unreceptive to a modern form of Colbertism? Was it the personality of Jacques Delors which spread neo-liberalism to southern Europe?

Market-Based Policies for Industry

Free-market policies have been used as weapons against national arrangements with the Commission relying on the law to force open markets. Frontiers have been opened in some previously protected sectors (as under the Japanese–European agreement on cars). European competition policy has been developed (repressing cartels and dominant positions and vetting mergers, as in the de Haviland case). The anti-competition aspects of public-sector activities (such as public procurement, state aids, and public service monopolies in telecommunications and rail transport) have been challenged; and state-owned companies have been subjected to surveillance.

It should be no surprise that this policy has unleashed the passions of those who see their tools for industrial intervention being removed. In several cases the Commission has demonstrated impressively the effectiveness of European mechanisms. In crafting the Japanese–European 'consensus' on automobiles the Commission apparently succeeded in unleashing a process designed to end European protectionism by the year 2000. In the de Haviland case, the Commission blocked a major acquisition outside Europe by a Franco–Italian aeronautical consortium. The general rules of competition have been used to force open certain highly regulated sectors, such as telecommunications.[2] The supervision of state aids seems to have pressured governments to privatize state-owned companies.

---

[2] The Terminals Directive (88/301/EEC) was adopted under Articles 90–3 of the Treaty of Rome. The ECJ upheld this action, confirming that in was not necessary to use Article 100a.

Publicly Directed Industrial Policies

Every EC decision on industrial policy revolves around three axes: the member governments and their national bureaucracies, and the various links among them; firms and their associations; and the EC institutions, with their own internal dynamics and hierarchies of power and influence. This makes for a system of multi-level governance in which a multiplicity of stakes and stakeholders organize around the three axes (see Fig. 7.1).

Each set of actors has a policy perspective driven by the nature of its stake in the process: sovereignty for the governments; legitimacy for the EC; and competitiveness for the firms. The actors nurture relationships at all levels in order to promote their concerns and to bolster their positions in the institutional hierarchy. They also have relations with actors in the other sets.

A full understanding of the process requires a close examination of who is involved in decision-making in each arena. Just to take the French case, the legislative function depends partly on the government and administration, which also exercise executive powers, while the judicial function is dispersed between civil and administrative tribunals. Hence one can understand the reluctance of the French to make real transfers of legislative power to the European Parliament (EP), and their insistence on the prerogatives of the Council. The Commission is not viewed as an admin-

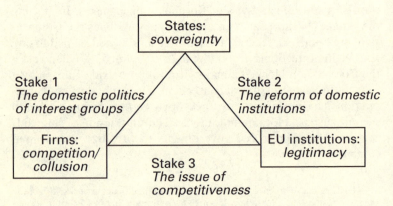

Fig. 7.1. *The EC system of multi-level governance*

istrative instrument in the traditional French sense, that is as able to take initiatives, and subject to a legitimate political authority.

EUROPEAN MARKET-LED POLICIES FOR INDUSTRY: CASES

Analysis of the 1991 EC–Japan agreement on automobile imports and the liberalization of telecommunications services will help us to understand better the politics of the European free-market economy and in particular the increasing reliance on the rule of law.

The EC–Japan Agreement on Automobiles

The EC–Japan arrangement on car imports is a remarkable endeavour. It constitutes the defeat of the protectionists, not only because the Europeans have committed themselves to abandon national forms of protection, but also because they have done so without obtaining any tangible improvement in access to the Japanese market. The Commission has thus proved that it can use the EC's exclusive competence in trade policy to outlaw the temptation to 'administer' trade, and to evade the risks implicit in the notion of reciprocity. Curiously the agreement, which commits the Japanese to restrain their exports, is in the form of a 'non-paper', not a formal contract, based on two parallel declarations, which cover different points. Hence, Jacques Calvet, Peugeot's chief executive, in denouncing the agreement as backtracking on earlier commitments, was paying homage to the EC.

Yet the reality that emerges below the surface is more varied.[3] The Commission had to negotiate with the Japanese precisely because it could not simply require that all goods circulate freely within the SEM. That the Japanese committed themselves to market-sharing is proof that they have, despite their denials, accepted a form of administered trade. The Japanese and the Commission, in agreeing to prohibit the targeting of particular

---

[3] Little reliable information is publicly available, and the story of the negotiations can be reconstructed only through interviews. For the general background see Ch. 8.

national markets and to retain country quotas, recognized that member governments had the power to resist threats to the equilibrium of their markets.

For a long time the automobile lobby oscillated between efforts to maximize its interests and the search for compromise (Gandillot, 1992). The lobby had traditionally been dominated by south European producers of middle- and bottom-of-the-range models, but also came to embrace north European producers of top-of-the-range models, as they in turn faced a Japanese challenge. The lobby achieved a common front on Japanese imports only by excluding Peugeot, which sought relentlessly to torpedo agreement (see Chapter 8). Unity was forged in the new European Automobile Manufacturers Association (ACEA), which included American subsidiaries and adopted a majority voting rule. Raymond Lévy, chairman of Renault, drew on his leadership role in the ACEA to shift his industrial group towards privatization, using an external constraint to achieve internal transition.

The fragmentation of the European policy process explains the hesitation, the sibylline language, and the confusion in the steps taken. Frans Andriessen, the external relations commissioner at the time, left the negotiations to his officials, particularly Gianluigi Giola, on condition that they did not make too many waves. Martin Bangemann, the industry commissioner, deputed his concerns to Robert Verue, his only task being to prevent Germany from appearing protectionist. Sir Leon Brittan, then competition commissioner, became the self-appointed scourge of the mercantilists. The resulting process left the negotiators a considerable margin of manœuvre to strike a compromise acceptable to member governments, the industry, and the Japanese; a compromise for which each participant claimed credit.

In her successive pronouncements as prime minister, Édith Cresson shifted the French position from the discourse of excommunication to invitations to invest in France. The French producers' conflicting positions made the government's stance difficult; and Bangemann's strategy of isolating Calvet was unacceptable. Also the French government withheld acceptance of the trade agreement in the hope of winning support from the EC for research and development (R&D), retraining the labour force, and converting threatened factories.

The member governments' positions clashed with each other and some were internally contradictory; hence the Commission had to pick its way through a political minefield. It faced the invective of those who were free traders in speech, but protectionist in deeds; the British automobile industry had reached a self-restraint agreement with the Japanese. It also had to contend with the stentorian liberalism of those with national restraint arrangements; Japanese import penetration was frozen in Germany. It had to grapple with the treaty-accepted protection of the Italian market, based on a 50-year-old agreement with Japan to neutralize changes in each other's markets, as well as the aggressive protectionism of the French, which had no legal foundation.

The instruments of the agreement capture perfectly the nature of the negotiation and of the commitments undertaken by the contracting parties. The only contractual document, the 'Elements of Consensus', sets out vague principles, which were filled out in a telephone conversation between Andriessen and the Japanese Minister for International Trade and Industry, Eiichi Nakao. Andriessen then spelled out the substantive commitments to the member governments. This formula allowed governments to adopt contradictory positions in their speeches to domestic audiences, without having to face thunderbolts from either the Commission or producers.[4] Moreover, the sectoral implications of the SEM obliged the Commission to negotiate with itself; with member governments, subject to strong electoral pressures; and with the Japanese. The latter held strong trump cards, given both the divisions on the European side and the tenuous legality of national measures, particularly France's, *vis-à-vis* the General Agreement on Tariffs and Trade (GATT).

The resulting agreement, with its ambiguities and scope for selective interpretation, is a diplomatic work of art, although also potentially open to recurrent criticism. In a process that engages several levels of governance, firms can use the constraints negotiated in Brussels to settle domestic issues, while denouncing them at home in order to improve their political and economic capabilities. Governments, like firms, play strategic games. At the national level

---

[4] Some of the clauses in supplementary protocols to the agreement—such as Japan cutting imports by two-thirds of any reduction in demand—soon proved inoperable.

they act as if they were the decisive political agents, and at the European level they behave like lobbyists, promoting the cause of their domestic firms. Eventually, they reappear as national political agents searching for an elusive domestic consensus by dissociating themselves from the collective position and demonizing their European partners.

State Aids and Public Services: The Case of Telecommunications

The Commission boasts that it contributed decisively to the opening up of the telecommunications sector. It claims to have woken up lazy and inefficient public monopolies by introducing open competition where previously there had been collusion between suppliers and consumers. The Commission also argues that it invented information highways, which promise a technological leap forwards, lower prices, and job creation. Moreover, it claims to have preserved public services in respecting the letter of the Treaty of Rome; this obliges the Commission neither to create obstacles to services in the general economic interest nor to discriminate on the basis of ownership. But what is the real story?

The liberalization process in telecommunications may instead be explained by the declining costs of equipment and components and by the pressure exerted by corporate users. These had made both possible and desirable alternatives to the traditional companies. These were pursued first in the US and the UK, then imitated in other countries, each determined to resolve its own specific problems.

The French industry had considerable success in the mid-1970s. It was helped by technological innovation in the form of time-division electronic switching systems, the expansion of domestic manufacturing capabilities, the huge Minitel programme (a successful collaboration with the national champion), and self-financing. None the less a cyclical downturn in the 1980s, and a series of other factors served to discredit the Colbertist model. The 'large industrial project' model failed to develop appropriate cable and satellite technology; the state found itself with an ill-considered industrial policy; and the costs became too high. From 1988 France Telecom started to expand into foreign markets, including Argentina, Greece, Mexico, and Poland, and to gain autonomy, developing video and data-processing services. The Ministry for Posts and

Telecommunications, deprived of its sponsorship responsibility, found a new role as a regulator.

The way liberalization has been pursued has varied between countries. In the UK an independent regulatory body, the Office of Telecommunications (OFTEL), imposed asymmetrical regulation, pressuring one dominant operator, British Telecommunications (BT), while prohibiting it from expanding into cable. In Germany liberalization made possible an extraordinary development of cartels around DBTelekon, the world's largest cable operator; one of the leading satellite operators (SES Astra), organizer of collaboration among video services; and Daimler-Benz's partner in software development (Debis). In France regulation remains under the authority of the government; liberalization has been gradual and the question of public services has yet to be resolved.

The Commission has thus not really played the role that is often attributed to it. Its Green Paper (Commission, 1987*b*) was published after the initial wave of liberalization, and its principles served more to delineate the conditions for liberalization than to accelerate the process. The Directorate General for Competition (DGIV) attempted to emulate the British model of separate networks for telephony and cable, but failed to accelerate the liberalization of cross-border communications in 1991.

European telecommunications companies today operate on two different levels. At the national level they justify reorganization, restructuring, diversification, and internationalization on the grounds of European pressure. They can portray measures that call into question historical and legally established forms of social protection as if they were externally imposed. At the European level, they invoke the American challenge, the absence of Japanese reciprocity, and the internal contradictions of EC policies. Liberalization of the infrastructure and alignment of open network provisions (ONP), without prior settlement of the issue of access charges, potentially threaten European firms. Thus the issues of universal service and internationalization influence how the infrastructure is liberalized. What remains pivotal is the relation between firms and 'their' national governments. The issue of rates, for example, is extremely sensitive in some countries, including France, because of the need to find mechanisms that can compensate for the current system of cross-subsidization. The commercial value of firms being privatized is difficult to assess, especially given the blackmail traditionally deployed on the issue of employment. Such factors give the telecommunications firms considerable leverage in their dealings with governments.

Hence the Commission could have run into fierce resistance from some member governments. It therefore very skilfully opted for vagueness in assessing 'public service' charges, and left it to member governments, in the name of subsidiarity, to calculate and allocate them. Such an approach could not on its own have produced so apparently large a change in sectors so long protected. What made the difference was that liberalization went hand-in-hand with assaults on state aids, often disguised as recapitalization of public enterprises, and on national preferences in public procurement.

Public utilities have thus found themselves constrained to keep their public service obligations to a minimum. To survive competition meant accepting a commitment to privatization. Thus articles of the Treaty of Rome, phrased in vague terms and drafted in a quite different context, acquired new meaning through a process of judicial expansion. Whether or not this happened as the result of a power-play by the Commission or through concessions from the member governments, the net effect was to externalize problems that were politically sensitive at the national level by making them appear technical.

The Treaty of Rome stipulated that the EC be neutral on the question of ownership. States could nationalize or privatize enterprises and the EC was not at liberty to interfere in the financial structures of national capitalism. None the less, the opening of markets—as well as the prevention of cartels, collusion, and other restrictive practices—was at the base of the European process. Hence public enterprises were, like private firms, susceptible to EC investigation if an abuse of dominant position was suspected. The limitation, however, was that these powers did not extend to the so-called natural monopolies, since the Treaty accepted that these provided public services or promoted some other general economic interest.

The absence of a clear definition of public interest or public service provided the champions of competitive markets with their window of opportunity. The European Court of Justice (ECJ) was able to assert that a notion of Community interest should predominate. By the late 1980s this meant, *inter alia*, the free circulation of goods and services. Thus a series of gradual but cumulative shifts of definition brought public utilities under close scrutiny. A member government needed only to recapitalize a public enterprise, whether or not it provided a public service, to provoke an investigation by the Commission. A loss-making private firm raises no issue for the regulators, who can assume that the market will sort out any malfunctions, but this is not the case for public enterprises with exclusive rights. What then should the stake-holding government do? As far as the Commission is concerned, the state should behave like an ordinary shareholder and look for a profitable return on its investment. Carried to its logical conclusion this leaves no place for the public enterprise save as a clone of a private firm; the public enterprise as such is destined to disappear. Public service is being called on to redefine itself, first as a universal service, then as a delegated service, and eventually as a market service. Deregulation leads inexorably to privatization, which in turn leads public service to be redefined as the provision of only basic services.

The EC's judicial mechanism has proved extraordinarily powerful because it is nurtured by its own internal logic, by market principles, by the actions of economic actors, and even by the concealed intentions of national governments. It constitutes an impressive expansion from a few treaty articles that had fallen into disuse. It would take a determined and widely shared political effort to roll this back, an effort that is beyond the Council because of its internal divisions.

Thus the Commission, appointed by the member governments, has acquired its own authority and has the results to prove it, in spite of the arrangements negotiated to cushion the transition in troubled sectors. The weaker the political determination of the member governments, the greater the implicit political consent and the more the process outlined above operates mechanically. Numerous forms of accommodation are possible, but they depend on the constellation of forces within the Commission, on how the relevant commissioners and their services judge the context, and on the policy preferences of the member governments.

POLITICALLY DIRECTED POLICIES FOR INDUSTRY: CASES

Governments have taken a range of collective measures at the European level to promote their industries: support for R&D and various forms of sectoral intervention.[5] Some programmes, such as Ariane and Airbus, involve only some member governments and are based upon the concept of *juste retour*. The governments involved have pursued aggressive financing strategies, based on reimbursable advances;[6] protectionist measures; and export promotion. Such an approach was deliberately designed to break the domination of Boeing, not so much by the use of normal market mechanisms as by making a political choice.[7] Such policies, whether through the EC or via intergovernmental collaboration, have proved relative failures; the European Strategic Programme of Research and Development in Information Technology (Esprit) and HDTV (see also Chater 9) are cases in point.[8]

Esprit

There seems to be a curse on co-operative projects launched by the EC. It is hard to deny that the few European successes have owed little to the Commission, but rather have resulted from intergovernmental co-operation and alliances between the firms concerned. Efforts to build European information technology (IT) programmes have persisted, but with meagre results.

The first Esprit programme, launched in 1982, sought to establish a leading position for Europe in IT. In two sectors in particular, data processing and electronic components, competition risked being overwhelming. Ten years later the results are mediocre. Europe's imports of IT products from the US are three times greater than its exports; imports from Japan are 14 times greater; and from the East Asian 'tigers' 10 times greater. Europe has a trade surplus in the sector only with the developing nations and with eastern Europe. Intra-EC exports are six times greater than those to the

[5] Only 3.4% of the EC budget is spent on R&D, compared with 51.7% on agriculture and 31% on regional development. Of the 13 billion ecu Fourth Framework Programme for research (1994–8) 28% is devoted to information technology.
[6] Such advances accounted for up to 60% of financing until a 1992 agreement among the members of the Airbus consortium limited them to 33%. R&D aid is limited to 3% of the industry's turnover and to 4% of that of the recipient company. France provides the equivalent of only 0.5% of Aerospatiale's turnover.
[7] See Esambert (1994) for a detailed description of the role of politics in the Airbus and CFM56 aircraft engine projects.
[8] This view is supported by the Commission's evaluations (Commission, 1987*a*), the work of the Callon team at the École des Mines (Laredo and Callon, 1990), and the findings of Mytelka (1989; 1991; 1992).

US, Japan, and the 'tigers' combined. Europeans have witnessed the advance of Japan, the US's return to pre-eminence, and the explosive growth of Korea (EITO, 1993). The 12 major European IT firms, victims of successive reorganizations, have largely failed to gain a position in world markets.

Though Esprit failed in its main aim, it did serve to promote the emergence of a European high technology club, albeit with only a marginal impact on the structure of the industry. Co-operation was fostered among small and large companies across Europe, research networks were established, institutions were forced out of isolation, advances were made in fundamental technological research, and even some commercial opportunities emerged (for example, Bull's Distributed Computing Model (DCM), Philips's interactive compact disk (CD-i), and flat-screen televisions) (Commission, 1991*c*). Nevertheless, the sector as a whole has continued to decline, with some notable failures, such as Nixdorf; technology has been acquired abroad; and a shifting pattern of alliances has developed, including GEC's bid for Plessy, Siemens's purchase of GPT, and Fujisu's purchase of ICL.

One reason for Esprit's relative failure is the obsession with commercial competition. This led to the privileging of pre-competitive research, albeit with a scattering of 'egalitarian' measures, and hostility to national policies of support, unless they also promoted the European cause. Yet the sector, particularly the electronic components industry, experienced a rapid transformation. The speed at which new products came to the market, as well the shortening of their life-spans, were challenges to which European business leaders proved unable to respond. Traditional rivalries between firms, such as those between Siemens and Alcatel-Alsthom and Thomson and Philips, were a further obstacle. Despite a series of reorganizations, European companies were able to survive at the global level only through alliances with American and Japanese firms.

Much the same was true of the second Esprit programme, the programme for Research and Development in Advanced Communications Technology for Europe (Race), and even the European Research Cooperation Agency (Eureka). Were it not for the commercial determination of Siemens and the efforts of the French government to support SGS-Thomson there would be no European electronic components industry.

High-Definition Television (HDTV)

The development of European HDTV is another telling case of the limits of European industrial policy (see Cohen, 1992; 1993; and Chapter 9). It was another effort to revive the consumer electronics sector, which was hampered by the existence of numerous divergent transmission standards in Europe (Secam and the different forms of Pal). HDTV also appeared to offer scope for the development of new services and new markets, both through 'at home' movie services and by rendering more dynamic the 'cultural' industries, which might stop the advance of the Japanese in the industry. It could provide opportunities for Europeans to develop productions in European languages other than English, a crucial symbol in Germany and France of European industrial, political, and cultural revival.

Between 1985 and 1990 a global strategy was attempted, successfully in so far as it prevented Japanese dominance in standard setting; the Japanese Muse standard was not adopted at the international meeting in Dubrovnik to allocate radio frequencies due to lobbying by France supported by other Europeans and some Africans. Co-operation was also stimulated among European firms—Bosch, Philips, and Thomson—through the 'Eureka 95' programme. The EC Council decided to insist on a common standard for direct transmission satellites (D2Mac, analog, and then digital HDMac) and to fund European television programmes. The 1992 Winter Olympics in Albertville provided a forum for live demonstrations, while the DCMac-Eurocrypt standard was used to support Filmnet, a Nordic private pay-television company.

Despite all this, failure was obvious from the start. The EC discretely abandoned all of its initial resolutions. First, it refused to extend to telecommunication satellites the requirement to transmit in accordance to the standards D2Mac/HDMac, thus giving weight to the critical arguments of the new lobby of satellite broadcasters, including Rupert Murdoch's Sky, Canal+, and Radio Luxembourg (see Chapter 9). Second, the EC refused to honour its commitment to support the distribution and the production of European television programmes. The UK had objected to setting a strict limit on programmes from outside Europe apparently on free-market grounds, though this position conveniently coincided with Murdoch's interests. Third, the HDMac standard fell by the wayside during 1993–5, during which time EC support shifted to the 'all-digital' solution (see Chapter 9). This last retreat was justified by the need to save what could be saved; the wide screen (16 × 9). The predictable outcome of all these changes were Thomson and Philips's decisions to abandon work on the HDMac standard.

Many factors account for these policy reversals. As in the case of automobiles, the fragmentation of the European policy process led to policy incoherence. There was no clear strategy for technology policy, though perhaps the crucial failing was that the technical solutions proposed to improve image definition were unrealistic. Objectives were set through a political process in which the proponents of specific technologies co-opted politicians to support their causes, without a serious assessment of the potential outlets and markets for the resulting products. The new DCMac-Eurocrypt standard would have increased the number of programmes offered at a lower cost, which consumers wanted, but mainly to the advantage of broadcasters aiming to occupy a monopoly position in the lucrative pay-television sector. Indeed the entire strategy of the French channel, Canal+, was focused on protecting its market by resisting regulations that would permit access control systems which would offer open access to pay-TV channels, in the hope of benefiting from increases in cable or satellite demand.

The HDTV project was based on a panoply of weapons. The rejection of Muse, the adoption of a European standard, and the joint European R&D programme added up to a plainly aggressive strategy of protection. To succeed required financial and regulatory commitments from member governments, firms with the capability and incentive to engage in so large a project, and the sustained support of politicians. The objective of producing a standardized technical object seemed straightforward.

However, a single standard was not enough to get the broadcasters and the producers of programmes on board, let alone to induce consumers to purchase new equipment. The EC tried to produce a new pattern of consumer demand by linking the provision of new programmes by satellite to the new standard, only to discover that those involved could not manage the process. EC policy-makers could not impose their plan on broadcasters and programme-makers, and the equipment manufacturers could not take the initiative any further. With programme-makers reluctant to produce the new material, broadcasters found themselves engaged in a war of attrition. Broadcasters turned instead to the standard being developed in the US as a means to retain their monopoly over pay-television. The adoption by the US Federal Communication Commission (FCC) of an all-digital standard resulted in the *de facto* creation of a universal standard. Thus the Europeans, after investing in their own standards, were caught between pressure to comply with the US standard and competition from the Japanese consumer electronics industry. Philips and Thomson therefore transferred their hopes to the American market, and opted for the digital standard. European governments, in an effort to retain some political consistency, attempted to limit the damage by continuing to provide financial support to broadcasters and programme-makers.

HDTV was a project of engineers who thought in terms of networks and integrated standards. It was not a project for broadcasters, who were well aware that what counted was a wider choice of programming, through a multiplicity of channels. Nor was HDTV a project for programme-makers, who took the costs of cinema production as their basis of comparison with HDTV. Moreover, the regulators were well aware that limits on the available broadcasting frequencies were bound to end up favouring cable and satellite.

The HDTV episode none the less enabled Thomson and Philips to acquire greater technical knowledge and expertise. It led to the mobilization of programme-makers, broadcasters, and the holders of distribution rights and copyrights, into the policy process surrounding the audio-visual sector, which had previously been dominated by engineers and regulators.

THE NATURE OF THE EUROPEAN POLICY PROCESS

We are left with two puzzles to resolve. First, why are the results of the European policy process so uneven? Relative success in promoting market liberalization has been accompanied by the relative failure of interventionist efforts to promote the European industry. Second, how does one explain the role of the Commission? It is partly dependent on the member governments' preferences, yet also partly autonomous in formulating European public policy. From our evidence we can derive a series of observations.

- *The Commission exercises only delegated authority.* The Commission is, as Giandomenico Majone (1994) has argued, neither already a European government nor one in embryo. Rather, the Commission is an independent administrative authority, to which national governments have given competences and expertise in a narrow field, but not renounced their sovereignty. Within its field of competence and expertise the Commission can and does influence policy, but it is always constrained.
- *The delegation of powers has a ratchet effect, but also produces uneven results.* When policy flows from a predominantly political initiative, as in the case of the SEM, its operations can embed a doctrine and a method, while its legitimation can be achieved through the jurisprudence of the ECJ. But when policy is left to unfold over the long term, it demands continuity, coherence, and scope for periodic discretion, features that the Commission can produce only with difficulty. Consequently, it has proved incapable of taking on really large collaborative projects, such as Airbus or Ariane, and has found it hard to establish a successful basis for sectoral R&D programmes.
- *Yet the notion of Europe reinforces the powers of EC institutions.* There are distinct European interests and a political dynamic has been stimulated by the relaunching of integration since 1985. Yet this dynamic is reversible and in periods of stress European policy-makers in the Commission tend to be timid and those in the Council are cautious. During periods of activism, there is a competition between these institutions to claim the credit.
- *The Commission has resources to exploit.* The authority of the Commission is greatest when it can rely upon the dynamics of the market and prior agreement from the cartel of national bureaucracies. European law and the market provide the bases of a kind of functional ideology for the EC process, and a vector of influence for the Commission. This also explains the redrawing of the hierarchies of influence within national administrations as they respond to the European process.
- *European policies can ease domestic reforms.* European constraints are a resource in the national political game, facilitating certain reforms, which have been resisted by powerful domestic actors. The whole apparatus of market policies represents a self-imposed constraint on member governments' use of industrial policy instruments, especially relevant for the Latin member

states: France, Italy, and Spain. In accepting such constraints on their own behaviour, the member governments have endowed the Commission with real power, which it has used well in its capacities of introducing initiatives and brokering compromises. The external constraints from Brussels have thus gradually become a lever for modernization in the face of all sorts of lobbies, and despite a political class that is the stubborn defender of vested social rights.

• *The democratic deficit is thus a false problem.* Sometimes decisions emerge through the Council, with national parliaments exercising a form of political control over their legitimately elected governments. Sometimes decisions are the product of the direct power exercised by the Commission, but are then applied through regulations or executive actions operated by the administrations in the member states, with the explicit acceptance of national governments.

CONCLUSION

During the 1980s all the Western countries privatized, liberalized, and deregulated their economies. How far did this evolution rest on the convergence of national models of industrial intervention? My conclusion is that there remains a plurality of national routes towards a more liberal approach to the market, but that the EC framework has much encouraged this European deregulatory pattern. The EC has absorbed the constraints imposed by global competition and the relative decline of Europe by transforming them into the categories of the SEM.

8

The Changing Dynamic of EU–Industry Relations: Lessons from the Liberalization of European Car and Airline Markets

PETER HOLMES AND FRANCIS MCGOWAN[1]

This paper explores how the relationship between European firms and their associations, on the one hand, and European institutions (specifically the Commission), on the other, has been changed by market liberalization. It does so by examining the dynamic between policy proposals, the lobbying process, and industry structure in two industries: cars and airlines. Although very different in most respects (manufacturing vs. service, predominantly public vs. predominantly private), both sectors have a history of close relations with government and of market structures that have been subject to a degree of regulation or protection, characteristics which have come under pressure as attempts to develop European policies have gathered pace. The paper considers whether the prospect and reality of such policies has contributed to changes in both the organization of these industries and their subsequent attempts to influence policy; it stresses the two-way process at work in the relationship between industry and the European Union (EU).

Our concern is with liberalization and, though there have been important changes in the way these industries are organized, it would be wrong to imply that EU policies have been wholly effective in achieving their objectives. Change has been limited in many respects, and both cases illustrate the extent to which firms in these

[1] The authors are grateful to Alasdair Young and other participants at the 1994 workshop for helpful comments. They also acknowledge the support of the ESRC's Single Market Initiatives, which funded the research on which this article is based.

sectors (either in their own right or through their privileged links to governments) have constrained the ability and the willingness of the Commission to embark upon and enforce reform, despite the apparent incompatibility between the conduct of business in the sectors and the principles underlying EU rules. The outcome has in each case been characterized by a degree of compromise: markets have become more open, more perhaps than industry lobbies initially wanted but not as much as the Commission might have wished. The paper looks at the factors which have shaped Commission strategy towards these sectors and considers three in particular: the strength and cohesion of the industries and their associations, the fear of member state backlash if a tough line were adopted by the Commission, and internal differences within the Commission.

THE EUROPEAN CAR INDUSTRY

The car industry in Europe is politically visible and sensitive. It is estimated that value-added in the automobile and component industry itself is just under 2 per cent of EU gross national product (GNP). EU car producers employed around 1.13 million workers in 1990, with another 900,000 in the components industry. If all indirect suppliers are added in, it is estimated that about 4.5 million workers, or 15 per cent of industrial employment, is involved in the industry (Vigier, 1992). Output is concentrated in a few producers, with six assemblers taking almost 75 per cent of EU car sales, mostly in their own home markets (see Table 8.1).

Japanese firms have been taking an increasing share of the market, more and more by foreign direct investment (FDI), though their share is well below that in electronics, and European firms have themselves been active exporters. Indeed, despite the increasing competition from Japan, the EU car industry was relatively prosperous in the late 1980s: the EU ran a trade surplus by value in cars, albeit a diminishing one, until 1992 (the industry was badly hit by the recession of the early 1990s).

Given its economic importance, and a widespread perception of the basic viability and competitiveness of the sector, many European governments have maintained a commitment to the industry. In some cases this has extended to direct ownership stakes, though

TABLE 8.1. *Market shares in the European car industry, 1995*

	Market share (%)	Cumulative share(%)	State ownership?
VW	15.4	15.4	Land minority
GM	12.0	27.4	
Ford	11.9	39.3	
PSA	11.7	51.0	
Fiat	10.8	61.8	
Renault	10.6	72.4	approx. 100%
BMW + Rover	6.0	78.4	
Mercedes Benz	4.3	82.7	
Volvo	1.7	84.4	
Japanese makes	10.9	95.3	
from Japan	6.5		
made in EU	3.9		
from US	0.2		
from elsewhere	0.3		
Korean	1.4	96.7	
US	0.5	97.2	
Others	2.6	99.8	

Source: Commission (1996*a*).

in recent years these have been eroded by privatizations and joint ventures. Whether public or private, however, the industry has maintained close links to government as well as organizing collect-ively at the European level (initially through the Committee of Common Market Car Manufacturers (CCMC), and later the Euro-pean Automobile Manufacturers Association (ACEA)).

While all governments have backed the sector, there has been a fundamental political divide between liberals and interventionists. Free traders believe that competition is good for the European industry; it is argued that the success of Japanese plants in the UK shows that Europe can produce efficiently. The opposite point of view holds that the playing-field must be tilted in favour of the European industry, in order to preserve in European hands an essential economic activity. Traditionally, the German government was more or less in favour of free trade, a stance made easier by the relative success of German industry in sustaining production in and exports from Germany. The UK government, believing the industry to be viable but in need of radical overhaul, encouraged inward investment. It allowed manufacturers to collude to restrict Japanese imports and to set prices high in the UK market, such that the UK consumer would in effect subsidize domestic and foreign producers alike. The French government, with Renault so long seen as one of the jewels in the crown of the state industrial sector, and suspicious of Japanese imports and investment, chose to subsidize local producers directly, while keeping prices lower, restricting imports by direct administrative controls that had no legal base, and discouraging inward investment. From the 1960s the Italian government maintained more or less legal and very restrictive import quotas (not contested by the Commission), leaving prices high and allowing no inward investment to compete with Fiat. Prices differed markedly across the EU, due both to market segmentation by firms and to the divergences in tax policies. Denmark and Greece, with no car industry, chose to set very high tax rates. Countries which produced cars chose to subsidize production, using very different instruments, while non-producers more often chose to tax heavily and showed less concern over the origin of imports. These different policies reflected both political factors and divergent social objectives.

EU Policy before 1991

Given these differences, it is not surprising that for many years the sector enjoyed special treatment under EU rules. The Commission was obliged to tolerate measures that struck at the heart of two of the principles of the Treaty of Rome: the basic rules of competition policy and the provision for a common commercial policy. It allowed member states to pursue individual policies on external trade and state aids and, in order to enable the regimes to coexist, it gave the industry a block exemption (Commission Decision 85/123/EEC) from competition rules with regard to distribution arrangements. In effect these allowed the manufacturers to segment markets as they wished. This was in stark contrast to the principles that had earlier led the Commission to invoke competition rules in rigorous opposition to intra-brand market segmentation in sectors where competition cases were used as an instrument for integration.

The Commission allowed Italy to invoke Article 115 of the Treaty of Rome: this provides for a member state to retain national controls on imports and thus restrict intra-EU flows of third-country goods where the member state has a valid derogation from the common commercial policy. France was not able to use this clause because its restrictions on Japanese cars fell outside this legal procedure. But the Commission none the less knew that openly to challenge the French government would have unthinkable political costs. The suspicion that arrangements were being made to restrict imports into Germany was ignored as was the agreement between the UK producers and the Japanese made in 1977, questionable under both competition and trade provisions of the treaty.[2] Subsidies to the car industry were known to be extensive, but separate national markets meant that the spill-over effects were arguably less. The Commission was dissatisfied with the situation, but recognized that the interests at stake were too great and too divergent to facilitate a common policy on cars, let alone one which respected both the rules of the Treaty of Rome and the Commission's inclination for a liberal solution.

Once the Commission decided that real steps had to be made towards a single market, the anomaly was called into question. The absence of a common market in cars was a symbolic affront to the '1992' programme: the Commission had a real problem to be solved if frontier controls were to be abolished. The White Paper of 1985 (Commission, 1985*a*) had merely suggested that a true single market would make separate national trade policies very hard to administer. Quietly the Commission set about trying to convince the member states and the industry that a common policy was unavoidable.

The Commission tried to negotiate a common external trade arrangement with Japan to begin on 2 January 1993. (Gandillot, 1992). The record shows that the Commission carried out the negotiations with an eye over its shoulder all the time to both the member states and the industry. The Commission's tactic seems to have been to negotiate essentially with representatives of the

---

[2] This arrangement was recently challenged by the European Consumers' Organization (BEUC), which asked the Directorate General for Competition (DGIV) to investigate the legality of the industry-to-industry agreement. Such agreements had previously been condemned by the Commission; only the public authorities have the right to control trade.

industry and the Japanese, in the expectation that, if a package could be found that was acceptable to both those parties, the member states would not object. In July 1991 the Commission announced it had achieved such a deal. It had persuaded the industry to agree that trade in cars should be subject to General Agreement on Tariffs and Trade (GATT) rules after 2000, while the Japanese had agreed an overall restraint in the mean time. On 31 July 1991 a 'consensus' with the Japanese Ministry of International Trade and Industry (MITI) was announced to the press. Member states agreed to abolish all their controls in exchange for an EU system.

The 'Elements of Consensus'

The arrangement with Japan was deliberately ambiguous. It set forecasts for car imports country by country for 1999, subject to various assumptions, linked to non-binding forecasts of total EU car demand and of output from Japanese 'transplant' production in Europe. The full agreement was never published. Instead Japanese Minister for Trade and Industry Eiichi Nakao and External Relations Commissioner Frans Andriessen made separate press statements, each indicating what he undertook to do. Ultimately, however, the core content of the 'consensus' was an agreement that there would be regular six-monthly negotiations between the Commission and MITI. It is these that set trade policy with Japan, not the wording of what was said or written in 1991. There are also almost certainly side deals with national governments. The main grey area concerns what would occur if demand falls below target or FDI production exceeds expectations. The Commission, the Japanese Government, and the UK Department of Trade and Industry (DTI) have all stated in the press that there is to be no automatic revision of import figures if transplant output exceeds the forecasts,[3] nor, according to Commission officials, was there any fixed agreement about how any fall in demand would be allocated among producers. French government officials, on the other hand, have stated that there was a firm agreement that import quotas would be modified to take account of changes in transplant

---

[3] This has been confirmed by interviews conducted by Peter Holmes with officials in DGs I and III during 1993–5.

output; and some have implied that the total market share figures were for imports and local production. Raymond Lévy of Renault told a parliamentary enquiry that there was some ambiguity on this (Assemblée Nationale, 1991). Renault staff and Élizabeth Guigou, the Minister for European Affairs, both insisted that the original agreement specified a formula for sharing falls in the market between suppliers (Assemblée Nationale, 1991). Commission officials deny this. They say that in any case transplant output was taken into account in terms of existing investment intentions. There can be no surprises. So there should be no need to modify import quotas for this reason. French officials acknowledge that their understanding of the agreement is different from that of the Commission and the British government, but are happy with their understanding of the deal. The implication is that Japan has given private assurances to France which could not be acknowledged by the other parties.

EU policy on cars is caught between attempts to regularize commercial policy and the political need for ambiguity, which means that it has to be decided in informal procedures. The Commission and Japan have notified the 1991 arrangement to GATT. It received a special exemption from the Uruguay Round ban on all voluntary export restraints.[4] The agreement was notified to the Committee of Permanent Representatives (Coreper) immediately before being announced to the press, but it was not formally adopted as a measure of commercial policy under Article 113 of the Treaty of Rome by the Council of Ministers. As such it has no legal force in the EU except what is provided by MITI's administrative guidance to Japanese firms.

The Commission has formally stated[5] that the EU had no 'agreement' with Japan and that no EU legislation restricts car imports from Japan. Privately, senior officials argue that the 'arrangement' with Japan rests on the self-interest of the Japanese in respecting it. If the Japanese do not satisfy the demands for 'moderation', the Commission can threaten the use of anti-dumping duties on cars, or, as one Commission official suggested, an unspecified threat in some other trade area.

---

[4] It was the only such agreement exempted in the Uruguay Round text on safeguards. When the Uruguay Round text came into force in 1995 the 1991 VER ceased to be a grey area under GATT law.
[5] Commission evidence in the BEUC case referred to in n. 2.

Whose Informal Politics?

Raymond Lévy said of the 1991 deal with Japan that it was not so much Europe negotiating with Japan but the Europeans negotiating amongst themselves. But who was negotiating with whom? Who were the main actors?

Clearly part of the political process took place inside the Commission. Gandillot (1992) reports vigorous disputes between the liberal and interventionist members of the college of Commissioners. However, the forces at stake were not simply votes in the Commission and it is not obvious that even Sir Leon Brittan acting alone would have acted differently. There clearly have been severe disagreements between the liberals in the Directorate General for Competition (DGIV), the sectoral teams in the Directorate General for Industry (DGIII), and increasingly those in DGIII who want to move away from sectoral support, including most recently, Stefano Micossi, the newly appointed director general of DGIII. But Martin Bangemann, the industry commissioner, played a very astute pragmatic game: he managed to make intra-Commission compromises more effectively than have occurred in some other sectors.

The battles inside the Commission reflected pressures from outside. But from whom? Consumer groups and some aggrieved traders cut out of the arbitrage business have had important cameo roles,[6] but the main actors have been producer interests. Can we distinguish between pressure from firms and from governments? As in the airlines case, the two are closely enmeshed. But even where industrial enterprises are formally part of the state one can usually identify separate actors.[7] Nevertheless a plausible reading of the events suggests that the industry itself was the key political force. The restructuring of the European motor industries' association appears here to have been a significant event. The CCMC, the

[6] There have been several legal actions challenging the block exemption enjoyed by producers, notably the BEUC case and Peugeot-EcoSystem, and restrictions on extra-EU imports, such as Automec and Asia Motors. In addition the consumer groups are consulted by DGIV on the block exemption.

[7] In earlier work at Sussex (Cawson *et al.*, 1990) we noted the sharp tensions between France Telecom as a commercial concern and those elements in the supervising ministry who wished to impose their own agenda, and the tensions that existed between Thomson and the French Industry Ministry on one side and the French Finance Ministry on the other.

original motor trade association included only those producers owned and controlled in the EU. Ford and GM, as well as Volvo and Saab, were excluded. It also required unanimity for the adoption of common positions. No common policy could be adopted by the EU if the CCMC refused to swallow it. The key player holding out against a deal was Jacques Calvet of Peugeot. Increasingly Peugeot's position came to diverge from that of Renault, where management had become convinced that, with the seeming inevitability of the single European market, national controls were becoming futile. For Renault, an EU–Japan deal of some sort was better than France trying to go it alone. Producers in the rest of Europe, many of whom had alliances with Japanese firms, were ready to seek an accommodation. When French firms agreed the stage was set. But Calvet had come round to the political position that in a choice between saving his firm or promoting the single market, Peugeot came first. A series of political manœuvres within France and the industry association led to Peugeot being marginalized.

At the end of 1990 it was agreed by all members except Peugeot that a new organization would be formed. The ACEA was created in May 1991. It included Ford, GM, Volvo, and Saab, and adopted a 75 per cent majority voting rule. The firms were in a very strong position to influence their governments if they could genuinely agree among themselves. The absence of Peugeot from the new ACEA helped the main players to agree on a common position with regard to Japanese imports (McLaughlin, 1994). It appears that once a consensus had been reached between all the firms bar Peugeot, each member sought to persuade its government to support the joint position. ACEA as an organization acted an as intermediary between the firms, as its principals, and the Commission (McLaughlin, 1994). So if the Commission could agree with ACEA, it was unlikely to have to renegotiate separately with the member governments.

The French National Assembly's December 1991 report (Assemblée Nationale, 1991) on the agreement gives an indication of the political process. In the committee hearings the main speaker presenting the agreement was not a minister, but Raymond Lévy, who stated he was speaking not merely as president of Renault, but also as president of ACEA. He stated that the agreement 'répondait, dans une certaine mesure aux demandes de l'ACEA'. He defended the agreement as the best possible in the circumstances: legal rulings had made French national measures harder to apply. He noted the ambiguity about the treatment of transplants, though said that the Japanese in private were more accommodating than in their public statements. Given French enthusiasm for the '1992' process, not yet dented by the Maastricht debate, it was possible for Raymond Lévy to argue publicly in 1991 that the commitment to Europe should override sectoral sensibilities.[8] In contrast, in his evidence, Jacques Calvet called for a renegotiation of everything, even the Single European Act (SEA) and the status of cars under the GATT!

The timetable suggests that Calvet's isolation within the European car lobby and Lévy's accommodation with the Germans, Volvo, Ford, and GM helped to swing the balance in favour of agreement. It is also worth noting that many of the members of ACEA had developed alliances with Japanese firms, most obviously Rover–Honda, but also Volvo–Renault–Mitsubishi, and VW–Toyota.

The politics of the industry have, however, altered since 1991. The Maastricht referendum and the recession brought Calvet into the mainstream of French politics, and the inter-firm alliances have markedly shifted. Peugeot has meanwhile rejoined ACEA. The producers remain a privileged interlocutor for the Commission.[9]

The Commission's margin of manœuvre is limited to what coalitions it can sustain. In the 'consensus' the Commission was able to get support from the member governments for a shorter transition period on Japanese imports than that asked for by the firms, but the nature of the deal is such that it lacks formal legal support from the Council.

This ambiguity suits the industry in many ways, as it facilitates

---

[8] In June 1990 P. Holmes witnessed Lévy addressing a committee of the European Parliament and antagonizing many members with his aggressive demand of reciprocity as a condition for allowing free trade in cars with Japan. He was rescued by the presence of a Japanese Automobile Manufacturers Association (JAMA) speaker, who annoyed his listeners even more by claiming that Japan had no trade barriers at all on cars.

[9] The producers succeeded in persuading the Commission to renew with only a few minor modifications the Block Exemption on motor vehicle distribution in 1995, despite opposition from BEUC and the new member states.

the use of informal procedures at which the industry has come to excel; but it has left a number of unexploded time-bombs (McLaughlin, 1994). Notable among these was the 'understanding' that the Japanese would cut imports back by two-thirds of any fall in EU car demand, which, if applied, would have meant no Japanese imports in 1993. Many Commission officials believe that it was unwise to circulate an unofficial Commission paper indicating that this was what they were expecting: the French firms saw both sides as bound by this, but the Commission and MITI did not. Fortunately the downturn was followed by an upturn in 1994 and the crisis was defused.

Was there a supranational element to the political process? The question of what is truly supranational is a difficult one. Mark Mason (1994) has argued that a compromise struck among national interests means that we should not see the outcome as 'supranational'. However, under the Treaty of Rome, trade policy is a matter for the Council as well as the Commission. Did the ministers allow discretion to the Commission? And, more importantly, did the member governments bind themselves by accepting the Commission's proposals? It would seem that the presence of the Commission in the negotiations did produce an outcome that was different from what would have occurred if there had been twelve separate bilateral negotiations with Japan. The Commission persuaded the member governments to drop all of their national measures and in effect to rely on Japanese goodwill to administer trade. Hitherto not even the British had indicated a willingness to do this. The fact is that now an EU measure puts genuine legal obstacles before member states tempted to apply their own grey measures, contrary to the situation when only bilateral national measures had been in place. The European Court of Justice (ECJ) and the Court of First Instance have shown an increasing willingness to act in this area. In addition, the negotiating process seems so far to leave all the key players (apart from Peugeot) feeling bound by the agreement. The disputes are not about renegotiating the accord, but what it meant and whether the Commission and the Japanese are actually respecting it. The Commission is firmly in control of the main negotiations with Japan, and the divergences between member governments' preferences make it hard for the Council to impose any alternative policies.

EUROPEAN AIRLINES

In contrast to the car industry case, the main focus of EU policy in the air transport industry has been to change the market structure of the industry rather than to address questions of market access by non-European firms.[10] Thus, for most of the 1980s, the main concern was with setting the rules redefining how European air transport markets were organized and regulated. While reform has been gradual, phased, and marked by derogations and exemptions, there have been real changes, and the 1990s have seen the Commission, national governments, and the industry negotiating over implementation.

The European airline industry accounts for approximately 1 per cent of EU GDP; it directly employs 300,000–400,000 staff, and indirectly a further million. In most years air services have run a trade surplus. However, the industry itself is characterized by low levels of profitability and, relative to some other regions, poor productivity performance. Some have argued that these shortcomings are at least partly a function of the special treatment which the industry has enjoyed on account of its perceived economic importance (McGowan, 1993).

The airline industry has been characterized by special regulatory arrangements, cartel-like behaviour on the part of airlines at the international level, and the predominance of single, often publicly owned, firms within countries. Taken together these factors render it hard to demarcate between government pressures, inter-firm collusion, and industry lobbying. In terms of the EU, the institutional legacy and the routines of industry conduct have rendered policy-making more difficult, leading to tensions not only between the Commission, on the one hand, and the Council and the industry, on the other, but also within the Commission itself.

The industry has a history of regulation, partly for safety reasons, but also because of the economic characteristics of the sector. Given the nature of the air transport industry, regulation in Europe, as elsewhere, has been carried out at the international as well as the national level. The international regime has involved mainly bilateral arrangements, but also some at the regional and international levels; it has comprised treaties between governments and

---

[10] That battle is in the process of being fought (*Financial Times*, 27 Apr. 1995).

agreements between firms. These have determined the prices at which air services are offered, the capacity available on routes, and the carriers which are allowed to operate. They have also involved conditions for revenue-pooling. In effect, these arrangements have allowed the industry to operate as a cartel, supported by a cluster of bilateral and multilateral agreements. Consequently, the scope for competition has been almost non-existent (Button and Swann, 1989).

The main industry associations are the International Air Transport Association (IATA), which plays a mixture of cartel, regulatory, and lobbying roles, and the Association of European Airlines (AEA). The AEA comprises the flag-carriers of all the EU states, plus those of European Free Trade Area (EFTA) and the eastern and Mediterranean European states; it is primarily a lobbying organization. In addition there is an organization representing the second-tier carriers (ACE) and various consumer organizations. For the most part, however, it has been the interests of the AEA and IATA which have received the most attention.

This environment of co-operation, even collusion, is reinforced by the similarity of industry structures across Europe. The Euro-

TABLE 8.2. *Market share and government ownership in the European airline industry, 1994*

	Market share (%)[a]	State ownership (%)
Sabena (Belgium)	100	23
SAS (Denmark[b])	92	50
Air France (France)	81	100
Lufthansa (Germany)	97	59
Aer Lingus (Ireland)	c.100	100
Alitalia (Italy)	c.100	85
Luxair (Luxembourg)	100	23
KLM (Netherlands)	99	38
TAP (Portugal)	99	100
Iberia (Spain)	88	100
British Airways (UK)	63	0

[a] Market share refers to the revenue passenger kilometres flown within Europe by a flag-carrier as a proportion of those flown by all scheduled airlines of that carrier's nationality.
[b] This refers to SAS's Danish activities.

Source: Author's calculations; Civil Aviation Authority.

pean industry has for the most part, been publicly owned, though there have been some privately owned 'secondary' carriers and private firms in the 'charter' market (and the trend in much of Europe is towards a larger role for private operators as a result of new regulatory policies and privatization). For many of the past forty years, the industry has been dominated by 'national champions', or flag-carriers. The importance of (and government stake in) flag-carriers has meant that national policies have been strongly oriented towards supporting and protecting the flag-carriers' interests. Governments have generally not pursued policies which seek to favour other carriers domestically or internationally (see Table 8.2). Since the early 1980s, however, differences between governments have begun to appear, reflecting divergent responses to liberalization: the UK was the main promoter of liberalization, though the Danish and Irish have also been sympathetic; the French and southern Europeans have been the most reluctant to accept change.

The EU and the Industry

Despite the identification of air transport as 'le secteur d'urgence' by the Spaak Committee, which laid the blueprint for the Treaty of Rome, it was only in the late 1980s that a specifically EU regime for the industry emerged. Although there was much debate on a policy in the early 1960s (which overlapped with proposals for even closer co-operation between airlines and governments in Europe (degli Abbati, 1985)), no substantial initiatives were taken by the Commission. Member governments allowed the existing framework of regulation to continue and left international discussions to international, regional, and industrial forums, such as the European Civil Aviation Conference. Efforts to formulate an aviation policy were made in the early 1970s; they were largely unsuccessful, despite an ECJ decision in 1974, which ruled that the general rules of the Treaty applied to the air transport sector. Over the next ten years, the Commission investigated the industry (in particular the compatibility of the sector with competition rules), but a first attempt at policy in 1979 came to very little (McGowan and Trengove, 1986).

Elsewhere, however, the 1970s were a decade of radical change in the airline industry, and, even if those changes did not immediately impinge upon the rules of the European game, they set in motion threats to the cartel, which responded by trying to contain the pace of reform. The most important change was the deregulation of the industry within the US. Although largely a domestic industry, with a small number of private operators, the regime governing the sector was not unlike that in other parts of the world: prices, entry, and capacity were controlled. Increasing dissatisfaction with the industry's performance made it a target for a wave of regulatory reform sweeping the US at that time. The abandonment of most of the economic controls upon the industry was achieved within a couple of years, and was followed by a longer period of radical restructuring.

While this was an internal reform, not directly affecting international services, deregulation was to prove a threat to the European industry. Airlines and their users could see that the US experiment was underway, which raised expectations for similar reforms in Europe. This required the airlines to emphasize the differences between the US and the European industry (IATA, 1984; *Agence Europe*, 16 Nov. 1983), while consumer groups preferred to emphasize the similarities (NCC, 1986; *Agence Europe*, 30 Oct. 1983).

The arguments of those who minimized the extent of similarities between the US and Europe wherever possible and emphasized the problems of the US experience otherwise appeared to have prevailed. In its Second Memorandum on Air Transport, the Commission (1984) stated at the outset that a US-style deregulation was not desirable, and couched its proposals for change very much within the context of the existing regulatory framework. None the less, it clearly signalled that, however gradual reform might be, it was moving in the direction of greater liberalization. The initial proposals in the package involved a modification of existing airline industry conduct, increasing the scope for competition, but at the same time permitting many prevailing practices to be continued by exempting them from EU competition rules. Reactions from outside the EU institutions to the second Memorandum replicated the attitudes adopted towards previous Commission proposals. The bulk of the industry sought to obtain exemption from competition rules, without offering concessions on greater flexibility and access. The AEA's response was seen as 'cautious and unresponsive' by one official (Pugh, 1986; AEA, 1985).

The trigger for securing agreement on the reforms was the ECJ's judgment in the Nouvelles Frontières case. This enabled the Commission to threaten legal action against member states and their airlines.[11] However, although a complete resistance to reform (favoured by some countries and airlines) was impossible, many airlines failed to comply with Commission requests for information, both before and after the ECJ's judgement (*Agence Europe*, 23 Sept. 1985; 11 July 1987; Commission, 1988). The dragging-out of the liberalization process can be seen as a victory of sorts for them and their governments (given the closeness of relationships between the two it is hard to distinguish between their interests in this period).

On the other hand, reform would probably not have succeeded had there not been governments and airlines in favour of, or at least not opposed to, change. The collective efforts of the flag-carriers were probably undermined by the emergence of major differences between the bulk of 'continental' operators and the British members of the AEA, as reflected in the refusal of the latter to endorse a number of policy statements and proposals made by the AEA (*Agence Europe*, 9 Oct. 1985).[12] These differences were reflected at a governmental level: the British authorities, who were already engaged in negotiating more liberal bilateral agreements, were the most supportive of the Commission's efforts. At the same time backing for liberalization from independent airlines seeking to take advantage of a more open market, and from national and European consumer groups, indicated that the producer interests of the main flag-carriers did not necessarily equate with those of the wider European interest (*Agence Europe*, 19 June 1986; 16 Feb. 1987; 21 Mar. 1987).

Liberalization was extended in two further packages of reforms, agreed in 1990 and 1992, the latter effectively opening up the industry by removing most controls on market entry and price setting (see Table 8.3). In contrast to the first set of reforms, these

---

[11] The case concerned a French travel firm which was taken to court over its discounting practices. The French Competition Court then referred the case to the ECJ: see Argyris (1989).

[12] It would be wrong to suggest that the British were the only members sympathetic to reform. Others, notably KLM, were in favour of liberalization, but the British were the only ones publicly to dissociate themselves from AEA statements.

measures were agreed relatively easily, though the limited scope of the second package owed something to the reluctance of some governments and some within the Commission to accept rapid reform (*Agence Europe*, 19 July 1989; 7 Oct. 1989; *Financial Times*, 18 July 1989; 20 June 1990). There was, however, no overnight reconciliation to liberalization by hitherto reluctant airlines and governments. The most hostile to reform remained those where government–industry links were closest—Greece, Italy, France—and there is no evidence to suggest that governments were using European policy to force change upon their carriers (indeed their subsequent support in the form of aid suggests the opposite). However, they were no longer able to hold back reform. The first package contained a time-limited exemption from competition rules: the Commission was therefore able to use this as an effective bargaining chip to secure liberalization. Moreover, the first package itself effectively undermined the idea that further reform could be stalled indefinitely. In addition, the anti-reform coalition was rather fragile, and defections and outside pressures rendered it impossible to sustain.

At the same time, however, the process of reform probably reassured a number of airlines and governments that they could sustain their incumbency. Stretched out over nearly ten years, liberalization was never going to entail the sort of shake-out experienced in the US. The European airlines used the period of transition to consolidate their activities, taking over potential rivals, entering joint ventures, and expanding fleet capacity. Such a response suggests that the legacy of collusion proved rather hard to shake off, and that perceptions of the consequences of liberalization had changed since the early period of negotiations. Such a view is reinforced by the shift in emphasis in industry lobbying away from resistance to reform: the airlines now called for the minimum of regulation (by which they meant the application of competition rules) and emphasized the competitiveness of the European industry, opposing any 'give-away' of rights to US carriers.[13]

Further shifts in emphasis can be seen in the industry's ambivalent response towards the Commission's on-going regulation of the industry. Based on existing reforms and the application of compe-

---

[13] They also successfully obtained a suspension of the rules during the Gulf War (*Financial Times*, 15 Feb. 1991).

TABLE 8.3. *Air transport reforms*

	First Package 1987	Second Package 1990	Third Package 1992
Prices	Zonal system (of standard, discount, and deep discount fares), providing limited scope for independent action	Mixture of zonal system, double disapproval for passengers, while free pricing for air cargo	Free pricing Block exemption from competition rules allows IATA fare consultations Limited scope for member states (and Commission) to intervene against excessive basic (economy) or predatory air fares.
Capacity Distribution	Capacity freedom only within a zone (55/45)	Capacity freedom only within a zone (60/40)	No capacity controls but safeguards for congestion and catastrophic conditions
Market Access	Full discretion on designation of rights to access a route subject to thresholds	Full discretion on designation subject to thresholds Limited 5th freedom (<50% of capacity) Limited public service obligations	No controls Full 7th freedom rights (if >300,000) Domestic services included Consecutive cabotage (full cabotage 1997) Developed public service obligations
Licensing of carriers	Full national discretion	Full national discretion	Technical and economic fitness rules EU ownership criteria replace national ownership rules

tition rules and related measures (notably the merger regulation), from 1987 onwards the Commission intervened in a number of cases involving anti-competitive behaviour; often reversing particular actions, and blocking proposed agreements or imposing conditions on them (see Table 8.4). For the most part these were relatively minor cases, though their importance in preventing further actions cannot be ignored. In a number of higher profile cases, mostly involving mergers or state aids, the Commission was less effective, giving the go-ahead in most cases with only limited conditions.[14] In both circumstances the airlines were generally hostile to the Commission as regulator, but individual carriers were not averse to taking advantage of the rules when they felt their interests would be served.

The industry's response to regulation raises the broader issue of the Commission's effectiveness. Why has the Commission's bark been worse than its bite in regulating the liberalized air transport market?

As in other areas of policy, the Commission's ability to pursue liberalization has been limited by internal differences. The most important has been that between the Transport Directorate General (DGVII) and DGIV. DGVII, like other sectoral DGs, is often seen as too ready to take the producer's perspective in European policy-making, whereas the orientation of DGIV, while often exaggerated, is geared towards applying the competition rules, particularly where the prevailing patterns of industrial structure and conduct are at variance with those rules. This difference undoubtedly affected the process of drafting air transport policy, with the commissioners responsible for transport and competition policy at the time, Stanley Clinton-Davis and Peter Sutherland, respectively, then responsible for competition, publicly differing on strategy during the negotiations on the first package. This difference reappeared in the 1990s as transport commissioner, Karel van Miert was more sympathetic to airline arguments on competitiveness than Leon Brittan, then responsible for competition (*Financial Times*, 30 Nov. 1991). He allowed a number of aid packages to go through despite Brittan's opposition (*Financial Times*, 21 Nov. 1991), while Brittan excluded van Miert from direct discussions

---

[14] In addition, there were a few cases in which the Commission's intervention contributed to the collapse of the proposed venture.

TABLE 8.4. *Application of competition rules to the European airline industry*

	1986	1987	1988	1989	1990	1991	1992	1993
Commission Action								
Virgin/BA case	Nouvelles Frontières	Threat of action on airline information provision	Code of conduct on CRS proposed	Block exemptions proposed following Ahmed Saeed case	Rules on interlining following Lufthansa–Air Europe row	Third package proposed	Approved aid to Air France and Iberia	Virgin/BA case
Block exemptions extended		Aid from BA for new regional services approved	BA–BCal link approved subject to conditions	Joint operations scrutinized	Revised block exemptions	Special treatment permitted due to Gulf War (to May 91)	Fined Aer Lingus for abuse of dominant position	Block exemptions extended
Viva Air decision			Fined Sabena over abuse of dominant position		Joint operations scrutinized	IATA Agency system allowed under 85.3	Air France–Sabena link investigated and approved	Viva Air decision
Initiatives on third-country relations.			Competition rules implemented		Air France–Lufthansa agreement approved subject to conditions	Amadeus–Sabre co-operation allowed under 85.3		Initiatives on third-country relations.
					BA–KLM–Sabena agreement queried	Approved aid to Air France and Sabena	Revised aid criteria	

Investigated airport support services	End of preference for flag-carriers by local civil servants	Air France–Air Inter–UTA link approved subject to conditions		Regulation on CRS code of conduct adopted	First package adopted
Decisions on UK fare complaints	KLM–Transavia link approved subject to conditions				
	Block exemptions extended				
Decision on London–Brussels frequencies					
	Accelerated complaints procedure	Adopted second package			
Council action Regulation on slot allocation	Regulation on air cargo services				
Third package adopted	Regulation on denied board compensation				

with the airlines involved in the abortive BA–KLM–Sabena merger (*Financial Times*, 28 June 1990).

Where such differences arose, moreover, it is clear that the commissioner responsible for competition was often outvoted by the rest of the college of Commissioners. In such cases it is reasonable to infer that Commissioners' positions reflected perceived national interests or fears of member state retaliation. It appears that in the wake of the Aerospatiale decision, the Commission's unwillingness to antagonize further member states, especially France, permitted a number of cases dealing with state aids for airlines to be approved. The French government's lobbying effort was by all accounts extremely vigorous in the debate on the aid package to Air France (*Financial Times*, 28 July 1994). The closeness of relations between member governments and their airlines makes it difficult to ascertain how far industry pressures have shaped the Commission's approach. It appears, however, that unilateral pressure (backed by a member government) is more important than industry-wide representation. This is not least because of the increasing divergences among industry interests. Although the Commission's actions can be criticized, it may be that the policy as a whole, as well as particular episodes, along with the admittedly slow process of adjustment within the industry, may change the way lobbying operates.

Whereas ten years ago, the industry was largely of one mind in its response to liberalization, it is now much harder to see such a consensus; airlines move at different paces and in different directions to adjust (as evidenced in their approaches to privatization, rationalization, and the choice of international partners). The opposition of initially BA and other British operators, and later some other flag-carriers (such as KLM and Lufthansa), to the subsidy programmes of a number of other carriers is one example (*Financial Times*, 5 Oct. 1995). The opposition of Air France and some others to BA's efforts to develop alliances is another. In the past, such developments would not have been opposed by other carriers, partly on the basis that one should not oppose what one may need to resort to at another time, but also because there was no competition. Now, such developments affect other airlines much more directly, as demonstrated by the decision of some airlines not only to challenge each other, but also to take the Commission before the ECJ.

CONCLUSIONS AND COMPARISONS

The car and airline cases illustrate the range of different problems which industrial networks and policy-makers confront: in the case of cars the main issue has been the negotiation and implementation of a single agreement with a foreign supplier; in the case of airlines the issue has been the evolution of an overall policy for the sector. Yet in their different ways they illustrate the fundamental issue of how industries react to attempts to incorporate them into a European policy framework.

In the car sector the Commission has relied very heavily on gradually extending its influence in trade and competition policy, while reassuring the main economic actors that it is willing to take their interests into account. Gradually it replaced the national governments as the industry's main interlocutor. The member governments have been reassured that any restrictions on national industrial policies are within the realm that national finance ministries are happy to accept. The Commission has sought to use its powers and discretion under competition rules to gain leverage.[15]

This means compromising on many principles. However, in brokering the deals among the main actors the Commission is continually trying to seek the most liberal solution from among those that it considers politically realistic. The net impact for the EU has clearly been to move in the direction of the disciplines called for by the treaties. So far the movement has been in one direction. But in seeking to use the leverage of political deals that do not have a clear foundation in the treaties, the Commission runs the risk that the informal political process that it has cleverly exploited might turn against it in a different constellation of forces.

We have argued that the nature of the informal political networks was very important in the case of the car industry. The industry (with the exception of Peugeot) took a common position in negotiating with the Commission. The governments seem to have played a supporting role. Obliged to compete with each other (more or less), the producers were aware of the need to act together politically in a way that was distinct from their economic

---

[15] Two recent cases—Automec and BEUC—before the ECJ have just begun to establish criteria for the exercise of discretion by the Commission, an area that is bound to become increasingly sensitive.

interaction. From a game-theoretic perspective the firms were playing a two-level game in which co-operation in the political sphere
created a set of incentives (e.g. the rules on distribution and the
'consensus') that made less than cut-throat competition a natural
outcome without collusion.

In the case of airlines the process seems to have been slightly
different. Accustomed as the airlines were to operating as a cartel,
they were not organized to engage in collective lobbying once the
cartel began to come unstuck. The very close ties between airlines
and governments seem to have led to a situation in which it was
considered 'normal' for the airlines to rely on their political representatives in governments. At the same time the interests of the
airlines seem to have been even more divided than in the case of
the car industry. As the maverick pro-deregulation company, BA
had the support of its home government and was closer to Commission thinking than was the rest of the industry. In the car case the
maverick Peugeot was fighting against the wishes of the Commission and the consensus established between the French government and Renault.

It is also worth observing that networks of alliances with external
competitors may have played a role in the car case. Although the
European car industry has had to pull in its horns in North America
in recent years, and is heavily centred on Europe, it is widely
acknowledged that the industry is global. Many alliances exist[16]—
some for technology transfer, some for joint marketing—which
give the impression of a certain common interest between Japanese
and western producers. Although, as we noted earlier, some of
these alliances have proved unstable,[17] there have been spectacular
rises in foreign penetration of the Japanese market, sometimes
through links with Japanese firms.

Such alliances may be important in the future with airlines. Certainly if the Commission were involved in the negotiation of EU-
wide bilateral agreements with third-countries (something several
member governments oppose), the different partnerships and
equity stakes which European carriers enjoy would be a powerful
influence on the shape of any such agreements. Alliances between

[16] In addition to those referred to above: GM–NUMMI and GM–Isuzu in
Europe, Ford–Mazda, Chrysler–Mitsubishi in the US.
[17] For example, Ford–Mazda, Rover–Honda, and the Renault–Mitsubishi link via
Volvo.

carriers within the EU are already a source of tension amongst different factions (see, for example, the complaints by Air France and Sabena over the takeover of Dan Air by BA and by Air France over BA's stake in TAT). Indeed, it may be that divisions among the producers will provide the Commission with its main opportunity to intervene: carriers which are largely privately owned and self-financing may press much harder for controls on state-owned carriers receiving government subsidies.

By contrast the role of consumers appears relatively weak in both cases. While consumers' associations have been allies of the Commission in liberalization, their practical role has been modest. In the car industry they have been an active pressure group on the block exemption. They were officially given confidential drafts by DGIV but appear to have had very little influence, except in securing publication of price information. They have been legal gadflies, especially in the JAMA–SMMT case (*Financial Times*, 18 May 1994; Frazer and Holmes, 1995), but so far this has been treated as a minor inconvenience by the Commission and has served to highlight the minor role for consumers' organizations in both trade and competition policy.

What of our three explanations for the Commission's limited success: fear of intergovernmental backlash, intra-Commission disputes, and industry capture? The first point to note is that we are not describing outright failures in either case. It may have been that without the Commission's initiatives the chances of reconciling these industries with treaty rules would have been non-existent. Moreover, one could argue that it is too early to judge: the regimes in question have only recently been established and it may take some time for the past special treatment and expectations of such treatment to fade.

On the whole the Commission seems to be subtly reading the runes of what it can get away with, carrying on internal negotiations at the same time as those with its interlocutors. This makes it hard to distinguish reluctance to take on vested interests from a calculation of inability to do so. In the airline case the divisions within the Commission and the considerable involvement of governments were more evident brakes to liberalization; in the car case Commission coherence was preserved by a pragmatic commissioner for industry (Bangemann, 1992) faced by an industry used to living just at arm's length from governments.

Reluctance to offend member governments may well become more acute in the future. Hostility to the Commission is building in France, due to nationalist sentiment and even among pragmatic pro-Europeans who consider that the Commission has exceeded its political legitimacy and legal authority in a number of competition cases. One basic reason for this is that the emergence of a true single market in many sectors increases the need for something resembling a coherent industrial policy at the European level, even if this only means coherence between the existing measures of regulation and intervention. So long as the Council is unable to adopt a common view, the Commission will find itself making policy in those areas in which it can act alone, namely the exercise of discretion in competition policy and in informal trade policy. However, there are political risks in leaving major policy decisions, such as the degree of competition among airlines and the policy towards Japanese car firms, to such informal processes.

9

Big Firms as Political Actors: Corporate Power and the Governance of the European Consumer Electronics Industry

ALAN CAWSON

INTRODUCTION

The relationships between firms in an industrial sector can be analysed on a number of levels. On the face of it, and according to the economics textbooks, the firms are competitors subject to the operation of market pressures, and the concept of 'power' is unnecessary in relation to market transactions. Firms are recognized to make different strategic choices in how to respond to market pressures, but ultimately are constrained by the operation of the market. According to economic orthodoxy, firms enter into power relationships only when they enter the political arena as lobbyists.

Alternative approaches which explore the political and social dynamics of industrial sectors have, however, become increasingly prominent in recent years, especially since the publication of seminal articles by authors such as Harrison White (1981) and Mark Granovetter (1985). A new literature on economic governance has grown up, which explores empirically the structure of relationships between firms, employing concepts drawn from sociology, political science, and political economy. Much more attention has now been given to the relationship between firms and governments, and to the way in which public policies shape sectoral governance.

This chapter seeks to develop this approach further in two ways. It explores in more detail the effects on sectoral governance of differences in national ownership between firms in a sector, using the case of the European consumer electronics industry, and in particular the examples of the Dutch-owned firm Philips and the Japanese-owned firm Matsushita, to highlight the different roles played by these firms in the sector, and the way in which European Community (EC) public policy which favours European firms has constrained the ability of the incoming firms to exert political power commensurate with their economic strength as global producers. Secondly, it examines the nature of the governance structure in European consumer electronics, as revealed in the shift from the analogue high definition television (HDTV) technology of the 1980s to the fully digital technologies being developed in the work of the digital video broadcasting (DVB) group.

The chapter can be seen as a sequel to earlier work (Cawson, 1992; Cawson *et al.*, 1990) which explored the changing structure of governance of the British consumer electronics industry as inward investing firms came to dominate that industry, at the same time that public policy determination was shifting from London to Brussels. In this chapter I focus more directly on the European level, since the processes we analysed in the period up to 1989 in *Hostile Brothers* have continued to erode the boundaries between different national markets in consumer electronics, and the major producers have moved towards reorganizing their own corporate governance structures at the European level. The chapter draws on continuing research on the impact of the single market process on the consumer electronics industry, with particular reference to the development of advanced television technologies.[1]

THE THREE DIMENSIONS OF THE POLITICAL ROLE OF FIRMS

Market Power

The first aspect of the political role of firms to be considered here derives from power relationships within market transactions. As we argued in *Hostile Brothers*, drawing on the work of Max Weber, there is a logic within market relationships towards the

[1] Support from the Economic and Social Research Council's Single European Market Programme (Award L113251007) and the Department of Trade and Industry is gratefully acknowledged.

socialization of impersonal relationships, and a tendency towards closure, whereby firms seek to insulate themselves from the unpredictable nature of market relationships. In the absence of effective regulations to prevent mergers and takeovers, market competition leads towards a small number of winners, and the competition terminates when the number of winners is small enough to negotiate non-market allocations, i.e. cartels, in which the rights of sellers with respect to buyers are determined by agreement.[2]

In most contemporary sectors formal cartels have been eliminated, although we have recently seen the temptation towards cartelization in bulk commodity industries such as chemicals, where there is little scope for achieving a dominant position in the market through innovation, and where price competition might become cut-throat. In the electronics industry the dynamic of competition has tended to be driven by innovation. The Japanese firms achieved their market position initially through innovations in manufacturing techniques, in organizational innovations such as 'just-in-time' production and quality circles, and in successive incremental product innovations such as those in television.

In our earlier analysis of the displacement of British firms by Japanese firms in the television industry, we argued that by the mid-1970s competition had reduced the number of manufacturers to around a dozen firms, and that these firms adopted informal cartel-like behaviour, which enabled them not to follow through on the initial innovation of colour television (CTV). The sector was loosely governed through informal relationships between the firms, in part carried on through the trade association, which acted as a forum for brokering informal 'understandings' between producers. The British firms were cushioned by the TV rental industry from pressure to improve quality and reliability, and were uninterested in developments in television manufacturing in other countries, especially Japan. Different technical standards divided national markets, so that British firms were initially largely untroubled by imports, and uninterested in exports. They bought component parts in 'spot' markets, on the basis of price and delivery, and accepted an arm's length relationship with suppliers; this was based on a manufacturing philosophy of accepting a certain percentage of

---

[2] Dai (1996) has shown how the early growth of Philips in the incandescent light business was dominated by its cartel with Siemens.

faults, and eliminating them through testing and repair at the end of the production process. Thus the power-structure of their market was a dual one with a non-competitive oligopoly in relation to final consumers, and a competitive and atomistic structure in relation to component suppliers.

In Japan the power structure of the market was the exact inverse. There was considerable rivalry between producers, with competitive strategies based on product and process innovations, and attempts to increase market share (rather than enhance or defend short-term profitability). In terms of their relationship with suppliers, Japanese firms sought long-term stable relationships based on an asymmetrical power relationship. Components suppliers were encouraged to adopt manufacturing practices to ensure quality (failures were measured as low as one part per million), and more of the process of manufacture was sub-contracted to these suppliers. In addition Japanese producers had undertaken incremental innovations to reduce the number of component parts required for a television set, and invested in automatic insertion equipment, which assembled the reduced number of parts more economically.

The result of this manufacturing system in the television industry was that the Japanese firms were able to supply better quality sets to British consumers at prices comparable to or lower than the British producers. The response of the British producers was to cry foul, and allege that the sets were being dumped onto the British market. The firms faced a usurpation of their power in the market, so they responded by entering the political process as complainants.

Firms as Interest Groups

This brings us to the second dimension of power, that of firms as interest groups. The conventional pressure group literature, as it developed in the US and Britain in the 1950s and 1960s, almost completely ignored the role of firms as presenters of their own interests. Firms were seen as members of associations, and associations were seen as the relevant actors in any discussion of lobbying. This approach, ironically, carried through to the mainstream of the literature on neo-corporatism, which in other respects recognized the tendency towards interdependencies between industrial interests and the state, in contrast to the emphasis on inputs into the policy-making process which is characteristic of pluralist theories of pressure group politics. Those who followed Philippe Schmitter's pioneering work (Lehmbruch and Schmitter, 1982; Schmitter, 1974; Schmitter and Lehmbruch, 1979) refused to include negotiated policy-making between individual firms and the state within the compass of corporatism. The oligopolistic structure of many product markets, including consumer electronics, makes trade associations more important as legitimators of firms' political activity than as orchestrators of sectoral interests. It made sense to me (Cawson, 1986) to see such firms as functional equivalents of associations in corporatist arrangements, and to recognize the possibility of micro-corporatism, as well as meso- and macro-corporatism.

In the light of the corporatist critique of pluralist approaches to interest-group politics we can distinguish two ways in which firms act as interest groups. The first is where firms are potential partners in corporatist bargaining; the second where they are lobbyists seeking to influence public policies, but not sufficiently powerful to be indispensable to successful policy implementation. The role that firms are able to play in the political process is plainly dependent on two factors: the extent of their market power, and the potential contribution of their sector to meeting the policy goals of governments. In the HDTV case discussed below, Philips and Thomson were the only two European-owned firms with power in the international market in consumer electronics products—the only two capable of mounting an effective challenge to the Japanese—and HDTV was seen as a 'strategic' technology.[3] As argued within the corporatist tradition, firms become lobbyists (pressuring governments from outside) when they lack the structural power to have their interests routinely considered by policy-makers.

Firms may seek to protect themselves from uncertainty in a number of different ways. The first way is through effective competition. Market power confers a degree of predictability through the exercise of domination, and this tends to be the preferred strategy. This may be increasingly difficult to achieve, however, as the organization of the firm expands and matures, and the internal

---

[3] For a discussion of what 'strategic' means in the context of HDTV, see Dai *et al.* (1994).

politics of the firms becomes dominated by bureaucratic behaviour (as discussed below). In *Hostile Brothers* we argued that the alternative strategies open to firms were to form associations or to seek the protection of the state. In the case of a very large multinational firm—such as Philips—the actual situation at any given time was a mixture of these three strategies, with any one of them dominant at a particular time. Thus when Philips's financial position became critical in the wake of the video-cassette recorder (VCR) disaster, when it was forced to abandon its own technology and adopt that of its Japanese rival, the dominant strategy switched from innovation to lobbying for protection, and then to incorporation into the European programme to develop HDTV.

The Internal Politics of Firms

In the course of the period from 1986 to 1992 the political role of Philips was largely determined by the third of our types of politics of the firm; power relations within firms. Internal conflicts can arise over political strategies, and these conflicts can lead to a loss of focus on the firm's commercial strategies, leading to an erosion of market power. This view of the three kinds of power as interconnected helps to explain the responses of Philips to the severe threats to its business in the 1980s, although data about external activities is more readily available.

Large firms are complex organizations, and their governance is an important area of research which has been largely neglected, in part because of problem of access to information which is commercially confidential.[4] In some cases (Metze, 1993) there is useful material published by journalists, but with obvious problems of verifiability. Firms like Philips and Matsushita are so large that it is impossible to obtain even a fuzzy picture without multiple interviews.[5] Written materials, such as board minutes, are rarely avail-

---

[4] It is for this reason that we do not identify informants when using interview material in our published work. Since 1985 we have been afforded exceptional access to information, especially by Philips, for which we are extremely grateful. In many cases this information has been given to us on expressed conditions of confidentiality.

[5] It is necessary at this point to stress that this paper draws on more than 35 interviews with Philips managers in London, Redhill, Croydon, Eindhoven, and Brussels, but with rather fewer (around 15) interviews with Matsushita officials in Tokyo, Osaka, Slough, Bracknell, and Brussels.

able until long after the events to which they refer.[6] Despite these problems, however, it is possible to piece together some important parts of the story as it relates to the innovation of new television technologies (which has been our main focus).

I have shown in earlier work how organizational structure affects the way in which specific strategies evolve (Cawson *et al.*, 1995). In the case of Compact Disc Interactive (CD-i)—an entirely new product line derived from compact disc (CD) technology—I analysed the problem of fitting new technologies within existing organizational boundaries, and showed how external consultants could be used within the internal process of a firm's decision-making to persuade the main board to adopt the technology as a priority in determining its strategies. In this respect parts of a firm behave in relation to the main board in exactly the same way as the whole firm behaves in relation to public authorities, that is as a faction or pressure group. In the CD-i case Philips Interactive Media Systems division employed a firm of consultants to present its own internal data to its own board. Only by that route was it possible to persuade the main board to give long-term backing to CD-i.

In the case of Matsushita, a partner of Philips in CD-i, a significant internal struggle led it to abandon CD-i. The board member responsible for the firm's business systems division persuaded Matsushita's president to invest in a rival technology that was being developed by the brains behind that successful American computer games software house, Electronic Arts. Trip Hawkins recruited Matsushita as a founding investor in 3DO, which had developed a new architecture for domestic interactive multimedia technology, and in addition the firm invested heavily as the first manufacturer of 3DO machines. This entrepreneurial, pioneer role is most uncharacteristic of Matsushita, which normally plays the role of follower, achieving market share through efficient manufacturing and marketing. 3DO continues to be handled through Matsushita's business systems division, separate from the audio-visual division which had been responsible for CD-i.[7]

---

[6] Again we must acknowledge the exceptional co-operation we have received from Philips in the UK and in Eindhoven, which has included privileged access to confidential documents.

[7] Both CD-i and 3DO have proved to be mass-market failures. CD-i struggles on as a system for professional and industrial applications, mainly training, whereas 3DO has fared poorly as a games machine, especially against Sony's PlayStation.

There were much more intense struggles than these within Philips over the future of television technology. The 'official' strategy—secured in a multi-million pound collaboration within the Eureka programme (a European programme of research and development (R&D) in close-to-the-market civil technologies)—was to back a satellite-based path involving a transition from improved standard definition technology (MAC) to high definition technology (HD-MAC). At exactly the same time that this was being developed, another group within Philips was co-operating with the German public broadcaster's (ZDF) research laboratory to develop a rival technology (PALplus) which was a potential competitor to MAC. The manager in charge of Philips's R&D on PALplus was extremely unpopular with the HD-MAC team; his work was seen as directly subversive to mainstream activities.[8] Despite Philips's (minor) activities in the PALplus grouping, RACE (Research and Development in Advanced Communications Technologies for Europe) projects, and other Eureka projects such as Digital Terrestrial Television Broadcasting (dTTb), the principal focus of its lobbying efforts was the HDTV project Eureka-95. The campaign for subsidies for wide-screen broadcasting was focused initially on HD-MAC and not PALplus, and the initial resistance to fully digital television reflected the priority accorded within Philips to the EU-95 (HDTV) programme. I would suggest that the internal politics of the firms is the best explanation for why Philips continued to cling to the MAC/HD-MAC strategy long after many neutrals (including this author) (Cawson *et al.*, 1990) had decided that the future of television was likely to be fully digital.

THE GOVERNANCE OF EUROPEAN CONSUMER ELECTRONICS

So far this paper has emphasized the politics of the firm rather than the industry or sector. We have looked at this in relation to market power, pressure politics, and the internal politics within the firm. It

[8] Now that HD-MAC R&D has come to an end the manager responsible for PALplus has been put in charge of all advanced (including digital HDTV) television technologies within Philips and is the main Philips voice within the DVB Group. The manager in charge of HDTV was given responsibility for Digital Compact Cassette (DCC); another failure!

is just as important, however, to stress that industries or sectors are also important arenas for political activities by firms. Up to now we have confined this dimension to the possibility that firms use associations as one among three principal strategies of influence. It is now time to consider sectoral governance in its own right.

Many studies have pointed to a variety of institutions whose activities and inter-relationships can be seen as a structure of governance for an industry. These include, besides the producing firms, institutions such as trade and employer associations, trade unions, research institutes and sometimes universities, relations with government departments and other public bodies. Our previous research on the consumer electronics industry has shown the relative *un*importance of many of those institutions, and especially trade associations and trade unions, some of which, however, do play an important role in the governance of other sectors. The actors who count in the consumer electronics industry are the major producing firms, national governments, the Commission, and the Council of Ministers.[9] It is in the intense and often conflictual relationships between big firms and public bodies that we find the processes by which the sector is governed. In the 1970s and 1980s the major Japanese firms played only a small part in sectoral governance, despite the growing importance of their activities to the European industry as a whole. They dutifully joined, in so far as they were able to, the national trade associations and, through those, the European Association of Consumer Electronics Manufacturers (EACEM). But as I have shown elsewhere (Cawson, 1995*a*), the national trade associations have generally been weak organizations and EACEM is a tiny outfit which operates as a fig-leaf to conceal from casual inspection the substantial influence of the major European-owned firms.[10]

In part this bipolar structure has arisen because of the peculiar level of concentration in the industry. Three firms account for the bulk of European-owned production of the major products of the

---

[9] The European Parliament began in 1991–2 to play a significant, if minor, role in the controversy over the European HDTV programme, discussed below.

[10] EACEM has taken the lead in anti-dumping complaints made by European producers against Japanese and other East Asian producers. The Japanese members of its national member associations have thus on occasion been complainants against themselves! Their reluctance to engage in anti-dumping politics in the national associations can be seen as part of the stance of 'good corporate citizenship' explored below.

industry, CTVs and VCRs. One of them, Philips, is the world's biggest CTV producer; the second, Thomson, is owned by the French government, but scheduled for privatization; and the third, Nokia, is Finnish-owned, but with substantial manufacturing interests in Germany and France.

The bipolar structure also arises because of the unwillingness of the Japanese producers up to now to involve themselves directly in the governance of the sector. Conscious of the hostility of the European firms towards their locating manufacturing plants in Europe in the 1970s, which was itself a process caused in part by the introduction of protectionist measures against them (Belderbos, 1994), the Japanese firms have tended to concentrate almost exclusively on production and marketing issues, and avoided raising political issues, even to the extent of colluding in anti-dumping complaints against themselves. The Japanese firms tend to send their European managers to represent them in trade associations, and have viewed their membership of the latter as a badge of good corporate citizenship. They wanted recognition of the long-term nature of their investments in the UK, and avoided antagonizing the remaining British-owned firms in the industry. They have not expected to benefit in practical ways from association membership.[11]

In contrast to the relative weakness of EACEM, since 1962 the Japanese industry has maintained a European office of its powerful domestic trade association, the Electronic Industries Association of Japan (EIAJ), in Dusseldorf. The EIAJ has had the same European director Takao Negishi, for 30 years, and he has in effect organized a parallel system of representation for the Japanese firms in helping them to deal with European governments. This role was critically important in the early days, but has become much less significant now that the firms are well established and have developed their own expertise in dealing with the complexities of the European political economy, in effect moving from associationalism to independent political lobbying but not (yet) to micro-corporatism.

In practice, from the mid-1970s until the early 1990s, the most powerful voices in the industry were those coming from Philips and Thomson, and from the French and German governments, which,

---

[11] This is based on interviews conducted in 1985–6.

unlike the British government, were willing to consider using public policy measures to protect indigenous firms. Philips and Thomson sought to protect themselves from the effects of intensifying Japanese competition by a variety of political and economic strategies. Some of these were straightforward pleas for protection, justified by the endlessly repeated mantra of the need for a 'level playing-field'. In large part those efforts were successful: the 'standard' tariff level for consumer electronics products remains high at 14 per cent, and special measures, such as the temporary tariff of 19 per cent on CD players in the 1980s, or the voluntary export restraint agreement between the EC and the Japanese Ministry for International Trade and Industry (MITI) on the export of VCRs to Europe, have been a constant feature of European policy.[12]

The most important manifestation of the power exerted by Philips and Thomson over the governance of the sector and European public policy towards it can be seen in the history of the project to develop a European high definition television (HDTV) system in competition with that pioneered by the Japanese industry. I have written extensively on this project, and will not repeat that material here (Cawson, 1995*b*). I will, however, say something about its successor, the DVB project, below, since it shows clearly how the governance structure has changed from the bipolar mode which characterized the HDTV episode.

This bipolar mode survived for so long because the major firms were accorded privileges in return for investing in areas, such as HDTV, which were seen by European governments and EC policy-makers as critical for the survival of the industry. This corporatist tryst effectively delegated responsibility for the implementation of policy to the firms. Ultimately it failed because, although the set-making firms like Philips and Thomson could create the technology (after all, at a technical level the HDTV programme was a resounding success), they alone could not ensure that it was adopted by the broadcasting organizations or bought by the public. In this respect the consumer electronics industry is different from Airbus or the TGV: only in the case of state-owned broadcasters like the BBC, TDF in France, and ZDF in Germany could the political nature of the project be extended into purchasing decisions. That was exactly

---

[12] Ironically, the high tariff levels are now affecting Philips and Thomson themselves, because they have moved a significant proportion of their production of audio products and low-end CTVs and VCRs to East Asia.

what had happened with the previous transition from monochrome to colour television in the 1960s, which was managed and subsidized by governments. But the economic climate of the 1990s was very different, not only because the public broadcasters were generally strapped for cash, and governments unwilling to raise licence fees, but also because of the entry of private broadcasters like BSkyB, based in Britain, Canal+ in France, and RTL in Germany.

This issue raises important questions for the study of economic governance in general, especially those concerning the boundaries of the sector. In the case of national governments, it is possible to define the boundaries of the political system as the territory within which a single political institution exercises an effective monopoly on the legitimate use of force. In the case of sectoral governance, the boundaries are largely arbitrary. When analysing the bipolar structure of the 'sector', I was defining the latter in terms of the production of key products (CTVs and VCRs). In choosing to privilege Philips and Thomson in the HDTV project, European governments and the EC were adopting the same sectoral definition, but seeking to apply it to broadcasting and not just to television manufacturing. With the advantage of hindsight, we can see that this was a crucial mistake. The EC had mandated by directive the adoption of a specific technology developed by specific firms; the satellite broadcasters (largely new, mostly private) were expected to accept this, at the same time that the existing public-sector terrestrial broadcasters were left out of the party altogether.

It is therefore not at all surprising that they chose to rebel, the satellite broadcasters by refusing to adopt the new technology (taking advantage of a 'loophole' in the directive, which made MAC mandatory for high-powered direct broadcast satellites, but not for medium-powered telecommunications satellites), and the terrestrial broadcasters by developing a rival technology (PALplus). The policies developed within the governance structure of the set-making industry, powerful though it was, were not capable of withstanding the strain of being applied to the broadcasting industry, the governance structure of which was quite different; although clearly the two structures overlap, given the importance of Philips and Thomson as producers of professional equipment (bought by broadcasters) as well as CTVs and VCRs (bought by consumers).

THE WEB OF CORPORATE INFLUENCE

Most studies of firms as political actors emphasize their activities as lobbyists and as members of associations; few studies go beyond this to examine structural ties between public authorities and private firms, or the extent to which the activities of governments affect corporate power.[13] Nowhere is this more true than in the recent literature on lobbying at the European level (Mazey and Richardson, 1993c; Van Schendelen, 1993), where analysts tend to read off power from the proliferation of lobbying activity (thus assuming that the more organizations there are, the more that power is dispersed among them). The studies assume that, because there is more activity, firms are exerting more influence; because there is more lobbying than ever, power is more dispersed.

The curious aspect of this 'Euro-pluralist' literature is that it almost entirely ignores the theoretical debates over pluralism at the national level in the 1970s, and fails to learn from the extensive literature on power and decision-making. The problem is not simply that there are few empirical studies as yet, although this is a problem, but that the research agendas and the questions posed are so superficial. As in the early literature on pressure groups, the focus is almost exclusively on the input side of government, and on the groups themselves, with much energy expended on nominalist classification and exclusive emphasis on overt behaviour. Very few studies attempt to use the decisional approach pioneered by Robert Dahl (1961); in fact most are pre-theoretical, with classification the most ambitious goal. None of the studies of Euro-lobbying even begin to approach the sophistication of the work on sectoral governance; theoretical frameworks are skeletal, and the conclusions are unhelpful.

The power of interest associations and the role of lobbying in the wider structures of economic governance require detailed and painstaking research into the histories of the sectors, and a comprehensive account of their dynamics, including technological, market, and political aspects. Only through such research can we begin to trace the complex patterns of lines of influence. In the absence of research, it is tempting to rely on practitioner evidence. Valuable as

---

[13] See Ch. 3 for a sophisticated statement of the relationship between public institutions, policy definitions, and the role of interest groups.

this can be in some cases, it carried dangers with it, as when a Commission official, in attempting to characterize the process of lobbying at the European level, gave stress to the importance of lobbying at the initial stages of a proposal: 'At the beginning he or she is a very lonely official with a blank piece of paper, wondering what to put on it. Lobbying at this very early stage therefore offers the greatest opportunity to shape thinking and ultimately to shape policy' (Hull, 1993: 83).

The idea that any policy begins with a blank sheet is absurd, and the notion that the formative influences on policy will be those who get their word in first is equally wrong. In this case the author is confusing the marginal effect that lobbyists can have over a policy with the determinants of policy, and equating policy-making with the process of creating a policy text. If we look at policy-making in the electronics sector, we can see that there is a good chance that the official staring at the 'blank piece of paper' is actually on secondment as an 'expert' from one of the big firms. Even if he is not, it would be impossible to write even the first word without considering the likely effects of policy on such companies as Siemens, Philips, or Thomson.[14] This power through anticipated reaction, ably analysed over 30 years ago by Matthew Crenson (1971), is still of major importance in assessing corporate influence. George Ross's blow-by-blow account of the drafting of a policy statement on the industry shows clearly how different officials represent views which are coloured by their anticipation of the effects of the policy on 'the industry' (Ross, 1993). The officials' own interest in these matters is clearly a factor—like the Japanese MITI bureaucrats, they may hope one day to 'descend from heaven' to a well-paid position as industry consultant—but their individual interests cannot outweigh the power exercized by the major firms.

Philips has maintained an office in Brussels devoted to relations with the Commission for many years. In the 1980s my interviewees in the firm referred to the director of the office as 'our Ambassador to Brussels'. This office is far more than a lobbying organization or a listening-post, although it is both of those. It is a means through

[14] It should be stressed, however, that the privileged position of firms is a relatively recent phenomenon, and is caught up with the recognition of a 'technology gap' in the 1980s and the consequent need for a European technology policy: see Ch. 6.

which the intimate and intense relationship between company managers and European officials can be constantly renewed. The office organizes part of the training for new officials and *stagières* by arranging briefing sessions on the industry. It also ensures that Commission officials fully understand the Philips position. In early 1994 the company arranged for a visit to Philips's Eastern European plants by officials from the Commission's Directorate General for Industry (DGIII) to show them how the company was helping to bolster the EC's policy of strengthening the former communist countries' economies. (I am sure it did not escape these officials' attention that production costs in the Philips VCR plant in Hungary are actually lower than at their plant in Singapore.)

Philips's closest counterpart amongst the Japanese firms— Matsushita—also maintains a Brussels Liaison Office, and it tries to do some of the same things that Philips does. But a comparison of the two shows up several important differences which highlight the extent to which the political context and culture of the European institutions works to minimize the influence that non-European firms are able to exert, despite their critical economic importance.[15]

Matsushita ruefully point out that, after the closure of the Philips VCR plant in Germany, and before the entry of Austria into the European Union, no European-owned firm was manufacturing VCRs in the EU, whereas several Japanese firms were.[16] With the departure of Philips's CD player production from Belgium to Singapore and China, there is no European-owned firm which makes CD players in Europe, whereas several Japanese firms do so. Yet the Commission continues to view European firms as 'indigenous' and Japanese firms as 'foreigners', a situation which Matsushita's patient efforts at diplomacy are intended to correct. Yet Matsushita, unlike Philips, does not have any employees seconded to the Commission, which denies it an 'inside track' to Commission thinking; nor does that firm get invited so frequently as Philips to present its views to officials.

---

[15] The following is based in part on interviews conducted with the two holders of these positions in Brussels in July 1994.

[16] It is important to note that the bulk of VCR imports into Europe are made by European-owned firms from their plants in East Asia. The bulk of VCR production in Europe is by Japanese-owned firms.

We can see that Matsushita approaches the Commission as an outsider and a lobbyist, whereas Philips is an insider in the policy process and has enjoyed a substantial measure of privilege. Philips was able to exercise an influence on policy for the electronics sector well ahead of its power in the market-place, especially during the late 1980s and early 1990s, because of the importance the Commission attached to HDTV technology as a defence against the competitive pressures from the Japanese industry. Once it became clear that the technological innovation of fully digital television was going to make the European HDTV system obsolete, and that the policy of trying to legislate for the market success of MAC had failed, then Philips's position at the heart of the bipolar governance was at risk.

It is important to emphasize that structural privileges of the kind that Philips enjoyed do bear some relationship to market power. What we have tried to show is that there is no simple relationship between market power and political influence, and that the determinants of the political power exercised by firms are in part shaped by the policy agenda of the state or the public authorities. In the mid-1990s Philips's influence has been weakened by the collapse of the HDTV strategy, and by the movement away from industrial policy solutions for the sector (Cawson and Holmes, 1995). As we shall see in the next section, the emergence of the DVB coalition represents a strikingly different pattern of sectoral governance for the electronics industry.

DVB: FROM EXCLUSIVE TO INCLUSIVE COALITION

The privileges accorded to Philips and Thomson in determining policy for HDTV were opposed by the major European broadcasters, and effectively usurped by Murdoch's BSkyB, which killed off the MAC satellite broadcasting system. As we have seen, the German public broadcaster ZDF was involved in developing a rival technology, and it was a senior official at the German Federal Ministry of Posts and Telecommunications, Peter Kahl, who initiated the moves which eventually led to the Digital Video Broadcasting Group. Kahl had been among the first to recognize the implications of the announcement in June 1990 by General Instrument Corp. in the United States that it had succeeded in developing a technology to compress and transmit fully digital HDTV pictures within the bandwidth occupied by a single conventional definition analogue television channel.[17] The implications were that essentially the same technology would allow digital television to be transmitted via satellite, cable, or terrestrial transmitters. Whereas HD-MAC was restricted to satellite transmission and new services, existing terrestrial broadcasters and cable operators would be able to exploit the advantages of digital technology. These advantages include the economy which will permit broadcasters to squeeze up to six standard definition channels within the space now occupied by one, and the flexibility which will allow broadcasters to trade off picture quality against the number of services they offer according to the demands of the market rather than the requirements of the technology.

In 1991 Kahl invited broadcasters, consumer electronics manufacturers, and regulatory authorities to join a European Launching Group (ELG) for digital television (DVB, 1995). Broadcasters had been outspoken in their opposition to the Commission's attempts to renew the directive which obliged new satellite services to use MAC technology, and were enthusiastic about the more consensual approach which Kahl was proposing for digital television. The opening of a new market for digital television would require the careful co-ordination of decisions by a wide range of actors, many of whom were suspicious about the Commission's close relationship with manufacturing interests. Kahl was ideally placed to play the role of an honest broker within an organization which was seen as open and neutral. In the course of 1992 a number of other players joined the coalition, including media groups and telecommunications operators, reflecting the emergent view that digital television is part of a process of convergence which will affect all forms of communication.

In September 1993, 87 organizations signed a memorandum of understanding which recognized the common interests of the different participants in a self-regulated process through which com-

---

[17] The Japanese and European HDTV technologies required approximately three times as much bandwidth and could only be delivered via satellite.

mon standards would be determined, and issues concerned with introducing digital television could be debated, and at least some of them resolved. The ELG was re-named DVB, and by mid-1996 had attracted over 200 members from 25 different countries.[18] DVB has succeeded in developing standards for digital television for distribution by satellite, cable, satellite master antenna (SMATV), terrestrial, and digital multipoint video distributions systems (MVDS). These standards have been agreed in a series of technical committees or 'modules', chaired by leading figures from the industry, which have then been formally adopted by DVB, and then proposed to and accepted by the relevant European and international standards bodies such as the European Telecommunications Standards Institute (ETSI), the European Committee for Electrotechnical Standards (CENELEC), and the International Telecommunications Union (ITU).

The DVB is governed by a steering board, chaired by Peter Kahl, within which have been constituted a series of *ad hoc* groups, such as those for intellectual property rights, regulation aspects, and rules of procedure. Reporting to the steering board, in addition to the technical modules mentioned above, are commercial modules which deal with the problems of market opening in different service areas, including cable and satellite, terrestrial, and interactive services. The DVB as a whole meets annually as a General Assembly, which provides an opportunity for the proposals coming out of the modules and endorsed by the steering board to be legitimated by the overall membership.

The technical aspects of digital television have proved much easier to resolve than the issues involved in commercializing services. At the heart of a digital television system is the 'set-top box', which receives the encrypted and compressed signal and decrypts and decodes it for display on the television receiver. In addition the set-top box contains circuitry to authorize the display of the picture for the particular receiver, according to whether the equipment is recognized, and whether the subscriber has paid for or agreed to be billed for the service. The encryption and conditional access systems within the set-top box have proved to be contentious, because no consumer is going to want to buy more than one box, and the

---

[18] Information is available from the DVB World Wide Web site at http://www.ebu.ch/dvb_home1.html.

supplier of the first box is in a strong position to control the access of rival service providers to the consumer, unless the technology of the system is non-proprietary, or there is effective regulation to provide access for all service providers on a fair and non-discriminatory basis.

The conditional access *ad hoc* group of the DVB, chaired by an official from the Commission's Directorate General for Telecommunications, the Information Market, and the Exploitation of Research (DGXIII), sought to gain agreement from all DVB members to a non-proprietary interface to be included in all set-top boxes. After a series of heated meetings, where a major split appeared between the terrestrial broadcasters and the new satellite operators such as BSkyB and Canal+, the DVB agreed to a compromise which fell short of requiring open access to the set-top box. It agreed to standardize a common interface, but its incorporation into set-top boxes or televisions was to be optional, so that broadcasters could continue to use proprietary conditional access technology so long as they abide by a code of conduct to allow other broadcasters access to their subscribers on fair and reasonable terms. Responsibility for ensuring that broadcasters do not exploit proprietary technologies to engage in anti-competitive practice will be placed in the hands of national regulatory bodies.

Compared to the system of governance which characterized the HDTV project, dominated by a close and privileged relationship between the major European-owned set-makers and the Commission, the DVB is more open, more inclusive, and more consensual. The power of the major manufacturing firms has been balanced by the inclusion of both broadcasters and network operators (principally the telecommunications providers), and non-European firms have been admitted into membership.

CONCLUSIONS

This chapter has sought to explore the development of public policy in the European consumer electronics industry from the perspective of the power exerted by firms. It explored three different dimensions of the exercise of power: power exercised in relation to other firms through the process of competition; power exercised in relation to governments and public authorities; and power relations within firms. These dimensions of power are exercised within quite complex systems of governance, involving interrelationships between public bodies and private firms, and this chapter has provided some case material for the analysis of sectoral governance from the efforts to develop advanced television technologies in Europe over the last ten years.

The consumer electronics industry in Europe is a combination of European-owned firms (dominated by Philips, Thomson, and Nokia) and foreign-owned firms (dominated by the major Japanese producers). The chapter showed how the incoming Japanese firms were at first careful to keep a low political profile, and behave as 'good corporate citizens', but are now, at least in the case of Matsushita, frustrated that their contribution to the European manufacturing industry is not reflected in their influence over public policy. By contrast, Philips and Thomson were able to achieve a privileged position at the heart of policy-making in the sector as key participants in the HDTV programme.

The failure of that programme, and the shift of policy towards fostering fully digital television technology for Europe, was accompanied by a major change in the governance of the sector. From attempting to mandate the use of specific technologies in order to protect European-owned firms, the Commission has moved towards a policy of encouraging industrial co-operation between a wide range of firms, and seeking to achieve its objectives through competition policy rather than industrial policy. This policy shift is a reflection of the increased uncertainty about the immediate future of particular industry segments and specific technologies, which would have made the continuation of earlier policies even more risky. The shift to fully digital technologies has also had the effect of bringing into electronics policy-making a much wider range of firms which see digital television as part of a wider process of the convergence of communications technologies. Firms such as BT and Bertelsmann have ensured that the field is not left to equipment manufacturers, as it had been with HDTV.

In the television sector at least, developments in the last five or six years suggest that corporate power is no longer caught up in closed and exclusive relationships with governments and public authorities. The impact of technological change has been to increase the level of uncertainty in existing product markets, and to increase the risk associated with new product development.[19] Firms are looking for co-operative solutions to minimize that risk, but they have to do so amongst a much larger number of players, as we have seen in the case of DVB. But so far the Japanese producers, which form such an important part of the manufacturing industry, have yet to play a commensurate role within the governance of the sector.

---

[19] Witness the case of Digital Video Disc (DVD), the next generation of optical disc products to follow the CD. Philips and Sony, on the one hand, and a coalition of firms led by Toshiba and Time Warner, on the other, had been developing incompatible products, but decided in 1995 to pool their technologies around a single standard to prevent a replay of the format battles which characterized the introduction of the VCR in the 1980s.

10

Consumption without Representation? Consumers in the Single Market[1]

ALASDAIR R. YOUNG

The Single European Market (SEM) programme poses challenges and creates opportunities for the European Union's (EU) nearly 370 million consumers. By reducing impediments to trade the creation of the single market should facilitate competition and thereby increase consumer choice and reduce prices. Creating a single market, however, also raises the related issues of how to handle the consequences of economic integration for consumers and what is the appropriate level of governance for consumer protection. Even if economic integration has increased consumer welfare overall, it has not necessarily translated into economic gains that consumers recognize as such. Nor do they feel engaged in the accompanying policy process.

The EU's consumer policy has two principal components: measures intended, directly or indirectly, to ease the free circulation of goods, and legislation meant to facilitate the movement of consumers. The first dimension addresses the protection of consumer health and safety, and the second the advancement of consumers' economic and legal rights. Both dimensions are buttressed by efforts to promote consumer education and information. Many measures that fall within the first dimension are not formally part of EU consumer policy, although that is their effect. In addition, a number of other non-consumer EU policies—particularly agriculture, com-

[1] This chapter is based on research funded by Phase II of the Economic and Social Research Council's Single European Market Initiative (Award L113251029). I would like to thank all of the representatives of consumer organizations and trade associations and Commission and national government officials who took the time to talk with me and comment on drafts of this chapter.

petition, and trade—are highly relevant to consumers in that they affect the prices they pay for goods.

Differences in the dynamics affecting these areas of EU policy largely explain why European policy is most developed with regard to the approximation of national health and safety measures and why consumer interests tend to play only a limited direct role in non-consumer policies that affect them. To a significant extent, these dynamics are structured by the *acquis communautaire*, which both shapes the power relations among the European institutions and influences the policy preferences of the actors. The reluctance of member governments to cede responsibility for consumer protection to the EU has restrained the development of a fully fledged common consumer policy and is the key element in explaining the shape that European policy has taken.

The dynamics that shape EU consumer policy are not static and have changed over time. These changes, some specific to consumer policy, others not, have contributed recently to greater European involvement in consumer policy. In addition, the growing concern of the EU's leaders that the general population feels left out of the process of integration is contributing to greater attention being paid to delivering benefits to citizens. This may be contributing to consumer interests being more fully considered in the EU policy process (see Chapter 3 for a more general discussion of the importance of prevailing ideas in the policy process).

THE CONTEXT OF CONSUMER POLICY

The political dynamics differ between EU policies of relevance to consumers in three principal ways: the applicable legal framework, the institutional actors involved, and the type and level of involvement of producers and consumers. First, the *acquis* creates pressures to align national measures that impede trade, but provides less impetus for EU policies to address the other implications for consumers of economic integration. The virtual prohibition against national measures equivalent in effect to quotas is contained in the Treaty of Rome (Art. 30), while a treaty foundation for a common consumer policy was not established until the (Maastricht) Treaty on European Union (TEU), and even so still leaves the lead largely to the member governments.

Second, the fragmented nature of the EU's policy-making structures means that different institutions or parts of institutions take the lead on different types of policy. As a consequence, while the Directorate General for Consumer Policy (DGXXIV) is responsible for developing proposals on consumers' access to justice, the Directorate General for Industry (DGIII) takes the lead on proposals for car safety requirements and the Directorate General for Agriculture (DGVI) oversees food prices. This is significant because government departments differ in their degree of autonomy from interest groups (Atkinson and Coleman, 1989). In particular, those departments with functional, as opposed to sectoral, mandates tend to be more independent from industrial interests. In addition, the type of policy at issue also influences which European institutions are involved. Although the European Court of Justice (ECJ), for instance, plays an important role in assessing whether a national measure that impedes trade is justified on public health and safety grounds, it has no role in advancing common policies.

Third, as Theodore Lowi (1964) observed, policy makes politics, and the way in which societal interests respond to a proposed policy is affected by their expectations about its likely effects. James Q. Wilson (1980*a*) carries Lowi's analysis a step further, arguing that the anticipated distribution of costs and benefits of a regulatory policy shapes which and how interests in society mobilize. When the expected benefits are widely dispersed and the costs narrowly concentrated, as is usually the case with consumer safety measures, there is a place for a policy entrepreneur to publicize the issue and move it into more public arenas of policy-making. This is a role often played by the European consumer associations and by the European Parliament (EP), particularly its Committee on the Environment, Public Health, and Consumer Protection. When benefits of a proposed policy are likely to be concentrated and costs dispersed—as is the case with agricultural price support, external trade barriers, and exemptions from competition rules—clientele politics are likely to dominate. In addition, many of the EU's non-consumer policies affect consumers' economic interests, about which consumers tend to be less inclined to mobilize compared with health and safety issues. Although such policies have significant implications for the welfare of European consumers, this discussion is largely confined to the EU's consumer policy proper.

THE DEVELOPMENT OF A EUROPEAN CONSUMER POLICY

From Humble Beginnings

The Treaty of Rome was adopted before the burgeoning of national consumer protection measures during the 1960s and 1970s. The attitude of the treaty's framers would appear to have been that consumer interests, to the extent that they were viewed in the European project, would be adequately catered for by increased production, free movement of goods and services, and increased competition (Bourgoignie, 1987; Close, 1984). Consequently, consumer interests were considered largely as a by-product of more fundamental European policies and concerns (Bourgoignie, 1987).

Given the lack of explicit legal basis in the treaty, the early development of a common consumer policy depended, as did that of environmental policy, on a 'generous' reading of Article 2 of the treaty (Hildebrand, 1992: 19). In addition, Articles 100 and 235, in particular, offered the possibility of EU action in policy areas not expressly identified in the treaty. The absence of a clear basis for consumer protection policy, however, contributed to disagreements among the member governments about the appropriateness of a common consumer policy (Close, 1984) and impeded the policy's development.

National Policies and Barriers to Trade

Consumer policies, however, began to emerge in several member states in the 1960s. During the 1950s the market-place became both more exciting and more threatening, as the number and complexity of consumer goods available increased; marketing techniques became more sophisticated; and complicated purchasing transactions began to emerge (OECD, 1983). At the same time, the prolonged economic boom had brought both prosperity and higher expectations about the quality of life more broadly defined (Vogel, 1989; Weale, 1992). High levels of education and affluence helped to channel these social changes into political pressure for consumer protection measures, and a number of Western governments responded by developing explicit consumer protection policies (OECD, 1983).

As Ernesto Previdi discusses elsewhere in this volume (Chapter 4), governments perceive different risks and respond to them in divergent ways. Because most consumer protection legislation, particularly in the early days, was related to product safety, divergent national regulations could serve as non-tariff barriers to trade (NTBs). The impact of such NTBs became particularly apparent within the then European Community (EC) after the establishment of the customs union in 1968 eliminated tariffs and quotas on trade among the members.

The first step to institutionalize consumer policy at the EC level came in April 1968 when the Commission, under some pressure from the EP, established a small service for questions relevant to consumers in the Directorate General for Competition Policy (DGIV). In 1971 the Council of Ministers adopted the first directive that sought to harmonize divergent national consumer regulations, in this case the names of textiles. In October the following year at their Paris Summit the heads of state and government of the member states and the three applicant countries launched an EC consumer protection policy, along with common environmental, social, and regional policies (see Table 10.1 for an extended chronology).

The impending accession of Denmark, Ireland, and the United Kingdom heightened the need for common measures to reduce the impact of divergent national consumer regulations on trade, as Denmark and the UK had significantly higher levels of consumer protection than the then member states (Bourgoignie, 1987; DGXXIV, 1995). In addition, by bringing consumer, environmental, and social policies into the EC's competence, the leaders of the member states hoped to make the EC more relevant to the people of Europe and lend it a 'human face' (Johnson and Corcelle, 1989: 2).

Slow and Uneven Policy Development

Despite the adoption of EC consumer programmes in 1975 and 1981, little came of this new policy. By mid-1985, apart from a number of technical implementing measures, the Council had adopted only four substantial proposals arising directly out of the two consumer programmes. Three other proposals had been awaiting decisions for from six to eight years. Consequently, the Com-

TABLE 10.1. *Significant events in EU consumer policy*

June 1961	Commissioner Mansholt convened consumer organizations for first time at the European level
Apr. 1962	Contact Committee for Consumer Questions established
Apr. 1968	Consumer affairs unit established in DGIV (competition policy)
July 1971	Council adopted first directive harmonizing consumer regulations
Oct. 1972	Heads of state and government approved EC consumer policy
Jan. 1973	Denmark, Ireland, and the United Kingdom joined EEC Environment and Consumer Protection Service created
Apr. 1975	Preliminary programme for a consumer protection policy adopted
Feb. 1979	*Cassis de Dijon* judgment
Jan. 1981	DGXI (environment, consumer protection, and nuclear safety) created
May 1981	Second programme for a consumer protection policy adopted
Dec. 1982	First consumer observers participated in European standard body committees (CEN)
Dec. 1983	First consumer council met
May 1985	'New approach' to regulation adopted
June 1985	Single market programme adopted Commission proposed a 'new impetus' for consumer protection policy
Feb. 1986	SEA signed
Feb. 1989	Consumer Policy Service separated from DGXI
May 1990	Three-year action plan of consumer policy (1990–2) adopted
Feb. 1992	TEU signed
July 1993	Second three-year action plan (1993–5) adopted
Nov. 1993	TEU came into effect
Jan. 1995	Austria, Finland, and Sweden joined the EU
Feb. 1995	ANEC established
Mar. 1995	DGXXIV (consumer policy) created
Jun. 1995	Consumer Consultative Council abolished, framework established for Consumer Committee
Oct. 1995	Priorities for Consumer Policy, 1996–8, adopted
Jan. 1996	Consumer Committee appointed

mission (1985*b*) concluded that the achievements of EC consumer policy had fallen far below expectations.

A number of factors not specific to consumer policy contributed to the poor performance of the EC's consumer programmes. The deep economic recessions that followed the oil shocks in 1973 and 1979 made the member governments very reluctant to impose additional burdens on already struggling industries (Commission,

1985*b*). That is not to say that the member governments stopped adopting new regulations during the 1970s, rather that the substantial number that were adopted often protected domestic industries from competition from other member states (Dashwood, 1983). Many of these protectionist regulations masqueraded as consumer protection measures (Venables, 1986). Consequently, member governments were not only reluctant to adopt strict, and therefore costly, standards, but they were strongly disinclined to accept harmonized measures that would strip their national industries of protection.

The reluctance of member governments to embrace EC regulations had a devastating effect on EC consumer policy. The requirement that all decisions be reached unanimously meant that any one member government could impede legislation indefinitely. Consequently, measures tended to be adopted only after protracted negotiations in which the various member governments' concerns were soothed. This does not mean, however, that the agreed measures necessarily reflected the lowest common denominator (see Chapter 3). In fact, member governments with high domestic levels of protection had a strong incentive to resist low standards, as in the absence of common measures both their consumers and their industries would be protected by national regulations.

Other factors that impeded the development of a more active consumer policy were more specific to the nature of the policy itself. Many member governments did not consider consumer policy a legitimate EC concern, particularly with regard to the legal and economic interests of consumers, which tend not to impede the free movement of goods (Commission, 1985*b*). Perhaps as a consequence, the Environment and Consumer Protection Service (ECPS) of the Commission, which was established in 1973, was poorly resourced. Even after the ECPS was elevated to a full directorate general (DGXI) in 1981, it paid particular attention to environmental matters and the directorate responsible for consumer policy remained under-funded and inadequately staffed (Goyens, 1992). In addition, concern for consumers' interests was largely isolated within this small service. The substantial influence of the industrial lobbies, bolstered by the political imperative to combat unemployment, also impeded the development of a strong EC consumer policy (Goldman, 1980; Weiler, 1991). Consequently, the few significant measures—most notably the directives on food-stuff labelling, misleading advertising, and product liability—that were adopted during the late 1970s and early 1980s required years of negotiation among the member governments.

The Single European Market Programme: Boon to Consumer Choice or Threat to Consumer Protection?

In the mid-1980s the new approach to technical harmonization, the SEM programme, and the Single European Act (SEA) reinvigorated European integration. By increasing choice and reducing prices through heightened competition and the exploitation of economies of scale, the creation of the SEM promised to benefit consumers. The new approach, however, encouraged mutual recognition of some national rules, which meant that the free movement of goods and the freedom to provide services could pose problems for national consumer protection measures. In particular, it meant that imports and services provided by foreign firms would not have to meet the same standards as did domestic firms in countries with high levels of protection. As long as consumers are aware of the differences, this benefits consumers by giving them greater choice. Under such circumstances, consumers' preference for a familiar standard could penalize foreign firms that fail to comply with the higher national standards (Sun and Pelkmans, 1995; Woolcock, 1994). Such an influence of consumer taste is illustrated by the fact that Swedish bakers continue to list the baking date as well as the 'sell by' date on bread, despite this erstwhile requirement having been abolished upon accession to the EU. When consumers are not fully aware of the significant differences between national regulatory regimes, however, they might assume that competing goods had been produced to comparable standards and choose the cheaper, perhaps less safe, product.

Under such circumstances, mutual recognition could undermine consumer confidence in non-domestic goods and might prevent the SEM from functioning properly (ESC, 1991; Sutherland *et al.*, 1992). Recognizing this, the Commission (1985*b*) identified a 'new impetus' for consumer protection policy. In addition, at the insistence of some member governments, particularly the Danish and German, the SEA (Art. 100*a*(3)) required that all Commission proposals for SEM measures concerning consumers 'take as a base a high level of protection'.

The introduction of qualified majority voting (QMV) also raised the spectre of a national government being forced to adopt standards that were unacceptable to its population. The threat of being outvoted on consumer issues particularly concerned the Danish government and was a more general issue for the British and Irish governments. To address this concern, the European Council adopted a safeguard clause that allowed member governments to retain higher national standards in specified spheres, including the protection of public health and safety (Art. 100a(4)) (Ehlermann, 1987).

The performance, however, did not live up to its promise. In 1990 Karel Van Miert (1991: 5), then the commissioner responsible for consumer policy, observed that, 'consumer policy is lagging behind in the march towards the single market'. The reason he gave for this was that the inclusion of consumer issues in the Commission's legislative programme would have 'overloaded the already ambitious single market agenda'. The Economic and Social Committee (ESC, 1991: 18) also observed that the phrasing of Article 100a indicates that consumer policy remains 'subsidiary, secondary, and indirect'. This is not entirely surprising as the SEM programme was intended to address problems of production, particularly unemployment and competitiveness (Pelkmans and Winters, 1988). As a result of the emphasis on the supply side of the economy, few specific consumer protection measures were adopted in the years immediately following the launch of the SEM programme (see Fig. 10.1), although numerous measures with implications for consumer safety were agreed. These measures were largely adopted with an emphasis on removing barriers to trade rather than ensuring consumer safety.

Consumer safety was largely preserved in the absence of a vigorous consumer policy, however, by the interaction of three factors. First, member governments with strict domestic consumer safety measures were, at least to an extent, able to ensure that the 'essential requirements' required by new approach directives provided an adequate level of protection (Woolcock, 1994). Second, the alignment of national standards meant setting new, European standards. This revision of standards, due to technical progress, tended to confer higher standards of consumer protection than the older

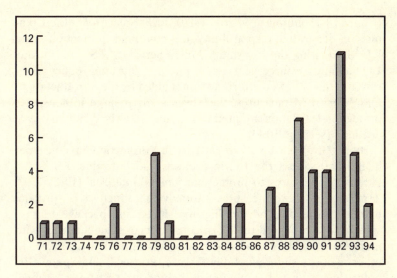

FIG. 10.1. *Number of major EU consumer protection measures adopted per year*

Note: This is an indicative rather than a comprehensive list. The CPS, for example, does not include the four directives on food additives that were adopted in 1994.
Source: CPS (1995).

standards they replaced. In addition, consumer confidence was required for the new standards to be effective. Therefore, they had to require fairly high levels of consumer protection. Third, the free circulation of goods did not prevent the member governments from maintaining post-market control of product safety. If an unsafe product is found, the member government can ban its sale and order a recall. National market surveillance is bolstered by an EC system for exchanging information on dangerous products among the member governments. Participation in this system was seen by Swedish consumer protection officials as one of the main benefits of joining the European Economic Area (EEA).

Although consumer protection had not suffered unduly, the lack of progress in developing an EC consumer policy presented problems as the completion of the SEM approached: some consumer-related trade barriers remained and regulatory gaps loomed as national measures were scaled back. In response there were renewed efforts to 'relaunch' the EC's consumer protection policy

(Council Resolution of 9 Nov. 1989). In February 1989 the Commission separated responsibility for consumer protection from DGXI, creating the Consumer Policy Service (CPS) and in May 1990 adopted a three-year action plan for consumer policy. As a result of this renewed effort, no doubt aided by the introduction of QMV for SEM measures, there was a sharp surge in consumer protection legislation adopted in the run up to the 1 January 1993 deadline (see Fig. 10.1).

By 1993, at least with regard to the protection of consumer health and safety, the EC institutions had 'introduced a whole battery of measures to protect consumers' interests' (ESC, 1993: 23). Some of these measures—notably the directives on product liability, misleading advertising, toy safety, and package tours—significantly improved the lot of consumers even in countries with more developed consumer protection regimes (ESC, 1993). In other member states—notably Greece, Portugal, and Spain—EC policy has been the driving-force behind strengthening national consumer protection measures (Commission, 1991*a*; Dehousse, 1992).

This renewed activism in EC consumer policy, however, was largely concentrated in areas relevant to the free circulation of goods and services. The ESC (1991: 25) criticized the Commission's first three-year action plan on consumer policy (1990–3) for assuming that 'the final objective [of EC consumer policy] is the achievement of a single market'. As a result, the wave of legislation in the early 1990s left gaps, most notably in the areas of consumers' economic and legal rights (ESC, 1993). As a consequence of these shortcomings, consumers have largely failed to recognize the promised benefits of the SEM (BEUC, 1995*b*; ESC, 1995). The resulting lack of consumer confidence in the SEM contributed to popular concern about the impacts of economic integration (see Fig. 10.2).

In order to bolster the EU's ability to introduce a comprehensive consumer policy, the TEU established a common consumer policy (Art. 129a) and identified strengthening consumer protection as one of the EU's activities (Art. 3s). Since the TEU came into force in November 1993 there have been some signs of change. The Commission's second three-year plan (Commission, 1993*c*) acknowledged the importance of integrating consumer policy considerations into other EU policies and began to address some of the

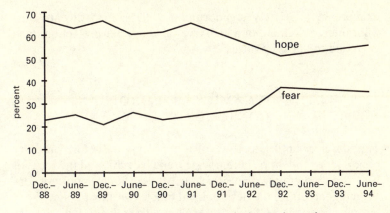

FIG. 10.2. *Public attitudes towards the single market*
Source: *Eurobarometer*, 41, July 1994.

EU consumer policy's shortcomings with regard to the protection of consumers' economic and legal rights. In addition, in March 1995, at least in part due to the efforts of the commissioner for consumer affairs, Emma Bonino, the Commission elevated the CPS to the status of a full directorate general (DGXXIV).

None the less, the TEU has had only a modest impact on consumer protection in the EU. As of the end of 1995 the only measure adopted on the basis of Article 129a was a 1994 Parliament and Council decision to make permanent the European Home and Leisure Accident Surveillance System (EHLASS), which facilitates the exchange of information on accidents involving consumer products. It was not until July 1995 that the Commission advanced the first proposal for a directive (on unit pricing) under the new legal basis. As a consequence, shortcomings in EU consumer policy remain. In particular, measures regarding guarantees, after-sales service, and access to justice, which would facilitate cross-border shopping, have been slow in coming. Regulatory gaps persist with regard to financial services, and significant differences in the rigour of national surveillance of food quality standards pose problems for consumer safety and are a source of public concern (Commission, 1995*c*).

To address adequately these issues, some member governments want Article 129a strengthened in the 1996 Intergovernmental

Conference (IGC) (Westendorp *et al.*, 1995). In particular, they want the requirement of a high level of consumer protection to be extended to all EU policies.

THE DYNAMICS OF EUROPEAN
CONSUMER POLICY

The absence, until late 1993, of a firm legal basis for consumer policy, independent from removing trade barriers, and the focus of European integration on production, were certainly important constraining factors on the development of EU consumer policy. They are not, however, sufficient to explain its relatively slow and uneven development. EU environmental policy, which to a substantial degree shares those impediments, is far better developed than is consumer policy. The *acquis* and the producer orientation of EU policy in general provide the context for and shape a number of interrelated factors that are responsible for the relatively poor development of the EU consumer policy. These are:

- the absence of an influential advocacy coalition of member governments;
- the weakness of institutional advocacy; and
- problems with consumer representation.

The Absence of an Advocacy Coalition

The support of influential member governments has proved essential in advancing a number of EU policies, ranging from tax harmonization (Puchala, 1983) to environmental protection (Weale and Williams, 1992). Such an advocacy coalition is largely lacking with regard to EU consumer policy, because a number of influential member governments are ambivalent about the value of common approaches in this area.

This ambivalence is shared by Europe's consumers. Although consumer protection is a significant source of concern for EU citizens (see Fig. 10.3), they are almost evenly divided regarding which level of governance (national or EU) is the most appropriate for ensuring it (see Fig. 10.4). Only in Belgium, Germany, the Netherlands, and Spain do pluralities prefer EU measures.

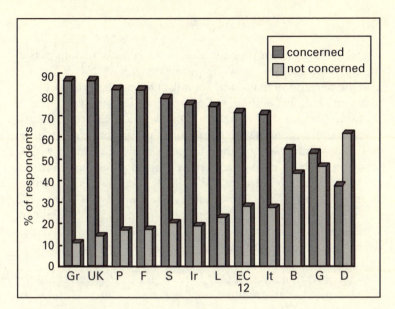

FIG. 10.3. *Public concern about the safety of products and services, 1992*

Note: 'concerned' = very concerned and somewhat concerned; 'not concerned' = not very concerned and not at all concerned.

Source: *Eurobarometer*, 38, Dec. 1992.

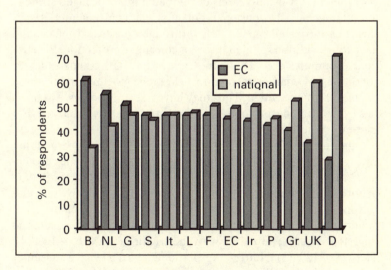

FIG. 10.4. *Public perceptions of the appropriate level of governance for consumer protection, 1993*
Source: *Eurobarometer*, 39, July 1993.

This ambivalence is probably due to the complicated impacts of the SEM on consumers. While promising greater choice there is also the perception that trade liberalization creates greater uncertainty and risk. In addition, at least in countries with high levels of protection, national measures are a known and treasured quantity. Consequently, some national consumer groups have resisted the shift of consumer policy to the European level because they wish to maintain the high levels of consumer protection they have secured at the national level (Huyse *et al.*, 1992). The UK's Consumers in Europe Group (CEG), for example, does not always favour EU action, and when it does, it seeks directives that set only minimum standards (for a more general discussion of the interactions between national and European interests associations, see Chapters 2 and 3).

What government support there is for European consumer policy comes largely from the smaller member states. Historically, the Belgian and Danish governments have been the only vigorous supporters of a more aggressive EU consumer policy, although the three new member governments also seem likely to advocate high levels of consumer protection at the European level. The Swedish government, for example, has developed a multi-pronged strategy for influencing EU consumer policy (Civildepartementet, 1995). These countries all pursue policy through consensual means and have long traditions of high levels of consumer protection. Because their economies are very open, trade with other countries under conditions of mutual recognition threatens to undermine these high levels of protection. Thus they have a strong incentive to try to raise their trading partners' standards, an objective that the EU framework at least makes possible.

Other member governments, however, are more concerned that European integration might undermine national consumer protection measures. As mentioned earlier, at the insistence of some member governments, both the SEA and TEU explicitly state that European action shall not prohibit member governments from maintaining or introducing more stringent protective measures so long as they are compatible with the treaties (SEA, Art. 100a(4); TEU, Art. 129a(3)). Further, even though the TEU gave consumer policy explicit standing as a common policy, it did so in a rather lukewarm fashion, indicating the persistence of the member governments' caution with regard to ceding too much authority to the

EU in this area. Article 129a(1b) states that the EU will contribute to the attainment of a high level of consumer protection through 'specific action which supports and supplements the policy pursued by the Member States . . .'.

Both Germany and the UK have well developed national consumer protection regimes, but resist the development of EU consumer policy. The UK has traditionally been wary of transferring authority to Brussels, while the German government's reservations about the value of EU action are more specific to consumer policy itself. It tends to believe that German consumers would be better served by national consumer protection measures. Even the Swedish government would be inclined to invoke subsidiarity if it felt that Swedish consumers would be better protected by national measures. Because of these reservations, agreement on many 'common' policies has been possible only on the basis of minimum harmonization, which permits governments to retain or introduce more stringent national measures so long as they are compatible with the treaties.

Member governments' reluctance to cede consumer policy to the EU also has a dark side for consumers. Subsidiarity is also sometimes abused as a principle by member governments that simply want to block European action without undertaking national measures instead (CEG, 1994).

Where member government advocacy of common policies has occurred, it has focused more on health and safety issues, which are both of great concern to consumers and pose significant impediment to the free circulation of goods. Government advocacy also tends to concentrate on protecting domestic consumers rather than on safeguarding the rights of consumers engaged in cross-border transactions. Further, as EU consumer policy moves beyond health and safety issues into ensuring consumers' legal rights, it comes up against fundamental differences in the member states' legal traditions, which tend to reflect the countries' core values and which will therefore be difficult to align.

The member governments' limited advocacy of European consumer policy has been reinforced by the low status of consumer policy in the Council. Until 1983 consumer matters were addressed in the Council of Economics and Finance Ministers, and thus tended to have low priority (CEG, 1994). The creation in 1983 of a 'Consumer Affairs' Council was not, however, a panacea. In most member governments rather junior ministers are responsible for consumer matters and frequently even they do not attend Council meetings, sending officials instead. Some officials in DGXXIV, however, hope that the accession of the new member states will reinvigorate the Council by involving more senior politicians.

The Weakness of Institutional Advocacy

The EP has long had an interest in consumer affairs and even before the introduction of direct elections in 1979 sought to stake out a position for itself among the European institutions as the representative of the common man (Bourgoignie, 1987). As such, it was the first European institution to advocate a specific policy to protect consumers and has subsequently played an important role in shaping the development of consumer protection in the EU. Despite growing attention from business lobbies, consumer representatives still view the EP as the most consumer-friendly EU institution, although it does not always stand in the consumers' corner. With regard to the common agricultural policy (CAP), for example, it has traditionally supported farmers because of the importance of farm votes to national political parties in most of the national groups (NCC, 1988)

Given the general thrust of European policy, the EP's influence has been greatest on matters affecting consumer health and safety. It was influential in bringing about EC action on child safety, and its efforts contributed to the adoption of the general product safety directive in 1992 (Commission, 1991a; EP, 1994). The EP has also successfully amended numerous proposals—including those dealing with food hygiene, food colours, and food additives other than colours and sweeteners—to the consumer's advantage.

The Parliament also champions consumer interests in its annual battle with the Council over the consumer protection budget. In 1994, for example, the Commission proposed 16 mecu for the 1995 consumer protection budget. The Council, as usual, sought to reduce this amount. The EP fought hard to increase it, and the final budget allocated 20.75 mecu to consumer protection (BEUC, 1995a).

Despite these successes, the EP's capacity to promote consumer interests is constrained, despite the extension of its powers under the SEA and TEU. Its ability to exercise these powers is restricted by the need to muster absolute majorities to amend or reject proposals at their second reading, and is affected by the Commission's disposition towards its amendments and by the constellation of preferences in the Council (Tsebelis, 1994).

The Commission has a mixed view of consumer policy. On the one hand a common consumer policy is attractive to the Commission, because it both represents the broadening of its responsibilities (Bomberg and Peterson, 1993; Grant *et al.*, 1988) and appeals to its ethos of advancing the European project (see Chapter 5). In June 1961 the Commission brought national and European consumer organizations together in Brussels. Then Commission Vice-President and Commissioner for Agriculture Sicco Mansholt advised them to unite, noting that 'the general interest of consumers in the common market are not represented to the same extent as are those of producers' (quoted in Commission, 1991*a*: 13). On the other hand, consumer protection policy does not sit easily with the objective of promoting economic growth, which has underpinned European integration thus far. In addition, considerations, such as consumer protection, that apply across a broad range of policies do not fit neatly into the Commission's structure, which is largely divided along policy lines.

The Commission's focus on producers is reflected in its organization. DGIII and DGVI are much better resourced than is DGXXIV (Goyens, 1992). Until quite recently, its small staff has meant that DGXXIV has had to concentrate on the policy proposals for which it was directly responsible, rather than pursue the consumer implications of policies being developed elsewhere in the Commission. Two other directorates general, DGIV and DGXV (internal market), pursue policies that tend to be in the interests of consumers, but their primary concern is with the increased competition aspect of consumer policy rather than with consumer safety or the protection of consumers' economic and legal interests.

In addition, DGXXIV, in its attempts to develop policies that can carry the support of all member governments, at times proposes lower levels of protection than the European consumer associations would like. Its priorities and those of the consumer groups also do not always coincide: it tends to focus on specific policies, while the consumer organizations seek more fundamental reforms (Goyens, 1992). For these reasons, and because of DGXXIV's restricted ability to track all policies relevant to consumers, the

European consumer groups do not rely on it to represent their interests within the Commission and hence also cultivate bilateral contacts with other Commission services.

Overall, the Commission has become more attentive to consumer interests than it was in the early 1980s, when there was only a small pocket of consumer advocates in DGXI. Consideration of consumers' interests has not, however, pervaded the Commission to anything like the degree that environmental awareness has. Consequently, the reception given to consumer groups differs markedly from place to place within the Commission. In some parts of the Commission—such as DGIV, DGXV, and parts of DGI (external economic relations)—they are viewed as providing a valuable counter to producer interests; elsewhere—particularly in DGVI and to a lesser extent in DGIII—they tend to be considered an annoyance.

There are signs, however, that concern about consumers' interests is spreading within the Commission. Its report on the operation of the SEM in 1995, for instance, notes that improving consumer protection is an essential requirement for the achievement of the Commission's objective of creating a single market that benefits the citizen to the full (Commission, 1996*b*).

PATTERNS OF REPRESENTATION[2]

Its ambivalence about the appropriate level of consumer protection aside, the Commission has long recognized that consumer organizations can play an important role in the regulatory policy process. They can bring problems to the attention of officials and can serve as valuable additional sources of information to that provided by those being regulated (Barlebo-Larsen, 1991; OECD, 1991).

Consequently, the Commission has, at least to an extent, promoted consumer participation in the policy process. In 1962 it established the Contact Committee for Consumer Questions, composed of representatives of the existing European organizations with an interest in consumer issues, to provide input into Commis-

---

[2] For a more detailed discussion of consumer representation at the European level see Young (1997).

sion proposals. It also provides subsidies to the European consumer groups to support their core activities,[3] funds specific projects, and supports the development of regional and national consumer organizations in Greece, Ireland, Portugal, and Spain.

Currently five organizations represent consumer interests at the European level, each reflecting a different tradition of consumer organization. They are:

- co-operatives: EURO COOP (European Community of Consumer Cooperatives);
- trade unions: EURO-C (the consumer unit of the European Trade Union Confederation);
- independent consumer organizations: BEUC (the European Consumers' Organization);
- family organizations: COFACE (Confederation of Family Organizations in the European Community); and
- regional bodies: IEIC (the European Inter-regional Institute for Consumer Affairs).

These different traditions have enabled consumers to organize themselves politically at the national level. The differences between the traditions and the dissimilar interests and ideologies stemming from them mean, however, that the European consumer movement is fragmented. As a result, the European organizations do not always co-operate and sometimes even dramatically oppose each other.

BEUC

BEUC is the best resourced and probably most influential of the European consumer organizations. It expresses the most purely consumerist view of all of the European consumer organizations. Its support for increasing consumer choice through liberalizing trade and increasing competition meshes well with the objectives of the SEM programme, and it receives a receptive ear in parts of the Commission. BEUC's advocacy of liberalization is tempered by concern for consumer safety and consumer welfare.

BEUC's secretariat enjoys a fairly high degree of autonomy, within guidelines set at the biannual meetings of the General

---

[3] In 1994 the Commission gave BEUC 300,000 ecu towards its core funding. The other four groups each received 200,000 ecu.

Assembly and bimonthly meetings of the Executive. The secretariat drafts most position papers, which are only sometimes based on prior consultations with member organizations, and circulates the drafts to the members for comment. The director decides whether there is sufficient agreement among the members to advance an official position.

Even though its secretariat is larger than those of most European interest associations, BEUC relies heavily on its member organizations, several of which have large staffs, to help it cope with the breadth of its workload. Staff from its member organizations often represent it in Commission advisory and consultative bodies and sometimes help to track European legislation. They also provide the secretariat with information and technical expertise.

BEUC's preferences are occasionally congruent with those of business interests, and it will sometimes co-operate with them. In opposing the Commission's proposals for extending intellectual property protection on car spare parts, for example, BEUC co-operates with the representatives of independent producers and suppliers of car spare parts, insurance companies, and small and medium-sized enterprises within the loose association ECAR. The groups share information, co-ordinate activities, and occasionally make joint representations. BEUC, however, refuses to lose its identity or autonomy to collaborative exercises.

COFACE

COFACE is a different sort of organization altogether. Its more numerous members tend to be less affluent and have a wide range of social concerns. Consequently, consumer affairs is not its sole focus,[4] rather its concern is the family dimension of EU policies. None the less, a relatively large number of its member organizations are active with regard to consumer protection at the national level and participate in COFACE's consumers committee.

COFACE is less concerned than BEUC with the economic aspects of consumer policy, focusing rather on health and safety protection, informing and educating consumers, and ensuring their access to justice. COFACE also takes a more holistic approach to

---

[4] COFACE has seven 'commissions': Consumer and Economic Affairs, Housing, Health, Education, Standard of Living, Disabled Persons, and Rural Affairs.

consumer policy than BEUC, considering the side-effects of consumer regulation on families.

COFACE does not command the same degree of technical expertise as BEUC, but it has, through its members, the capacity to gather extensive information about consumer concerns and attitudes. For example, it has carried out cross-national studies on how well consumers understand the safety symbols on labels and conducts consumer education campaigns through its network of members.

COFACE also differs from BEUC in its policy-making structures. General policy guidelines are defined by the annual General Assembly and specific policy proposals are formulated in working groups, composed of representatives from interested member organizations, and must be approved by the administrative council, COFACE's most important deliberative body.

EURO-C

EURO-C is not a consumers' organization proper. It is the European Trade Union Confederation's (ETUC) 'voice on behalf of consumers'. Although other interested organizations can be associate members, all full EURO-C members are members of ETUC. Even the trade unions that have a strong interest in consumer policy are members of the ETUC first and EURO-C second.

Not surprisingly, therefore, EURO-C's approach to consumer policy can be dramatically different from those of BEUC or COFACE. EURO-C sees its niche in the European consumer movement to be 'social and solidarity-based consumer protection' (EURO-C, 1994*a*: 2). This means that it is rather sceptical about the benefits of increased competition through liberalization, although it favours reform of the CAP. With respect to ensuring consumer safety and guaranteeing consumers' economic and legal rights, however, it takes positions closer to those of the other European consumer groups.

Because it is not an independent organization, EURO-C's decision-making structure differs markedly from those of the other consumer organizations. One of the ETUC's confederal secretaries (appointees below the deputy secretary-general) provides general policy direction and approves specific EURO-C proposals, which are drafted by the EURO-C secretariat after a fairly informal process of consultation with interested members.

EURO COOP

As it is composed of consumer co-operatives, such as the UK's Cooperative Union, advocating consumer protection is not EURO COOP's only objective. Its member organizations' have their own interests as retailers as well as representing the interests of their consumer members. As its members are particularly active in food retailing, EURO COOP specializes in EU food issues and is an active proponent of CAP reform. Pending wholesale reform of the CAP, EURO COOP has focused its efforts on improving the quality of produce. In line with its members' interests, EURO COOP has also been active on product labelling and packaging and packaging waste.

The Members' Assembly, which meets at least once a year, sets general policy and reviews the performance and finances of EURO COOP. It also elects the Management Committee, which establishes policy guidelines and ensures the implementation of decisions taken by the Members' Assembly. The Management Committee appoints the Secretary General, who is responsible for pursuing EURO COOP's policy objectives.

IEIC

IEIC differs from the other European consumer organizations: it represents both public authorities, such as the South Ayrshire Council, and consumer organizations; and it has only sub-national organizations as members. The IEIC is the youngest of the European consumer organizations, having been founded by seven regional organizations in 1989.

The association is particularly active in the areas of consumer information, training, and education. In order to advance consumer knowledge, the association also regularly conducts and coordinates studies and surveys on prices and commercial practices in different European countries. Although active on a wide range of consumer policy issues, IEIC focuses on those associated with cross-border shopping, particularly with the settlement of cross-border disputes and access to justice.

IEIC's structure is more complex than those of the other European consumer associations. The annual General Assembly gives general direction to and elects the Board of Governors, which implements its resolutions and manages the association's working groups. The secretariat is responsible for the day-to-day management of the association.

PATTERNS OF PARTICIPATION

The diversity of the organizations that represent consumers' interests at the European level means that co-operation among them tends to be the exception rather than the rule and on occasion disputes have broken out between them. None the less, there are several participatory arenas, either established or encouraged by the Commission, that bring together all of the European consumer organizations, as well as national ones.

The Consumers' Consultative Council

Organized by the Commission, the Consumers' Consultative Council (CCC) brought together all of the European groups that represent consumers' interests for the purpose of providing a consumers' opinion on Commission proposals. It suffered from a number of shortcomings and despite numerous modifications failed to function properly.[5] Disagreements among its constituent groups, its slow response time, and a lack of regard for it within the Commission all impeded its influence. In an attempt to improve the effectiveness of consumer consultation the Commission disbanded the CCC on 13 June 1995 and established the more streamlined Consumer Committee (CC).

[5] The CCC's roots can be traced to the Contact Committee for Consumer Questions, which was created in 1962 and disbanded itself in 1972 after two years of inactivity. In 1973 the Consumers' Consultative Committee was established with a similar membership but with the addition of individual experts. In 1980 the balance among the European consumer groups was adjusted, reducing the influence of the ETUC. In 1989 it became the Consumers' Consultative Council and representatives of national consumer organizations were added. In 1994 BEUC was allocated twice as many seats as the other established European organizations and EIEC gained representation. Following an adjustment in early 1995 to the number of national representatives to account for enlargement the CCC was disbanded in June 1995 to be replaced by the Consumer Committee.

During much of the early 1990s the functioning of the CCC was badly disrupted by disagreements among the European consumer organizations which stem from their different traditions. Tensions between BEUC and ETUC came to a head after BEUC forced a discussion on reform of the CCC by refusing to nominate its representatives to the CCC, which was to be renewed on 1 January 1993. Although BEUC accepts that both ETUC and EURO COOP can do valuable work on behalf of consumers, it does not consider them to represent the interests only of consumers and, therefore, does not think that they should participate in a body that represents consumers' views. It, consequently, sought to have the former expelled from the CCC and the status of the latter reviewed. Both groups fought back. EURO COOP, for example, rallied its allies in the EP to put pressure on Christine Scrivener, then the commissioner for consumer affairs. In the end, neither group was expelled, but BEUC was awarded eight seats, twice as many seats as each of the other sitting European organizations; the ETUC had to nominate its representatives from the consumer organizations of trade unions; and IEIC was given two seats. These changes satisfied no one and did not resolve the problem, as ideological differences continued to impede agreement on important appointments within the CCC. EURO-C went so far as to accuse BEUC of being dominated by 'conservative forces' and using its additional seats to obstruct the running of the CCC (EURO-C, 1995: 5).

The CCC's other principal internal problem was that it had grown unwieldy. In early 1995 it had 48 members and functioned in a slow and bureaucratic fashion, with many decisions being taken only at three plenary sessions a year. Consequently, sometimes even when consulted during the drafting stage, the CCC was unable to deliver an opinion on a proposal until after the college of Commissioners had taken its decision. The new CC has a smaller membership, one representative from each of the five European associations and each member state; will be chaired by a Commission official; and is supposed to be more responsive to Commission requests for opinions (Commission, 1995a).

Although an improvement on the CCC (CEG, 1995), the latest reform still does not address the more fundamental issue of the place of such a body in the EU's policy structure. Some directorates general failed to consult the CCC, despite being regularly reminded to do so by DGXXIV, or did so only after the Commission had adopted the proposal (ESC, 1991). In addition, even though the CC is estimated to cost less that one-third what the CCC would have (CEG, 1995), DGXXIV does not intend to use the savings to increase the frequency of meetings or to provide experts to advise on technical issues. These are both reforms that consumer groups feel would significantly increase the effectiveness of consumer representation in the Commission by improving the quality and increasing the speed of the CC's opinions (CEG, 1995; EURO-C, 1994*b*).

Consumer Representation in Standardization

The Council's decision in May 1985 to delegate much of the detail of approximation to the European standards bodies—the European Standards Committee (CEN), the European Electrotechnical Standards Committee (CENELEC), and the European Telecommunications Standards Institute (ETSI)—dramatically increased the importance of consumer participation in their work. In some member states—particularly Germany, France, and the UK—consumers have been represented in the national standards bodies for quite a long time, and therefore indirectly participate in the European bodies. These consumer representatives even represent their national standards bodies in some CEN and CENELEC working groups and technical committees. Even in 1995, however, the standard bodies in six member states had no formal relationships with consumer representatives.

The first European consumer observers, with support from the Commission, gained direct access to CEN in December 1982 and to CENELEC in April 1983. These observers were appointed by the CCC and their activities were co-ordinated and supported by SECO (the European Secretariat for Coordination in Standardization).

The Commission's 1990 green paper on the development of European standardization (Commission, 1990*a*), among other things, noted that the participation of the social partners, including consumers, at every level of the standard bodies is a pre-condition for the acceptance and continued development of European standardization. The Consumer Consultative Councils of the EU and the

European Free Trade Area (EFTA)[6] responded with a joint proposal which ultimately led to the creation of ANEC (the European Association for the Coordination of Consumer Representation in Standardization), which replaced SECO in February 1995.

ANEC is composed of eighteen national members, one selected by the consumer organizations in each member country of the EU and EFTA, and four representatives from the CCC and two from the Consumer Consultative Council of the EFTA Secretariat. The General Assembly, *inter alia*, sets general policy objectives and decides to which committees to assign consumer observers. Consumer representation is organized by the Coordination Group, which is composed of representatives from each member country, the chairs of ANEC's working groups, and invited experts. ANEC's six working groups—child safety, electrical appliances, environment, gas appliances, machinery, and traffic safety—are composed of interested national representatives, the ANEC observers on the relevant technical committees, and invited experts. At which level decisions are taken about ANEC's position on a particular standard depends on how technical it is, with the more political and wide-ranging decisions being taken higher up in the hierarchy. At the time of writing these boundaries were still being finalized.

Consumers can influence European standards in essentially two ways: consumers represented on national standards bodies can seek to influence them to support the consumers' view and/or ANEC can present its opinion on draft standards. ANEC also participates in the General Assemblies of CEN and CENELEC, which means that it can propose new work items.

In 1995 there were more than 100 national consumer representatives and 44 ANEC observers active in 175 CEN and CENELEC technical committees and working groups (ANEC, 1995). In addition, ANEC supports the work of consumer representatives in key committees and working groups in the international standards bodies—the International Organization for Standardization (ISO) and the International Electro-technical Commission (IEC)—as European standards, particularly electrical ones, are increasingly being set at the international level.

---

[6] As the member states of both the EU and EFTA are members of CEN and CENELEC, consumer representation is likewise drawn from both groups of countries.

Bilateral Consultations

The European consumer groups also have extensive individual contact with the Commission. The different groups participate in a wide range of issue-specific Commission advisory bodies— including 25 Agricultural Advisory Committees, the Committee on Veterinary Medicinal Products, the Eco-Label Forum, and the Payment System Users Liaison Group—but these comprise only a tiny fraction of the constellation of advisory bodies that supply the Commission with expertise (see Chapter 2), many of which, admittedly are composed only of government officials. Consumer organizations are also consulted on an *ad hoc* basis by Commission officials. As mentioned earlier, all of the consumer organizations maintain bilateral contacts with the Commission and frequently initiate contacts on issues of concern to them. On such occasions consumer associations serve both as representatives of consumers' interests and as sources of information and expertise. Consequently, their ability to conduct authoritative studies through their member organizations is essential to their effective participation.

Participation, however, is not the same as influence. Consumer organizations feel that they are poorly represented on advisory committees and that consultations are often sporadic (CEG, 1993; NCC, 1988). Perhaps the most extreme example of representation with only marginal influence is in DGVI's agricultural advisory committees. On these committees representatives of producer organizations and agricultural co-operatives hold approximately 50 per cent of the seats; trade and industry occupy 25 per cent; and trade unions, consumers, and other interested parties take up the remainder. In all, consumers constitute only 10 per cent of the committees' memberships (NCC, 1988).

CONCLUSION

The SEM programme has not brought a substantial decline in consumer safety, and in some areas and in some countries has even augmented it. At the same time, it has not delivered benefits that consumers recognize as such. This is due to the uneven development of European consumer policy, which has developed furthest with respect to product safety, but has done relatively little to promote consumers' economic and legal rights, and to the failure to take adequate account of consumers' interests in all areas of EU policy-making.

This state of affairs is the result of policy following the path of least resistance. The *acquis*'s emphasis on the free circulation of goods made alignment of national measures a priority and provided mechanisms to facilitate its achievement. Even so progress was often possible only on the basis of minimum harmonization or required the establishment of opt-out clauses. The treaty-based imperatives and member government incentives for common policies in the areas of consumers' economic and legal rights have been much weaker. The EP and the European consumer organizations, although influential at times, were not sufficiently powerful to divert the momentum of the SEM programme into a more consumer-friendly orientation. In particular, they were thwarted by the EU's fragmented system which impeded the integration of consumer interests across the range of European policy.

None the less, a common consumer policy did begin to emerge during the 1980s and two important factors are propelling its further development. The first is the need to address the SEM programme's shortcomings, especially with regard to encouraging cross-border consumption, and the regulatory gaps, particularly in the areas of financial services and food quality, created by economic integration. The second, and closely related, element is the concern of Europe's leading politicians for the lack of popular support for European integration. Neither of these impetuses is entirely new; in fact they have underpinned the development of the European consumer policy thus far. But they have become of heightened importance both as other problems have been addressed and therefore become less pressing and as the EU's crisis of popularity and legitimacy has deepened.

11

The Kaleidoscope of European Policy-Making: Shifting Patterns of Participation and Influence

HELEN WALLACE AND ALASDAIR R. YOUNG

The essays in this volume show a kaleidoscope of changing patterns of participation in the collective process of European policy-making on issues of market regulation and policies for industry. Participation in the European arena constitutes a shift in two dimensions. First, the European policy model marks a distinct departure from patterns of policy-making in national arenas. Second, the European policy process is in flux, varying between policy areas and over time. The question is what kind of kaleidoscope is being created, and with what kinds of patterns? And, further, what light do they shed on the form of governance which is emerging in this *demi-monde* between the traditional West European state and the transnational policy arena.

These questions are put in a period when the character of West European integration is under intense scrutiny both from the academic community and in the public debate. In the academic community there is a flurry of welcome new theorizing about the nature of integration, especially with the development of approaches based on rational choice, new institutionalism, and comparative political economy (Hall and Taylor, 1996; Nørgaard, 1996; Olsen, 1996). In the practitioners' debate three considerations are in play: first, the assertion that there is a distinct mode of West European market regulation (Majone, 1996; McGowan and H. Wallace, 1996); second, the mood of persistent criticism over the weak legitimation of the integration process; and, third, the conundrum of whether the integration model is extendable to 'pan-Europe' (Smith *et al.*, 1996).

Our collection has assembled evidence relevant to both academic and practitioner debates. It has the merit of drawing its empirical subject-matter from the heart of the economic integration process. Issues to do with market regulation and industrial policies have always been at the centre of the European Community (EC). They continue to constitute the predominant focus of the first pillar of the redefined European Union (EU). The material on which we draw in this volume concerns the mainstream, and not the margins, of collective European public policy. The activities of the various actors whom we have portrayed and the array of forms of their participation in the EU are emblematic of a wider refashioning of institutions and of policy direction. That refashioning is, it must be stressed, not just about the relationships between national and transnational levels of governance. It is also about a redrawing of roles, responsibilities, and boundaries between public and private agents, as well as among public agents or among private agents. Our various case-studies shed light on each of these dimensions. In highlighting here some broad conclusions we also draw on material from other parallel studies (H. Wallace and Young, 1996).

Our focus has been on political and economic actors; the fluidity of their patterns of participation is to be expected in a period of changing public policy and economic adjustment. The Single European Market (SEM) process and the redefinition of industrial policies, to rest more on horizontal rules and policies, and less on sectoral championship, are both illustrative of responses by West Europeans to changing conditions in the international political economy. We can observe repositioning and reorientation within and between countries, as both political and economic élites endeavour to set in place arrangements that will permit a viable—and more flexible—form of coexistence between national, European, and broader international arenas of engagement. The persistence of these different arenas, none predominant, provides both constraints and opportunities, and these impact differentially on different actors.

THE INSTITUTIONAL CONTEXT

The participants in the European policy process operate through idiosyncratic European institutions. This is not intended as the familiar truism that they are *sui generis*. However, the persistence and evolution of the EU framework does reflect a series of efforts to create a policy framework that offers different options and opportunities from those available within either the traditional national polities or other forms of international regime. In this sense it is innovative, experimental, and exploratory. The participants are engaged simultaneously in shaping the rules of the game and in seeking particular policy outcomes. The emerging institutional patterns have a trajectory distinct from those of the component polities, each of which in any case retains individual features. Yet the European institutions are now sufficiently mature to have acquired contours that mould behaviour. These include: the strong legal regime; the underpinning of the *acquis communautaire*; and the presence of actors whose first loyalty is to the European arena rather than to the component polities. These features induce distinctive and constrained patterns of behaviour which are more densely and intensely expressed than in conventional international fora.

Thus these institutions and associated patterns of behaviour seem explicitly not to replicate national institutional patterns in crucial respects. Indeed we can draw some evidence from our studies to suggest that the European institutional arena has taken the form that it has precisely as an antidote to some of the embedded features of national polities. Certainly our cases suggest that some outcomes are different because they have been articulated through European institutions with features different from those that characterize the member states.

Moreover, the institutional character of European policy formation is unstable and incomplete. It is unstable, in so far as it is lacks the ingrained habits, traditions, and political boundaries that have characterized in the past its equivalents in the member states. In particular the switch within the EU to an emphasis on the policy tools of market regulation is still too recent to have created certainty about the contours of the process or about patterns of behaviour. It is for this reason that elsewhere (H. Wallace and W. Wallace, 1996) we have used the metaphor of a policy pendulum swinging between different arenas of policy-making.

The European institutions are also incomplete, in that they do not engage some of the actors who are involved in the more developed polities of the member states. Parliamentarians, parties, and organized labour are less visibly engaged. So far at least, the

European policy process is not nested in the interweaving of political, social, and economic arrangements that have, often with
strong national variations, been typical of West European states
(Esping-Anderson, 1990; Streeck, 1995).

Our studies add weight to the arguments of those who suggest
that institutional arrangements are partly the product of changing
policy contexts and socio-economic evolution. We also endorse
the corollary argument of those who believe that particular institutional formats influence patterns of participation, relationships between participants, and outcomes (as regards both relative power
or position and specific policies). In addition cultural factors play a
part in our cases, both leading particular players in this complex
game to adopt particular ideas and strategies and giving certain
kinds of characteristics to policy results.

WHO PARTICIPATES?

This volume demonstrates that there is a broad basis of participation in the European policy process. It also indicates that Theodore
Lowi's (1964) adage that 'policy makes politics' applies in the European arena. Different actors mobilize in different ways in response to different policy initiatives or predicaments. This helps to
explain variations in the patterns of participation across policy
issues and between the European and national levels. It also sheds
light on why some actors are more present than others.

Political Actors

Our studies reveal the familiar political actors: national politicians
and national officials, alongside European politicians (Commissioners are, in our view, politicians), and European officials. In
various of our chapters the dense labyrinth of committees that
locks these players into dialogue and negotiation is evident and
important. But two caveats must be mentioned. First, the informal
features of these committees seem more pertinent in practice than
their formal basis of constitution or decision rules. Second, in any
case the evidence that formal constitution and rules make a big
difference to outcomes from the 'comitology' procedures is actually scanty, or at least so the Commission has itself concluded, in

knappa

the different context of preparations for the Intergovernmental Conference (IGC).[1] It should also be noted that in the case of Japanese automobile imports, covered in Chapters 7 and 8, the crucial deal struck between Europeans and between Europeans and Japanese was in the form not of a publicly presented contract, but cast as the 'Elements of Consensus'. It was established by informal understandings, and is dependent on 'voluntary' restraints for its implementation.

Perhaps more importantly, it is hard to detect from our cases a clear cut-off point between the explicitly more pluralist forms of participation, evident in the shaping of agendas and in pre-negotiation in and around the Commission, and the more exclusivist predominance of mandated national representatives in the Council, in an 'intergovernmental' phase of negotiation and decision (see also Hayes-Renshaw and H. Wallace, 1997). Instead the two phases shade into each other, with persistent variations in participation and activity by a range of actors, and with opportunities recurring to shape and to reshape the definition and resolution of issues. Iteration of policy-making between levels and phases is typical. Though Council phases of negotiation in a sense constitute a form of closure, this should not be over-stated. Permanent representations of the member states in Brussels, for example, often designate advertised access points for firms 'requiring information' or 'advice'. Their officials, as well as nationally based officials, do not go into purdah simply because they are involved in a Council working group's deliberations. In the regulatory process of the SEM much of the detailed and industry-sensitive work is handled through the standards bodies, to which many private actors can, and do, make representations.

We should note that the increasing reliance on the instruments of competition policy in order to shape the context for industrial policy and to deal with particular instances takes this policy arena too away from 'intergovernmentalism' into a more mixed mode. Governments, to be sure, try to influence the outcomes here, but can do so only indirectly. The participation of lawyers and judges through the European Court of Justice (ECJ) is a powerful

---

[1] Unpublished study by the Commission in 1995, which revealed that the Commission's views tended to prevail in most of the comitology procedures, even those that apparently gave more formal power to the representatives of the member states.

counterweight to intergovernmentalism. And after all most of the litigation that affects market regulation and industrial policy is prompted by aggrieved firms, not by governments.

Economic Actors

Part of the explanation for this shading of levels and layers in the patterns of participation is because economic actors are participants in all phases of the policy process, often explicitly, sometimes implicitly, often relying on officials of the same nationality, but sometimes consorting with officials of other nationalities. Who are our economic actors? The simple answer is mainly firms. The more complicated answer is firms, but in an array of configurations. Some firms participate directly, and, unsurprisingly, most vigorously when the policy issue proposed or sought directly affects their immediate concerns. On sectoral issues, the sectoral trade or producer associations are also active, but note *also*, not instead. Indeed the trend seems to be for firms to be less reliant on their associations as the primary or monopoly representatives of their interests. In attempts at policy-influencing, as well as in the market-place, firms pursue mixed strategies of co-operation and competition.

On horizontal issues, that is those that deal with the conditions generally affecting the operations of the market or external trade conditions or the non-industrial corollaries of market and process regulation, peak associations continue to play an important part in defining and channelling industrial views. But over the past decade they have been deemed insufficient by big, and especially multinational, firms. These latter have sought both to increase their influence within the peak associations and to complement them by developing their own clubs. The predominant focus, especially as articulated through the European Round Table of Industrialists, has been on embedding core objectives for developing the SEM and the rules of the game, that is seeking to shape the institutional context as well as particular measures. Their concerns have spread beyond the direct industrial issues to include an active interest in the infrastructure for industry and the conditions that affect competitiveness. Such clubs of industrialists have also been organized around some sectoral industrial issues—the coalition promoting digital video broadcasting is an obvious illustration.

Thus the issue in our cases is not whether firms are engaged, but when they choose to act independently, when collectively, and which forms of collective representation are chosen. This volume shows the range of possibilities. In Chapters 7 and 9 we have seen individual firms engaged in promoting their individual concerns, and sometimes colluding in one or other form of policy cartel. In Chapter 8 we find the traces of sectoral associations and the remaking of sectoral associations, as among the European automobile manufacturers. In Chapters 6 and 9 we have seen the emergence of several groupings of 'big business', the large multinational firms, both European and American, learning to act together in increasingly strategic ways to influence the policy environment and institutional arrangements, as well as seeking to secure specific policy options.

Two complementary factors seem to be at work here. One lies in the simple observation that collective representation of business interests cannot be reasonably expected to be the sole form of participation, since firms are in competition with each other. The 'normal' pattern is one which mixes co-operation and competition. Secondly, developments in the global economy, combined with the shift in regulatory authority to the European from the national level, have made it easier for big firms in particular to escape from some of the confines of collective representation and social partnership that have been so powerful in some national polities.

Civic Interests

Also engaged in our cases is a variety of what we have called 'civic interests'. These are groups that organize to 'balance' or to offset the efforts of producers to shape market regulation and industrial policies. They include, in particular, the consumers and those groups that have been spawned in response to the new issues of industrial regulation, notably as regards industrial processes, hence the activism that we note of environmental groups.

A strong feature of our cases is that such groups and the views that they represent are very much present in the policy process. Two points stand out. First, such groups are indeed actively engaged in efforts to influence policy. The consumer organizations have become more and more active, even though their efforts are thinly spread across the range of relevant issues. Second, their access is encouraged, both by the Commission and by some governments, or sections of some governments. And these political actors often take on the mantle of the consumer interest. This finding is in contrast to the historical picture of consumers impinging rather scantily on either sectoral industrial issues or agricultural policy issues in the EU. The BSE story of course is now provoking a different picture even for agriculture with greater emphasis now being placed on food safety. This changing picture of consumer representation is in keeping with the widespread evidence (Mazey and Richardson, 1992; Rucht, 1993) of the engagement of environmental groups.

WHO APPEARS NOT TO PARTICIPATE?

Our cases also suggest a limited participation by some of the political actors who are among the most active in a traditional country-defined polity. Parties of opposition and national parliaments do not figure in our story directly. There is no surprise in this observation, but it reinforces the point that traditional channels of representation, and of interest aggregation and intermediation, are not much apparent in the definition of European market and industrial policies.

Instead we observe a kind of sanitized version of political engagement, in which some perspectives and interests are latent, or are expressed indirectly, or represented only implicitly. One key point that follows is that the scope for programmatic debate is severely limited, while the opportunity for doctrinal capture seems to be considerable. The debate over controlling air pollution from automobiles is a case in point. Only very recently has the strangle hold of technical 'end-of-the-pipe' solutions begun to loosen. The European Parliament, which figures occasionally in the case profiles in this volume (although more so in many other cases), hardly seems to provide a substitute forum for programmatic debate on the issues that we have covered. It does, however, contribute to the acceptance of received ideas and doctrines, whether on the commitment to market liberalization as a predominant and shared policy mode, or on the insertion of corollary considerations, such as the environmental dimension or the concerns of consumers.

Another point that needs to be emphasized is that the primary political actors involved are drawn from national governments and national agencies. Sub-national actors, in spite of being increasingly drawn into the transnational arena of activity in other policy fields (Marks *et al.*, 1996), seem not to find much opportunity for leverage on the core issues of market regulation. OBS!

✗ Moreover the shift of emphasis from vertical to horizontal policies for industry makes it harder for regional and local authorities to engage in support of 'their' sector or 'their' local firms. Instead their participation emerges 'downstream', in the implementing and buffering arrangements of structural adjustment and compensation, subjects that are not covered in detail in this volume.

Also strikingly absent from our cases are socially focused groups and the representative associations of labour. Although the period covered by our cases coincides with one in which there has been recurrent discussion of the scope for a 'social dimension' to European policies, this discussion seems to have been in parallel to, and not interwoven with, the development of market regulation and of industrial policies. Yes, there has been a debate on the challenge of competitiveness, growth and (un)employment, kick-started by the Commission's 1993 White Paper (Commission, 1993c). Yes, its publication has been followed by the establishment of the Ciampi Group, reporting periodically to European Councils, and including, alongside the business leaders, some voice for the organized labour movement. Yes, there is talk in the 1996 IGC of creating a new high-level forum for social partners to address employment issues.

All of these points notwithstanding, the role of organized labour is weak at the European level on the issues that this volume covers. Historically of course such groups have had an impact within countries, or at least within some member states. Their participation and their influence have been articulated through the institutions of social partnership and in specific sectoral contexts. The former are weak at the EU level, and rendered weaker by the fact that social partnership is weakly articulated in some of the member states. The ability of organized labour to engage has also been reduced as policy has shifted away from sectoral bargaining to horizontal regulatory issues.

WHAT SHAPES THE OPPORTUNITIES
FOR—AND BARRIERS TO—PARTICIPATION?

We have been careful so far not to confuse participation with influence, since the former does not necessarily imply the latter. None the less it is reasonable to assume that participation is generally pursued in the hope of exercising influence, and that repeated investments in the costs (not insignificant) of participation at least imply that the participants believe themselves to be having an impact. The considerable increase in activism and in lobbying around the Brussels policy process is therefore in itself important, as is pointed out in Chapters 2 and 3.

The EU policy process has a number of features that both encourage participation and encourage the belief that participation conveys a degree of influence. There are multiple access points to the process, in both the member states and around the European institutions. Information flows are extensive and most practitioners believe that information flows more freely around and through the European institutions than in many, even most, member states. The arrival of new Nordic members, to complement Danish and Dutch efforts, has strengthened this feature of the EU and begun to make information more accessible even on Council phases of negotiation. Iteration between the Council and the European Parliament on issues subject to co-decision increases the opportunities for others to interpose. Within the Commission it is considered 'appropriate' to facilitate information flows to, and access points for, the clients of policy, though there are concerns about excessive lobbying (McLaughlin and Greenwood, 1995). More than that, therefore, within the Commission it is considered 'appropriate' to give an extra boost to the efforts of some groups to engage; both consumer and environmental organizations have been the beneficiaries of this view.

None the less there are asymmetries of information, of access, and of skills. The diffuse character of the Brussels process within and between institutions means that to be a participant often requires covering several access points in order to find the most useful one. Small groups, and small firms, thus find it much harder to engage than the better resourced organizations or firms. The legalism of language and the role of litigation to test policy agreement put a premium on legal expertise, more achievable for firms with sophisticated corporate lawyers, or for those who can afford to retain a Brussels-based solicitor. Rather few of the 'civic interests' can make a mark here, though the European Consumers' Organization (BEUC) is an interesting example of one that has done so.

The traditional patterns of industrial policy in the EU, as in many member states, initially gave the edge, in terms of effective access, to sectorally focused interests, that needed only to follow 'their' subjects and to monitor 'their' policy-makers, both national and European. The shift towards more horizontal issues shifts the opportunity structure towards those who can either marshal more comprehensive expertise or deploy the same main argument across a broad swathe of topics. Here the consumers and the environmentalists have an inbuilt advantage, in so far as their main arguments tend to remain constant and pertinent. They can thus take advantage of critical 'focal points' in a policy discussion (Pierson, forthcoming) and avoid the risks of 'argument dilution' (Fisher and Ury, 1982). Such concentration of effort is much harder for organized labour or political parties.

These advantages of opportunity are, or can be, consolidated by those participants whose arguments seem to have a direct relevance to the proposal at hand. Necessarily most product regulations have a consumer dimension, making the incorporation of some consumer perspective more or less automatic for national and European policy-makers. Many have a direct environmental impact and thus force the policy-makers to make some kind of assessment of how to address this. Process regulations similarly often have an explicit environmental dimension, which provokes consideration of the environmental groups' points of view. This directness of relevance gives the environmentalists an initial advantage compared with those whose concerns are at two or three stages removed from the core of proposed legislation. Organized labour can thus, for example, more easily find toeholds for its arguments about health and safety at work than for those about the conditions in the labour market. These latter concerns require separate legislation, rather than a clause in a market regulation measure prompted for other reasons.

But it is not simply a question of direct relevance. Opportunities to engage also depend on how well the views being put forward chime with the emerging prevailing wisdoms of policy and with the quest of European policy-makers (including those from national governments) for a form of legitimation for their proposed actions. Thus we can observe a shift on the part of the Commission and many member governments away from consultations with the peak and sectoral organizations of business towards direct dialogue with individual firms.

The reasoning for this within the Commission seems to be based on two calculations. One has been the search for coalition partners in pressing the regulatory agenda forwards, sometimes against the declared preferences or inertia of governments. Note, however, that this does not necessarily produce a tendency towards 'capture'. As Grande (1996) argues in relation to European technology policy, closer dialogue can make the Commission tougher in resisting firms' claims for privileged treatment. A second factor has been the quest for credibility or 'economic legitimation'. To have senior industrialists or financiers speaking up for a Commission proposal is a means of demonstrating its relevance and significance. For those governments that have championed market liberalization it has been important to demonstrate the specific benefits to particular entrepreneurs. Even the more reluctant liberalizers among the member governments have often found themselves pulled along behind the arguments for opening up new market opportunities for firms from their own countries.

Interestingly it has not only been economic legitimation that has been cultivated. Social legitimation has been an additional concern. The paler reflection of this has permeated the debate about the social dimension. Our case-studies, however, reveal a different 'logic of appropriateness' in the inclusion of consumer and environmental dimensions to the market. One of the puzzles of European market regulation is that minimum essential standards have, on balance, been set higher rather than lower, even higher sometimes than the prior standards of the more 'advanced' member states. Explanations have been sought for this in the emergence of particularly effective policy networks or advocacy coalitions or the particular devices chosen to promote high standards, which determine how the costs of accommodating those are distributed (Héritier, 1996; Scharpf, 1996a). We suggest here one additional factor, namely that the concern of European policy-makers to make market liberalization socially more acceptable has tipped the balance of the argument towards higher standards and being seen to acknowledge environmental or consumer concerns.

This receptivity to high consumer and environmental standards at EU level is, of course, also found in some of the (especially northern) member states. But the EU process in some other respects parts company with the patterns in the member states. In particular it is a feature of the experience of individual countries and their domestic policy arrangements that the public arrangements for the operation of economic markets are embedded in a context of distributional and social understandings. These are differently composed in different countries: in Germany in the *Sozialwirtschaft* model; in France in the traditions of Colbertism; and so on. In each such case the particular national variant has struck a specific balance of interests and engagement across classes and across social groups, with the latter active participants in a process that facilitated, but also conditioned, the operations of the market. We find little trace of these habits in our case-studies. Instead, the patterns of participation in policy-making at the European level as regards the terms of the market for entrepreneurs have been freed from some of the obligations of social partnership.

One of several questions left hanging by our volume concerns how far patterns of industrial participation depend on the traditions, context, and ethos of different EU member states. We offer some glimpses into the variations. Cohen in Chapter 7 makes some observations on the French case, arguing that French firms producing cars and engaged in the consumer electronics industry have used their involvement in the European arena to leverage changes at home that would otherwise have been more difficult. In other words European resources have changed the balance of influence and argument within the national polity, and *vis-à-vis* other social and economic agents. Holmes and McGowan suggest in Chapter 8 that responses to and influences on European policy developments vary between countries, especially in the airlines case, where there are clearly distinctive patterns of relationship between governments and firms.

THE EUROPEAN POLICY MODEL

Our volume thus builds up a picture of the distinctive features of the European policy model that operates on issues of market regulation and industrial policy. The horizontal nature of so many of the policy measures and policy instruments favours certain kinds of participants and certain kinds of participation. It has not favoured the emergence of corporatism or neo-corporatism at the European level (Streeck and Schmitter, 1991; Grande, 1996), nor of closed policy communities (Mazey and Richardson, 1993*b*). On the contrary it may have disrupted some of the forms of interest intermediation that have been present historically within some member states.

The decoupling of regulatory issues from distributional ones at the European level is of long-term significance. It marks a break from West European habits of developing policies on a cross-class, cross-sectoral, social partnership basis of consensus-building. Not only does it disrupt the policy traditions in some member states, but it also probably reveals a growing division between European and country levels of governance. Majone (1996) and others have already pointed out that the European model, with its strong legal institutions, favours regulation, but deters the development of distributional policies.

Our additional observation is that we should expect a residual impact of those national traditions of social partnership and welfare arrangements. This is likely to be found in a tenacious insistence from within the relevant member states to preserve room for manœuvre at the national level in the sphere of distributional policies and measures to induce social cohesion. This would accord with much of the historical reality of the limits to European policy integration, a process in which some collective policies have coexisted with continuing diversity of national social and distributional policies. It is in this arena that we should expect to see efforts to reinforce subsidiarity and to insist on the acceptability of differentiation of certain policies between member states. The European model may well also generate some tensions between the European and national levels, as national politicians and social groups seek to retain their distinct trajectories of social adjustment to the pressures of the international political economy. Indeed this is, for example, now the explicitly stated objective of Dutch European policy.

The weakness of European instruments to provide the social corollaries for adjustment is, however, in contrast to the opportunities to achieve more stringent regulation. The European policy model seems to foster agreement on both product and process standards at higher rather than lower levels. This is more easily achieved on product regulation than on process regulation, but the tendency to go for rather stringent process regulation (impinging on both environmental and workplace standards) seems to be rather well entrenched. This reflects the engagements of some of the relevant representational groups, but often implicitly rather than explicitly. The incorporation of such concerns by the policy-makers themselves, as much as under the intensity of lobbying pressures, seems to be a feature of European institutional behaviour. The Commission has used these opportunities to frame legislation as a form of social legitimation, but also as a means to buttress its own influence on policy measures. In pleading the cause of consumer or environmental concerns, the Commission can tip the balance of the argument in negotiation and marshal a more broadly based coalition of support for high-standard member-state policies. Often this will include the concurrent concerns of particular member governments or accommodate positions expressed by European parliamentarians.

It would be wrong, however, to conclude that this produces even, consistent, and predictable policy outcomes. Results vary across cases. The policy communities are not stable: policy networks are open in composition, thus with varying characteristics, compared with networks or communities that coalesce around more sectoral policy issues. There is scope for advocacy coalitions to develop, especially around relatively distinct and simply stated civic preferences, but their presence should not be overstated.

The kaleidoscope of European policy-making thus continues to rearrange the patterns of participation and of opportunities for influence. On the one hand there is a drift towards the consolidation of regulatory policies through collective measures and with the extensive engagement of public officials, national and European, of economic actors, and of some civic interests. In this consolidation both public and private interests are articulated. Firms have, by and large, adjusted to, indeed encouraged, the relocation of policy authority, while also discovering the corollary imprint of consumer and environmental groups on the process of defining particular regulatory measures and doctrines to guide the approach to policy. Horizontal regulation lends itself to a plurality of participation in the process and to limits to the risks of iron triangles and capture.

On the other hand, those same political and economic actors which are so intensively engaged in the European arena persist in being involved in the national arena, not only to buttress their European activities, but also to pursue other objectives. Some of these may be complements to what is available through the European arena: a liberalization of national arrangements combined with a consolidation of transnational arrangements. But some nationally (or regionally) focused activities may be contrary to, even contradictory to, European engagements. Thus it is possible to argue the apparently strong neo-liberal case at the European level for a minimalist public control over market forces and strong competition yet to be strongly in favour of social intervention nationally to correct for imperfections in the market. Thus there are both congruences between the two arenas and concomitant paradoxes. The differently arranged institutional jigsaws in the two arenas make the paradoxes easier to manage as related, but distinctive. The opportunities to shape the European institutional arrangements, and thereby their consequences, are part of the explanation for the intensity of participation in the process by so wide a range of political and economic actors.

REFERENCES

Abélès, M. (1996), *En attente d'Europe* (Paris: Hachette).

——and Bellier, I. (1996), 'La Commission Européenne: du compromis culturel à la culture politique du compromis', *Revue Française de Science Politique*, 46/3, 431–56.

————and McDonald, M. (1993), *Approche anthropologique de la Commission européenne*, Report for the Commission, December.

AEA (1984), Association of European Airlines, *Comparison of Air Transport in Europe and the United States* (Brussels: AEA).

——(1985), 'European Air Transport Policy: AEA Proposals' (Brussels: AEA).

——(1991), 'White Paper on Air Transport Policy' (Brussels: AEA).

Altenstetter, C. (1994), 'European Union Responses to AIDS/HIV and Policy Networks in the pre-Maastricht Era', *Journal of European Public Policy*, 1/3, 413–40.

Andersen, S. S. and Eliassen, K. A. (1991), 'European Community Lobbying', *European Journal of Political Research*, 20, 173–87.

—— —— (1996) (eds.), *The European Union: How Democratic is It?* (London: Sage).

ANEC (1995), European Association for the Coordination of Consumer Representation in Standardization, 'Consumer Participation in Standardization', ANEC/95/GA/56 (Brussels: ANEC).

Argyris, N. (1989), 'The EEC Rules of Competition and the Air Transport Sector', *Common Market Law Review*, 26/1, 5–32.

Assemblée Nationale (1991), *Report of Hearings on Consensus with Japan* (Paris: Imprimerie Nationale).

Atkinson, M. M. and Coleman, W. D. (1989), *The State, Business, and Industrial Change in Canada* (Toronto: University of Toronto Press).

Bangemann, M. (1992), *Meeting the Global Challenge* (London: Kogan Page).

Barlebo-Larsen, P. K. (1991), 'La Politique européenne des consommateurs: une priorité du grand marché', *Revue du Marché Commun et de l'Union Européenne*, 345, 176–9.

Behrman, J. (1970), *National Interests and the Multinational Enterprise: Tensions Among the North Atlantic Countries* (Englewood Cliffs, NJ: Prentice-Hall).

Belderbos, R. (1994), 'Strategic Trade Policy and Multinational Enterprises', Tinbergen Institute Research Series No. 68 (Utrecht: Tinbergen Institute).

Bellier, I. (1995*a*), 'Une culture de la Commission Européenne? De la rencontre des cultures et du multilinguisme des fonctionnaires', in Mény *et al.* (1995), 49–60.

——(1995*b*), 'Morality, Language and Powers', *Social Anthropology*, 3/3, 235–50.

BEUC (1995*a*), The European Consumers' Organization, *Annual Report 1994*, BEUC/55/95 (Brussels: BEUC).

——(1995*b*), 'A European Union for Consumers: Priority Actions for the Commission's 1995 Work Programme' (Brussels: BEUC).

Blanpain, R., Blanquet, F., Herman, F., and Mouty, A. (1983), *The Vredeling Proposal: Information and Consultation of Employees in Multinational Enterprises* (Deventer: Kluwer).

Bomberg, E., and Peterson, J. (1993), 'Prevention from Above? The Role of the European Community', in Mills (1993), 140–60.

Bond, M., Smith, J., and Wallace, W. (1996) (eds.), *Eminent Europeans* (London: Greycoat Press).

Bourgoignie, T. M. (1987), 'Consumer Law and the European Community: Issues and Prospects', in Bourgoignie and Trubek (1987), 89–261.

——and Trubek, D. (1987), *Consumer Law, Common Markets and Federalism in Europe and the United States* (Berlin: Walter de Gruyter).

Braczyk, H.-J. and Scheinstock, G. (1996) (eds.), *Kurswechsel in der Industrie* (Stuttgart: Kohlhammer).

Bressand, A. and Nicolaïdis, K. (1990), 'Regional Integration in a Networked World Economy', in W. Wallace (1990), 27–49.

Buigues, P., Ilzkovitz, F., Lebrun, J. F., and Sapir, A. (1994) (eds.), *European Economy: Social Europe: Market Services and European Integration*, 3.

Bulmer, S. (1994), 'The Governance of the European Union: A New Institutionalist Approach', *Journal of Public Policy*, 13/4, 351–79.

Button, K. and Swann, D. (1989), 'European Community Airlines: Deregulation and Its Problems', *Journal of Common Market Studies*, 27/4, 259–82.

Cafruny, A. W. and Rosenthal, G. G. (1993) (eds.), *The State of the European Community*, ii. *The Maastricht Debates and Beyond* (Boulder, Colo.: Lynne Rienner).

Cawson, A. (1986), *Corporatism and Political Theory* (Oxford: Blackwell).

——(1992), 'Running a High-Tech Industry: Consumer Electronics', *Running the Country*, Unit 13 (Milton Keynes: Open University Press).

——(1994), 'Public Policies and Private Interests: The Role of Business Interests in Determining Europe's Future Television Systems', working paper of the Mannheimer Zentrum für Europäische Sozialforschung, (Mannheim: MZES).

——(1995a), 'Consumer Electronics', in Greenwood (1995).

——(1995b), 'High Definition Television in Europe', *Political Quarterly*, 66/2, 157–73.

——and Holmes, P. (1995), 'Technology Policy and Competition Issues in the Transition to Advanced Television Services in Europe', *Journal of European Public Policy*, 2/4, 650–71.

——Haddon, L. G., and Miles, I. (1995), *The Shape of Things to Consume: Delivering Information Technology into the Home* (Aldershot: Avebury).

——Morgan, K., Webber, D., Holmes, P., and Stevens, A. (1990), *Hostile Brothers: Competition and Closure in the European Consumer Electronics Industry* (Oxford: Clarendon Press).

CEG (1993), Consumers in Europe Group (formerly Consumers in the European Community Group), 'The Long-Term Operation of the Single Market', CECG 93/8 (London: CEG).

——(1994), 'European Union Consumer Protection Policy', CEG 94/11 (London: CEG).

——(1995), 'The European Commission's Consumer Committee', CEG 95/14 (London: CEG).

Civildepartementet (1995), *Svensk Konsumentpolitik i EU-Perspektiv*, Ds 1995:32 (Stockholm: Civildepartementet).

Clement, W. (1995), 'Der Ausschuß der Regionen: Kritik und Überblick— eine politische Bewertung', in Tomuschat (1995b), 97–116.

Close, G. (1984), 'The Legal Basis for the Consumer Protection Programme of the EEC and Priorities for Action', in Woodroffe (1984), 1–23.

Cohen, E. (1992), *Le Colbertisme high tech* (Paris: Hachette).

——(1993), 'TVHD: un échec exemplaire', *Les Annales des Mines*, May.

——(1995), 'National Champions in Search of a Mission', in Hayward (1995), 23–47.

Collins, K. (1995), 'Draft Opinion for the Committee on the Rules of Procedure, the Verification of Credentials and Immunities on Lobbying and the European Parliament', PK 212.031, 20 Feb.

Commission (1984), 'Civil Aviation Memorandum No. 2, Progress towards the Development of a Community Air Transport Policy', COM(84) 72 final.

——(1985a), 'Completing the Internal Market: White Paper from the Commission to the European Council (Milan, 28–9 June 1985)', COM(85) 310 final.

——(1985b), 'A New Impetus for Consumer Protection Policy', COM(85) 314 final.

——(1987), 'Towards a Dynamic European Economy: Green Paper on the Development of the Common Market for Telecommunications Services and Equipment', COM(87) 290 final.

——(1987a), *ESPRIT première phase: état d'avancement et résultats* (Luxembourg: Office for Official Publications of the European Communities).

——(1988), *Seventeenth Annual Report on Competition Policy* (Luxembourg: Office for Official Publications of the European Communities).

——(1990a), 'Commission Communication on the Development of European Standardization: Action for Faster Technological Integration in Europe', COM(90) 456 final.

——(1990b), 'Three Year Action Plan of Consumer Policy in the EEC: 1990–1992', COM(90) 98 final.

——(1991a), *Consumer Policy in the Single Market*, 2nd edn. (Luxembourg: Office for Official Publications of the European Communities).

——(1991b), 'The European Electronic and Information Technology Industry: State of Play, Issues at Stake and Proposals for Action', SEC(91) 565.

——(1991c), 'First Contributions of the Commission to the Intergovernmental Conference on "Political Union"', SEC(91) 500.

——(1992a), 'Increased Transparency in the Work of the Commission', SEC(92) 2274.

——(1992b), 'An Open and Structured Dialogue between the Commission and Interest Groups', SEC(92) 2272.

——(1993a), 'Growth, Competitiveness, Employment: The Challenges and Ways Forward into the 21st Century', COM(93) 700 final.

——(1993b), 'Openness in the Community: Communication to the Council, the Parliament and the Economic and Social Committee', COM(93) 258 final.

——(1993c), 'Second Commission Three-Year Action Plan: 1993–1995', COM(93) 378 final.

——(1995a), 'Commission Decision of 13 June 1995 Setting up a Consumer Committee', COM(95) 260 final.

——(1995b), *General Report on the Activities of the European Union 1994* (Luxembourg: Office for Official Publications of the European Communities).

——(1995c), 'Priorities for Consumer Policy, 1996–1998', COM(95) 519 final.

——(1996a), 'Communication to the Council, European Parliament, Economic and Social Committee, and the Committee of the Regions: European Automobile Industry 1996', COM(96) 327 final.

——(1996b), 'The Single Market in 1995: Report of the Commission to the Council and the European Parliament', COM(96) 51 final.

Cowles, M. G. (1994), 'The Politics of Big Business in the European Community: Setting the Agenda for a New Europe', Ph.D. thesis (The American University, Washington, DC).

——(1995), 'Setting the Agenda for a New Europe: The ERT and EC 1992', *Journal of Common Market Studies*, 33/4, 501–26.

——(1996*a*), 'Business Means Europe—Who Built the Market?', in Bond *et al.* (1996).

——(1996*b*), 'German Big Business: Learning to Play the European Game', *German Politics and Society*, 14/3.

——(1996*c*), 'The EU Committee of AmCham: The Powerful Voice of American Firms in Brussels', *Journal of European Public Policy*, 3/3, 339–58.

CPS (1995), Consumer Policy Service, 'Inventory of Community Acts Relating to Consumer Affairs' Jan.

Crenson, M. (1971), *The Unpolitics of Air Pollution* (Baltimore, Md.: Johns Hopkins University Press).

Dahl, R. A. (1961), *Who Governs?* (New Haven, Conn.: Yale University Press).

Dai, X. (1996), *Corporate Strategy, Public Policy and New Technologies: Philips and the European Consumer Electronics Industry* (Oxford: Pergamon).

——Cawson, A. and Holmes, P. (1994), 'Competition, Collaboration and Public Policy: A Case Study of the European HDTV Strategy', Sussex European Institute Working Paper No. 3 (Falmer: Sussex European Institute).

Dashwood, A. (1983), 'Hastening Slowly: The Communities' Path towards Harmonization', in H. Wallace *et al.* (1983), 177–208.

degli Abbati, C. (1987), *Transport and European Integration* (Luxembourg: Office for Official Publications of the European Communities).

Dehousse, R. (1992), 'Integration v. Regulation? On the Dynamics of Regulation in the European Community', *Journal of Common Market Studies*, 30/4, 383–402.

DGXXIV (1995), 'History of EC Consumer Protection', *INFO-C*, 4/3, 2.

DVB (1995), Digital Video Broadcasting, 'Going Ahead with Digital Television' (Geneva: DVB Project Office).

Easton, D. (1953), *The Political System: An Enquiry into the State of Political Science* (New York, NY: Knopf).

ECAC (1982), European Civil Aviation Conference, *Report on Competition in Intra European Air Services* (Paris: ECAC).

Ehlermann, C. D. (1987), 'The Internal Market Following the Single European Act', *Common Market Law Review*, 24, 361–409.

Ehrmann, H. (1957), *Organized Business in France* (Princeton, NJ: Princeton University Press).

Eichener, V. (1993), 'Social Dumping or Innovative Regulation? Processes and Outcomes of European Decision-Making in the Sector of Health and Safety at Work Regulation', EUI Working Paper SPS 92/28 (Florence: European University Institute).

——(1996), 'Die Rückwirkungen der europäischen Integration auf nationale Politikmuster', in Jachtenfuchs and Kohler-Koch (1996b), 249–80.

——and Voelzkow, H. (1994a), 'Ko-Evolution politisch-administrativer und verbandlicher Strukturen auf der europäischen Ebene am Beispiel der technischen Harmonisierung des Arbeits-, Verbraucher- und Umweltschutzes', in Streeck (1994), 256–90.

——and Voelzkow, H. (1994b) (eds.), *Europäische Integration und verbandliche Interessenvermittlung* (Marburg: Metropolis).

Eising, R. and Kohler-Koch, B. (1994), 'Inflation und Zerfaserung: Trends der Interessenvermittlung in der Europäischen Gemeinschaft', in Streeck (1994), 175–206.

EITO (1993), European Information Technology Observatory, *1993 Report (Luxembourg: Office for Official Publications of the European Communities)*.

Encarnation, D. and Mason, M. (1993), *Does Ownership Matter?* (Oxford: Oxford University Press).

EP (1994), European Parliament, 'Public Health and Consumer Protection: Activities of the Committee on the Environment, Public Health, and Consumer Protection, 1989–1994', Working Paper W-7 (Luxembourg: European Parliament).

ERT (1984), European Round Table of Industrialists, *Missing Links* (Brussels: ERT).

Esambert, B. (1994), *Pompidou Capitaine d'Industrie* (Paris: Odile Jacob).

ESC (1991), Economic and Social Committee, 'Opinion on Consumer Protection and Completion of the Internal Market', *Official Journal*, C339, 31 Dec.

——(1993), 'Opinion on the Consumer and the Internal Market', *Official Journal*, C19, 25 Jan.

——(1995), 'Opinion on the Single Market and Consumer Protection: Opportunities and Obstacles in the Internal Market', CES 1309/95 (Brussels: ESC), 22–23 Nov.

Esping-Andersen, G. (1990), *The Three Worlds of Welfare Capitalism* (Cambridge: Polity Press).

EURO-C (1994a), ' "EURO-C": The ETUC's Voice on Behalf of Consumers' (Brussels: EURO-C).

——(1994b), 'Reform of the CCC', *Euro-C Newsletter*, 0, February.

——(1995), 'Activities of the CCC: Developments Prove Commission Wrong!', *EURO-C Newsletter*, 5, Jan.

Fallik, A. (1994) (ed.), *The European Public Affairs Directory 1995* (Brussels: Landmarks Publications).

Fisher, R. and Ury, W. (1982), *Getting to Yes: How to Succeed in Negotiation Without Giving In* (London: Hutchinson).

Frazer, T. and Holmes P. M. (1995), 'Self-Restraint: Cars, Complaints and the Commission', *European Public Law*, 1/1, 85–95.

Gandillot, T. (1992), *La dernière bataille de l'automobile Européenne* (Paris: Fayard).

Garrett, G. and Weingast, B. R. (1993), 'Ideas, Interests, and Institutions: Constructing the European Community's Internal Market', in Goldstein and Keohane (1993).

Gilpin, R. (1975), *U.S. Power and the Multinational Corporation: The Political Economy of Foreign Direct Investment* (New York, NY: Basic Books).

Goldman, P. (1980), testimony to the European Parliament's Committee on the Environment, Public Health and Consumer Protection, 'Verbatim Report of the Public Hearing on the Consumer Action Programme', PE 63.673, (Luxembourg: European Parliament), 26, 27 Feb., 26–9.

Goldstein, J. and Keohane, R. O. (1993) (eds.), *Ideas and Foreign Policy: Beliefs, Institutions, and Political Change* (Ithaca, NY: Cornell University Press).

Gorges, M. J. (1993), 'Interest Intermediation in the EC After Maastricht', in Cafruny and Rosenthal (1993), 19–34.

Goyens, M. (1992), 'Consumer Protection in a Single European Market: What Challenge for the EC Agenda?', *Common Market Law Review*, 29, 71–92.

Grabitz, E., Schmuck, O., Steppacher, S., and Wessels, W. (1988), *Direktwahl und Demokratisierung: Eine Funktionenbilanz des Europäischen Parlaments nach der ersten Wahlperiode* (Bonn: Europa Union Verlag).

Grande, E. (1994), *Vom Nationalstaat zur europäischen Politikverflechtung. Expansion und Transformation moderner Staatlichkeit— untersucht am Beispiel der Forschungs- und Technologiepolitik* (Konstanz: Habilitationsschrift).

——(1995), 'Das Paradox der Schwäche: Forschungspolitik und die Einflußlogik europäischer Politikverflechtung', in Jachtenfuchs and Kohler-Koch (1996b), 371–97.

——(1996), 'The State and Interest Groups in a Framework of Multi-level Decision-Making: The Case of the European Union', *Journal of European Public Policy*, 3/3, 318–38.

Grant, W. (1993), 'Pressure Groups and the European Community', in Mazey and Richardson (1993c), 27–46.

——Paterson, W. E., and Whitston, C. (1988), *Government and the Chemical Industry* (Oxford: Clarendon Press).

Granovetter, M. (1985), 'Economic Action and Social Structure: The Problem of Embeddedness', *American Journal of Sociology*, 91/3, 481–510.

Greenwood, J. (1995) (ed.), *European Business Alliances* (Hemel Hempstead: Prentice-Hall).

——and Aspinwall, M. (1997) (eds.), *Collective Action in the European Union: Interests and the New Politics of Associability* (London: Routledge).

——and McLaughlin, A. M. (1995), 'The Management of Interest Representation in the European Union', *Journal of Common Market Studies*, 33/1, 143–56.

——and Ronit, K. (1994), 'Interest Groups in the European Community: Newly Emerging Dynamics and Forms', *West European Politics*, 17/1, 31–52.

——Grote, J., and Ronit, K. (1992*a*), 'Introduction: Organized Interests and the Transnational Dimension', in Greenwood *et al.* (1992*b*), 1–41.

————— (1992*b*) (eds.), *Organised Interests and the European Community* (London: Sage).

Gresch, N. (1978), *Transnationale Parteizusammenarbeit in der EG* (Baden-Baden: Nomosverlag).

Gustavsson, S. and Lewin, L. (1996) (eds.), *The Future of the Nation State*, (Stockholm: Nerenius and Santérus).

Gyllenhammar, P. (1982), 'Viewpoint', *International Management*, European edition, July.

—— (1983), 'What Europe Needs is a New "Marshall Plan" ', *Financial Times*, Jan.

Haas, E. B. (1964), *Beyond the Nation State: Functionalism and International Organization* (Stanford, Calif.: Stanford University Press).

—— (1968), *The Uniting of Europe: Political, Social, and Economic Forces 1950–1957*, 2nd edn. (Stanford, Calif.: Stanford University Press).

Haas, P. M. (1990), *Saving the Mediterranean: The Politics of International Environmental Cooperation* (New York, NY: Columbia University Press).

—— (1992), 'Introduction: Epistemic Communities and International Policy Coordination', *International Organization*, 46/1, 1–35.

Hall, P. A. and Taylor, R. C. R. (1996), 'Political Science and the Three Institutionalisms', *Political Studies*, 44/5, 936–57.

Hallstein, W. (1979), *Die Europäische Gemeinschaft* (Düsseldorf: Econ).

Hammerch, K. E. (1969), *L'Union des Industries de la Communauté Européenne du Marché Commun* (Stockholm: Fédération Suédoise).

Hayes-Renshaw, F. and Wallace, H. (1997), *The Council of Ministers* (London: Macmillan).

Hayward. J. (1995) (ed.), *Industrial Enterprise and European Integration* (Oxford: Oxford University Press).

Heclo, H. (1978), 'Issue Networks and the Executive Establishment', in King (1978), 87–124.

Héritier, A. (1993*a*), 'Einleitung, Policy Analyse: Elemente der Kritik und Perspektiven der Neurorientierung', in Héritier (1993*b*), 9–38.

——(1993*b*) (ed.), *Policy Analyse, Politische Vierteljahresschrift Sonderheft*, 24, (Opladen: Westdeutscher Verlag).

——*et al.* (1994), *Die Veränderung von Staatlichkeit in Europa. Ein regulativer Wettbewerb: Deutschland, Großbritannien und Frankreich in der Europäischen Union* (Opladen: Leske+Budrich).

——(1996), 'The Accommodation of Diversity in European Policy-Making and its Outcomes: Regulatory Policy as a Patchwork', *Journal of European Public Policy*, 3/2, 149–67.

Hildebrand, P. H. (1992), 'The European Community's Environmental Policy, 1957 to "1992": From Incidental Measures to an International Regime?', *Environmental Politics*, 1/4, 13–44.

Hodges, M. (1983), 'Industrial Policy: Hard Times or Great Expectations?', in H. Wallace *et al.* (1983), 265–93.

Hrbek, R. (1993) (ed.), *Der Vertrag von Maastricht in der wissenschaftlichen Kontroverse* (Baden-Baden: Nomos Verlag).

——(1995) (ed.), *Das Subsidaritätsprinzip in der Europäischen Union— Bedeutung und Wirkung für ausgewählte Politikbereiche* (Baden-Baden: Nomos Verlag).

Hull, R. (1993), 'Lobbying Brussels: A View from Within', in Mazey and Richardson (1993*c*), 82–92.

Huyse, L., Petré, L., and Parmentier, S. (1992), 'La politique européenne des consommateurs', *Courrier Hebdomadaire*, 1357, 1–26.

IATA (1984), International Air Transport Association, *US Domestic Deregulation Concepts and their Potential Application to International Aviation Companies* (London: IATA).

Inglehart, R. (1971), 'Public Opinion and Regional Integration', in Lindberg and Scheingold (1971), 160–91.

Jachtenfuchs, M. (1996), *International Policy-Making as a Learning Process? The European Union and the Greenhouse Effect* (Aldershot: Avebury).

——and Kohler-Koch, B. (1996*a*), 'Einleitung: Regieren im dynamischen Mehrebenensystem', in Jachtenfuchs and Kohler-Koch (1996*b*), 15–46.

————(1996*b*) (eds.), *Europäische Integration* (Opladen: Leske +Budrich).

Jamar, J. and Wessels, W. (1985) (eds.), *Community Bureaucracy at the Cross-roads* (Bruges: De Tempel, Tempelhof).

Jansen, T. (1995), 'Die europäischen Parteien', in Weidenfeld and Wessels (1995), 255–60.

Joerges, C. (1991), 'Markt ohne Staat? Die Wirtschaftsverfassung der Gemeinschaft und die regulative Politik', in Wildenmann (1991), 225–68.

Johnson, S. P. and Corcelle, G. (1989), *The Environmental Policy of the European Communities* (London: Graham & Trotman).

Keohane, R. O. and Hoffmann, S. (1990), 'Conclusions: Community Politics and Institutional Change', in W. Wallace (1990), 276–300.

——(1991*a*), 'Institutional Change in Europe in the 1980s', in Keohane and Hoffmann (1991*b*), 1–39.

——(1991*b*), *The New European Community: Decision-Making and Institutional Change* (Boulder, Colo.: Westview Press).

King, A. (1978) (ed.), *The New American Political System* (Washington, DC: American Enterprise Institute).

Kohler-Koch, B. (1992), 'Interessen und Integration, Die Rolle organisierter Interessen im westeuropäischen Integrationsprozeß', in Kreile (1992), 81–119.

——(1994), 'Patterns of Interest Intermediation in the European Union', *Government and Opposition*, 29/2, 166–80.

——(1996*b*), 'Die Gestaltungsmacht organisierter Interessen', in Jachtenfuchs and Kohler-Koch (1996*b*), 191–220.

——(1996*a*), 'Catching up with Change: The Transformation of Governance in the European Union', *Journal of European Public Policy*, 3/3, 359–80.

——and Schaber, T. (1996): *Pressures on the European Parliament (PEP)* (Oxford: European Centre for Public Affairs).

Krause, A. (1992), *Inside the New Europe* (New York, NY: Harper Collins).

Kreile, M. (1992) (ed.), *Die Integration Europas, Politische Vierteljahresschrift Sonderheft*, 23 (Opladen: Westdeutscher Verlag).

Laredo, P. and Callon, M. (1990), *L'impact des programmes communautaires sur le tissu scientifique et technique français* (Paris: La Documentation Française).

Lehmbruch, G. and Schmitter, P. C. (1982) (eds.), *Patterns of Corporatist Policy-Making* (London: Sage Publications).

Liefferink, J. D., Lowe, P. D., and Mol, A. P. J. (1993) (eds.), *European Integration and Environmental Policy* (London: Belhaven Press).

Lindberg, L. N. (1970), 'Political Integration as a Multidimensional Phenomenon Requiring Multivariate Measurement', *International Organization*, 24/4, 649–731.

——and Scheingold, S. A. (1970), *Europe's Would-Be Polity, Patterns of Change in the European Community* (Englewood Cliffs, NJ: Prentice Hall).

————(1971) (eds.), *Regional Integration, Theory and Research* (Cambridge, Mass.: Harvard University Press).

Loges, F. (1994), 'Freie Wohlfahrtspflege in der Bundesrepublik Deutschland zwischen Binnenmarkt und politischer Union: Anmerkungen zur Implementation wohlfahrtsstaatlicher Interessen', in Eichener and Voelzkow (1994*b*), 485–502.

Lowi, T. J. (1964), 'American Business, Public Policy, Case-Studies, and Political Theory', *World Politics*, 16/4, 677–715.

Ludlow, P. (1991), 'The European Commission', in Keohane and Hoffmann (1991*b*), 85–132.

McGowan, F. (1993), 'Air Transport', in Buigues *et al.* (1993), 259–86.

——and Seabright, P. (1989), 'Deregulating European Airlines', *Economic Policy: A European Forum*, 9 (Cambridge: Cambridge University Press), 283–344.

——and Trengrove, C. (1986), 'Towards a Common European Aviation Market' (London: Institute for Fiscal Studies).

——and Wallace, H. (1996), 'Towards a European Regulatory State', *Journal of European Public Policy*, 3/4.

McLaughlin, A. M. (1994), 'ACEA and the EU-Japan Car Dispute', in Pedler and Van Schendelen (1994), 149–65.

——and Greenwood, J. (1995), 'The Management of Interest Representation in the European Union', *Journal of Common Market Studies*, 33/1, 143–56.

Majone, G. (1994), 'The Rise of the Regulatory State in Europe', *West European Politics*, 17/3, 77–101.

——(1996), *La Communauté Européenne: un État régulateur* (Paris: Montchrestier).

Marks, G., Hooghe, L., and Blank, K. (1996), 'European Integration from the 1980s: State-Centric v. Multi-Level Governance', *Journal of Common Market Studies*, 34/3, 341–78.

——Scharpf, F. W., Schmitter, P. C., and Streeck, W. (1996) (eds.), *Governance in the European Union* (London: Sage Publications).

Mason, M. (1994), 'Elements of Consensus: Europe's Response to the Japanese Automobile Challenge', *Journal of Common Market Studies*, 32/4, 433–54.

Mattoo, A. and Mavroidis, P. (1995), 'The EC-Japan Consensus on Cars', *World Economy*, 8/3, 345–65.

Mazey, S. and Richardson, J. (1992), 'Environmental Groups and the EC: Challenges and Opportunities', *Environmental Politics*, 1/4, 109–28.

———— (1993*a*), 'Introduction: Transference of Power, Decision Rules, and Rules of the Game', in Mazey and Richardson (1993*c*), 3–26.

———— (1993*b*), 'Conclusion: A European Policy Style?', in Mazey and Richardson (1993*c*), 246–58.

———— (1993*c*) (eds.), *Lobbying in the European Community* (Oxford: Oxford University Press).

———— (1995), 'De la liberté des moeurs politiques à un style européen de politique publique?', in Mény *et al.* (1995), 95–115.

Mény, Y., Muller, P., and Quermonne J.-L. (1995) (eds.), *Politiques Publiques en Europe* (Paris: L'Harmattan)

Metcalfe, L. (1994), 'Reducing the European Management Deficit', paper presented to the Sussex European Institute and Economic and Social Research Council workshop on Regulating Europe, Falmer, Feb.

Metze, M. (1993), *Short Circuit* (London: Minerva).

Meynaud, J. and Sidjanski, D. (1974), *Les Groupes de Pression dans la Communauté Européenne: 1958–1968* (Brussels: Université Libre de Bruxelles).

Middlemas, K. (1995), *Orchestrating Europe, The Informal Politics of European Union 1973–1995* (London: Fontana Press).

Miller, G. (1995), 'Post-Maastricht Legislative Procedures: Is The Council "Institutionally Challenged"?', paper to the Fourth Biennial International Conference of ECSA, Charleston, SC, 11–14 May.

Mills, M. (1993) (ed.), *Prevention, Health and British Politics* (Aldershot: Avebury).

Monar, J. (1994), 'Interinstitutional Agreements: The Phenomenon and Its Dynamics after Maastricht', *Common Market Law Review*, 31, 693–719.

Monnet, J. (1976), *Mémoires* (Paris: Fayard).

Moravcsik, A. (1991), 'Negotiating the Single European Act: National Interests and Conventional Statecraft in the European Community', *International Organization*, 45/1, 19–56.

Morgan, R. (1991), 'The Consultative Function of the Economic and Social Committee of the European Community', EUI Working Paper 91/11 (Florence: European University Institute).

Mytelka, L. K. (1989), 'Les alliances stratégiques au sein du programme européen ESPRIT,' *Economie Prospective Internationale*, 37.

——(1991), *Strategic Partnerships and the World Economy* (London: Pinter).

——(1992), 'Dancing with the Wolves: Global Oligopolies and Strategic Partnerships', paper presented to the Colloquium of Merit, Maastricht, Dec.

NCC (1986), National Consumer Council, *Air Transport and the Consumer: A Need for Change?: A Report on Air Transport Regulation in Europe* (London: HMSO).

——(1988), *Consumers and the Common Agricultural Policy* (London: HMSO).

Niedermayer, O. (1985), 'Zehn Jahre europäische Parteienbünde: kein Integrationsschub', *Integration*, 4, 174–81.

Nørgaard, A. S. (1996), 'Rediscovering Reasonable Rationality in Institutional Analysis', *European Journal of Political Research*, 29, 31–57.

OECD (1983), Organization for Economic Co-operation and Development, *Consumer Policy During the Past Ten Years: Main Developments and Prospects* (Paris: OECD).

——(1991), *Consumers, Product Safety Standards and International Trade* (Paris: OECD).

——(1995), *Statistics Directorate: Historical Statistics 1960–1993* (Paris: OECD).

Olsen, J. P. (1996), 'Europeanisation and Nation-State Dynamics', in Gustavsson and Lewin (1996), 245–85.

Pappas, S. (1994) (ed.), *Procédures administratives nationales de préparation et de mise en oeuvre des décisions communautaires* (Maastricht: EIPA).

Pedler, R. H. and Van Schendelen, M. P. C. M. (1994) (eds.), *Lobbying the EU* (Aldershot: Dartmouth).

Pelkmans, J. (1990), 'Regulation and the Single Market: An Economic Perspective', in Siebert (1990), 91–125.

——and Vanheukelen, M. (1986) (eds.), *Coming to Grips with the Internal Market* (Maastricht: European Institute of Public Administration).

——and Winters, L. A. (1988), *Europe's Domestic Market* (London: Royal Institute of International Affairs).

Peninou, G., Holtus, M., Kebschull D., and Attali, J. (1978), *Multinational Corporations and European Public Opinion* (New York, NY: Praeger).

Peters, B. G. (1989), *The Politics of Bureaucracy* (New York, NY: Longman).

——(1992), 'Politics and Institutions in the EC', in Sbragia (1992), 75–122.

Petite, M. (1989), 'Les Lobbies Européens', *Pouvoirs*, 48, 95–103.

Philips (1984), 'Europe 1990: An Agenda for Action', 13 Nov., speech and report delivered by Wisse Dekker on 11 Jan. 1985, Brussels.

Pierson, P. (1996), 'The Path to European Integration: A Historical Institutionalist Analysis', *Comparative Political Studies*, 29/2, 123–63.

Poullet, E. and Deprez, G. (1976), *Struktur und Macht der EG-Kommission: Die Kommission im System der Europäischen Gemeinschaft* (Bonn: Europa Verlag).

Puchala, D. (1983), 'Worm Cans and Worth Taxes: Fiscal Harmonization and the European Policy Process', in H. Wallace *et al.* (1983), 237–64.

Pugh, A. T. (1987), 'The Challenge of the Market', in Institute of Civil Engineers, *European Transport* (London: Thomas Telford).

Putnam, R. D. (1988), 'Diplomacy and Domestic Politics: The Logic of Two-Level Games', *International Organization*, 42/3, 427–60.

Reif, K. H. (1993), 'Ein Ende des "permissive consensus"? Zum Wandel europapolitischer Einstellungen in der öffentlichen Meinung der EG-Mitgliedstaaten', in Hrbek (1993), 23–40.

Richardson, J. (1996*a*), 'Policy-Making in the EU: Interests, Ideas, and Garbage Cans of Primeval Soup', in Richardson (1996*b*), 3–23.

——(1996*b*) (ed.), *European Union: Power and Policy-Making* (London: Routledge).

Riggs, F. W. (1964), *Administration in Developing Countries* (Boston, Mass.: Houghton Mifflin).

Ringius, L. (1992), 'Radwaste Disposal and the Global Ocean Dumping Convention: The Politics of International Environmental Regimes', Ph.D. thesis (European University Institute, Florence).

Rittberger, V. (1994), *Internationale Organisationen, Politik und Geschichte* (Opladen: Leske & Buderich).

Robinson, J. (1979), *Multinationals in the 1980s: Trends in European Regulation and International Control* (Brussels: Agence Européenne d'Informations).

——(1983), *Multinationals and Political Control* (New York, NY: St. Martin's Press).

Rometsch, D. and Wessels, W. (1996) (eds.), *The European Union and Member States: Towards Institutional Fusion?* (Manchester: Manchester University Press).

Ross, G. (1993), 'Sliding into Industrial Policy: Inside the European Commission', *French Politics and Society*, 11.

Rousseau, M. (1993), 'Rapport d'information sur l'application de l'arrangement entre la Communauté et le Japon sur les importations d'automobiles de ce pays déposé' (Paris: Assemblée Nationale), 6 July.

Rucht, D. (1993), '"Think Globally Act Locally"? Needs, Forms and Problems of Cross-National Cooperation among Environmental Groups', in Liefferink *et al.* (1993), 75–95.

Ruigrok, W. van, Tulder, R., and Baven, G. (1991), 'Cars and Complexes', European Commission: FAST/MONITOR, FOP 285.

Sainsaulieu, R. (1988), *L'identité au travail* (Paris: Presses de la Fondation Nationale des Sciences Politiques).

Sandholtz, W. (1992), *High-Tech Europe: The Politics of International Cooperation* (Berkeley, Calif.: University of California Press).

——and Zysman, J. (1989), '1992: Recasting the European Bargain', *World Politics*, 42/1, 95–128.

Sbragia, A. (1992) (ed.), *Euro-Politics: Institutions and Policy-Making in the New European Community* (Washington, DC: Brookings Institution).

Scharpf, F. W. (1985), 'Die Politikverflechtungs-Falle: Europäische Integration und deutscher Föderalismus im Vergleich', *Politische Vierteljahresschrift*, 4, 323–56.

——(1988), 'The Joint-Decision Trap: Lessons from German Federalism and European Integration', *Public Administration*, 66/3, 239–78.

——(1994), *Optionen des Föderalismus in Deutschland und Europa* (Frankfurt: Campus).

——(1996*a*), 'Negative and Positive Integration in the Political Economy of European Welfare States', in Marks *et al.* (1996), 15–39.

——(1996*b*), 'Politische Optionen im vollendeten Binnenmarkt', in Jachtenfuchs and Kohler-Koch (1996*b*), 109–40.

Schmid, J. (1994), 'Der Wohlfahrtsstaat Europa und die deutschen Wohlfahrtsverbände: Zur politisch-ökonomischen Dialektik zwischen europäischer Integration und verbandsorganisatorischer Differenzierung', in Eichener and Voelzkow (1994*b*), 453–83.

Schmitter, P. C. (1974), 'Still the Century of Corporatism?', *Review of Politics*, 36, 85–131.

——and Lehmbruch, G. (1979) (eds.), *Trends Toward Corporatist Intermediation* (London: Sage Publications).

——and Streeck, W. (1981), 'The Organization of Business Interests: A Research Design to Study the Associate Action of Business in the Advanced Societies of Western Europe', Discussion Paper IIM/LMP 81–13 (Berlin: International Institute of Management).

Schubert, K. and Bandelow, N. (1994), 'Neue Netze und fremde Gewässer: "Networking" für eine europäische Kulturpolitik', in Eichener and Voelzkow (1994*b*), 597–615.

Schuman, R. (1950), 'Erklärung des französischen Außenministers Robert Schuman vom 9. Mai 1950', in *Europa-Archiv*, 5, 3091–2.

Schweitzer, C.-C. (1985), *Die nationalen Parlamente in der Gemeinschaft— ihr schwinder Einfluß in Bonn und Westminster auf die Europagesetzgebung* (Bonn: Europa Verlag).

Seele, G. (1991), *Der Kreis aus europäischer Sicht, Die übergemeindliche Kommunalverwaltung im Spiegel der nationalstaatlichen Verwaltungsstrukturen und der europäischen Gemeinschaftspolitik* (Cologne: Kohlhammer).

Servan-Schreiber, J.-J. (1968), *The American Challenge*, trans. R. Steel (New York, NY: Athenium).

Sidjanski, D. (1995), 'Nouvelles tendances des groupes de pression dans l'Union Européenne', in Mény *et al.* (1995), 77–93.

——and Ayberk, U. (1990*a*), 'Le Nouveau Visage des Groupes d'Intérêt Communautaires', in Sidjanski and Ayberk (1990*b*), 42–80.

————(1990*b*) (eds.), *L'Europe du Sud dans la Communauté Européenne, Analyse Comparative des Groupes d'Intérêt et leur insertion dans le réseau communautaire* (Paris: PUF).

Siebert, H. (1990) (ed.), *The Completion of the Internal Market* (Tübingen: J. C. B. Mohr).

Smith, A., Holmes, P., Sedelmeier, U., Smith, E., Wallace, H., and Young, A. R. (1996), 'The European Union and Central and Eastern Europe: Pre-Accession Strategies', SEI Working Paper 15 (Falmer: Sussex European Institute).

Spence, D. (1993), 'The Role of the National Civil Service in European Lobbying: The British Case', in Mazey and Richardson (1993*c*), 47–73

Strange, S. (1988), *States and Markets: An Introduction to International Political Economy* (New York, NY: Blackwell).

Streeck, W. (1994) (ed.), *Staat und Verbände, Politische Vierteljahresschrift Sonderheft* 25 (Opladen: Westdeutscher Verlag).

—— (1995), 'German Capitalism: Does it Exist? Can it Survive?', Paper 95/5 (Cologne: Max-Planck Institut für Gesellschaftsforschung).

—— and Schmitter, P. C. (1991), 'From National Corporatism to Transnational Pluralism: Organized Interests in the Single European Market', *Politics and Society*, 19/2, 133–64.

Sun, J.-M. and Pelkmans, J. (1995), 'Regulatory Competition and the Single Market', *Journal of Common Market Studies*, 33/1, 67–89.

Sutherland, P., Albrecht, E., Babusiaux, C., Corby, B., Green, P., and Tramontana, G. (High Level Group on the Operation of the Internal Market) (1992), *The Internal Market After 1992: Meeting the Challenge* (Luxembourg: Office for Official Publications of the European Communities).

Taddei D. and Coriat, B. (1993), *Made in France* (Paris: Livre de Poche)

Tiedemann, R. (1994), *Aufstieg oder Niedergang der Interessenverbände? Rent-seeking und europäische Integration* (Baden-Baden: Nomos).

Tomuschat, C. (1995*a*), 'Einleitung: Der Ausschuß der Regionen als Verfassungsorgan der Europäischen Gemeinschaft', in Tomuschat (1995*b*), 9–22.

—— (1995*b*) (ed.), *Mitsprache der dritten Ebene in der europäischen Integration: Der Ausschuß der Regionen* (Bonn: Europa Verlag).

Tsebelis, G. (1994), 'The Power of the European Parliament as a Conditional Agenda Setter', *American Political Science Review*, 88/1, 128–42.

UNICE (1996), Union of Industrial and Employers' Confederations of Europe, 'Advisory and Support Group: List of Member Companies', (Brussels: UNICE).

Van Miert, K. (1991), 'The Internal Market Needs the Confidence of Consumers', in Commission (1991*a*), 5–6.

Van Schendelen, M. P. C. M. (1993) (ed.), *National Public and Private EC Lobbying* (Aldershot: Dartmouth).

——(1995), 'De Raad Beslist. Beslist de Raad? Verslag van een onderzoek naar besluitvorming door de EU Landbouwraad', manuscript, Rotterdam.

Venables, T. (1986), 'Harmonization in the Food Sector: A Consumer Viewpoint', in Pelkmans and Vanheukelen (1986), 55–62.

Vernon, R. (1971), *Sovereignty at Bay* (New York, NY: Basic Books).

——(1977), *Storm Over the Multinationals: The Real Issues* (Cambridge, Mass.: Harvard University Press).

Vigier, P. (1992), 'La politique communautaire de l'automobile', *Revue du Marché Unique Européen*, 3, 73–126.

Voelzkow, H. (1993), 'Staatseingriff und Verbandsfunktion: Das verbandliche System technischer Regelsetzung als Gegenstand staatlicher Politik', Discussion paper 2/93 (Cologne: Max-Planck-Gesellschaft).

Vogel, D. (1989), *Fluctuating Fortunes: The Political Power of Business in America* (New York, NY: Basic Books).

Wallace, H. (1990), 'Making Multilateral Negotiations Work', in W. Wallace (1990), 213–28.

——(1995), 'Les relations entre la Communauté et l'Administration britannique', in Mény *et al.* (1995), 155–69.

——and Wallace, W. (1995), *Flying Together in a More Diverse European Union* (The Hague: Netherlands Scientific Council for Government Policy).

————(1996) (eds.), *Policy-Making in the European Union* (Oxford: Oxford University Press).

——and Young, A. R. (1996), 'Balancing Public and Private Interests Under Duress', end-of-project report to the Economic and Social Research Council (Falmer: Sussex European Institute).

————and Webb, C. (1983) (eds.), *Policy Making in the European Community*, 2nd edn. (Chichester: John Wiley & Sons).

Wallace, W. (1990) (ed.), *The Dynamics of European Integration* (London: Pinter).

Weale, A. (1992), *The New Politics of Pollution* (Manchester: University of Manchester Press).

——and Williams, A. (1992), 'Between Economy and Ecology? The Single Market and the Integration of Environmental Policy,' *Environmental Politics*, 1/4.

Weber, M. (1971 [1922]), *Economie et Société* (Paris: Plon).

Weidenfeld, W. and Wessels, W. (1995) (eds.), *Jahrbuch der Europäischen Integration 1994/1995* (Bonn: Europa Union Verlag).

Weiler, J. H. H. (1991), 'The Transformation of Europe', *Yale Law Journal*, 100/8, 2403–81.

Wessels, W. (1985), 'Community Bureaucracy in a Changing Environment: Criticism, Trends, Questions', in Jamar and Wessels (1985), 8–36.

—— (1990), 'Administrative Integration', in W. Wallace (1990), 229–41.

—— (1992), 'Staat und (westeuropäiische) Integration, Die Fusionsthese', in Kreile (1992), 36–61.

—— (1996a), 'The Modern West European State and the European Union: Democratic Erosion or a New Kind of Policy?', in Andersen and Eliassen (1996), 57–69.

—— (1996b), 'Verwaltung im EG-Mehrebenensystem: Auf dem Weg zur Megabürokratie', in Jachtenfuchs and Kohler-Koch (1996b), 165–92.

—— (1997), 'An Ever Closer Fusion? Trends of European Integration', *Journal of Common Market Studies*, June.

—— and Rometsch, D. (1996), 'Conclusion: European Union and National Institutions', in Rometsch and Wessels (1996).

Westendorp, C., *et al.* (1995), 'Reflection Group's Report', SN520/95, Brussels, 5 Dec.

White, H. (1981), 'Where do Markets Come From?', *American Journal of Sociology*, 87/3, 517–47.

Wildenmann, R. (1991) (ed.), *Staatswerdung Europas? Optionen für eine Europäische Union* (Baden-Baden: Nomos).

Williamson, D. (1995), 'European Parliament: Committee on the Rules of Procedure: The Verification of Credentials and Immunities', Summary Record, SP(95) 1773, 1 June.

Wilkins, M. (1974), *The Maturing of Multinational Enterprise: American Business Abroad from 1914 to 1970* (Cambridge, Mass.: Harvard University Press).

Wilson, J. Q. (1980a), 'The Politics of Regulation', in Wilson (1980b), 357–394.

—— (1980b) (ed.), *The Politics of Regulation* (New York, NY: Basic Books).

Woodroffe, G. (1984) (ed.), *Consumer Law in the EEC* (London: Sweet and Maxwell).

Woolcock, S. (1994), *The Single European Market: Centralization or Competition among National Rules?* (London: Royal Institute of International Affairs).

Young, A. R. (1997), 'European Consumer Groups: Multiple Levels of Governance and Multiple Logics of Collective Action', in Greenwood and Aspinwall (1997).

INDEX